T0304160

ROUTLEDGE LIBRARY EDITIONS:
INFLATION

Volume 1

PROBLEMS OF LABOUR AND INFLATION

PROBLEMS OF LABOUR AND INFLATION

HILDE BEHREND

Routledge
Taylor & Francis Group

LONDON AND NEW YORK

First published in 1984 by Croom Helm Ltd

This edition first published in 2016
by Routledge
2 Park Square, Milton Park, Abingdon, Oxon OX14 4RN

and by Routledge
711 Third Avenue, New York, NY 10017

Routledge is an imprint of the Taylor & Francis Group, an informa business

British Library Cataloguing in Publication Data
A catalogue record for this book is available from the British Library

ISBN: 978-1-138-65251-4 (Set)
ISBN: 978-1-315-62042-8 (Set) (ebk)
ISBN: 978-1-138-65311-5 (Volume 1) (hbk)
ISBN: 978-1-315-62379-5 (Volume 1) (ebk)

Publisher's Note
The publisher has gone to great lengths to ensure the quality of this reprint but
points out that some imperfections in the original copies may be apparent.

Disclaimer
The publisher has made every effort to trace copyright holders and would welcome
correspondence from those they have been unable to trace.

PROBLEMS OF LABOUR AND INFLATION

Hilde Behrend

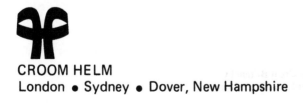

CROOM HELM
London • Sydney • Dover, New Hampshire

© 1984 Hilde Behrend
Croom Helm Ltd, Provident House, Burrell Row,
Beckenham, Kent BR3 1AT
Croom Helm Australia Pty Ltd, First Floor, 139 King St.,
Sydney, NSW 2001, Australia
Croom Helm, 51 Washington Strèet, Dover,
New Hampshire 03820, USA

British Library Cataloguing in Publication Data

Behrend, Hilda
    Problems of labour and inflation.
    1. Industrial relations—Great Britain
    I. Title
    331'.0941   HD8391
    ISBN 0-7099-3222-7

Library of Congress Cataloging in Publication Data

Behrend, Hilde.
    Problems of Labour and Inflation.

    Bibliography: p.
    Includes index.
    1. Labour and Laboring classes. 2. Work. 3. Infla-
tion (Finance) 4. Wages. 5. Industrial Relations.
I. Title.
HD4901.B43 1984   331   84-14263
ISBN 0-7099-3222-7

Printed and bound in Great Britain by
Biddles Ltd, Guildford and King's Lynn

Contents

Acknowledgments

Since this book brings together my major research contributions the list of people to whom I am indebted is long and I cannot name them all.

To begin with I must acknowledge my debt to Professor P Sargant Florence who provided me with the opportunity to enter academic life as a member of his research staff at the University of Birmingham. I also owe much in the way of early help and inspiration to Professor W Baldamus with whom I worked together at that time.

I would also like to express my gratitude to the University of Edinburgh for the facilities it provided (particularly in the Social Science Research Centre) and to Professor Norman Hunt, my head of department, for his unfailing interest and assistance.

I am greatly indebted to the Social Science Research Council for sponsoring the two projects 'Frames of Reference for Judging Incomes' and 'The Impact of Inflation on Conceptions of Earnings and Attitudes to Work' from 1965 to 1975.

My thanks are also due to the Irish Departments of Labour and Finance for sponsoring the 1969 Irish survey into attitudes to pay increases and pay differentials and for giving helpful advice. I am particularly grateful to Michael Fogarty, then Director of the Dublin Economic and Social Research Institute, for appointing me to direct the enquiry on the Institute's behalf and for his help in carrying it out.

For assistance with the two 1966 national sample surveys I am indebted to Dr Mark Abrams of Research Services and his staff, especially for the interest he showed in our work. The 1969, 1971 and 1973 surveys were carried out to our satisfaction by the staff of National Opinion Polls (NOP). To James

Acknowledgements

Spence (who worked at NOP at that time) I would like
to express my special thanks for his advice,
courtesy and efficiency in organising and
supervising the surveys.

In addition I am conscious of the debt I owe to
many managers in industry who have provided
information for my studies and to the respondents
who agreed to take part in our sample surveys.

Among academic colleagues I would like to thank
Professor Sir Henry Phelps Brown for the encouraging
and interesting comments I have received from him on
my work throughout my career which brought in his
labour economist's point of view. Frequent contacts
with Sylvia Shimmin, who was trained as a
psychologist, have been very important for my
interdisciplinary work. I would like to thank her
for the many stimulating discussions and exchanges
of ideas we have had and for very useful comments
and suggestions on the draft of chapter 15 of this
book.

In expressing my thanks to all the people who
have helped with my work in Edinburgh I would like
to thank first of all Harriet Lynch whose energy and
initiative got the first SSRC project off the ground
and Ann Knowles who took over from her at a critical
time; Jean Davies who stayed with the projects
throughout and whose unfailing support, energy and
application were key factors in the success of the
projects. On the more technical side my thanks are
due to Emily Paterson who dealt cheerfully and
competently with figure and data processing work for
nearly six years. I have also received help on many
occasions from William Watson of the Edinburgh
Regional Computing Centre and from John Nimmo and
Mrs Sheila Edgar of the Social Science Research
Centre.

I am grateful to my industrial relations
colleagues Phil White and Ian Sams who made it
possible for me to take up sabbatical term
entitlements and who provided me with constructive
criticism after reading some draft chapters of this
book; also to Colin Duncan for reading most of the
manuscript and for making useful comments and for
help with identifying word processor errors. Among
former Edinburgh colleagues I enjoyed working with
Stuart Pocock and Elisabeth Gould. I would also
like to thank our computer expert, Robin Day for his
advice and guidance in the use of the word
processor.

These acknowledgements would not be complete
without my expressing special thanks and
appreciation to Roseann Finn who has worked for me

as secretarial research assistant for 12 years. Her efficient and patient help with the wording, presentation and typing of often very untidy manuscripts, including all the drafts of the chapters in this book, and transforming them into finished products has been invaluable.

Finally, I also want to express my gratitude to Tricia Fraser for carrying out the word processing of the manuscript for this book in her spare time - a task which proved to be difficult and trying because our modern 'wonder machine' broke down frequently, causing many headaches and much extra work. She passed the endurance test with flying colours.

1 Introduction

In the period since the second world war many people in different spheres of life have been interested in, pre-occupied by, or confronted with problems of labour. Inflation has also been of major concern, particularly for successive governments.

These issues have been described and interpreted in various ways by different writers, commentators and researchers. This diversity finds expression in the choice of vocabulary; for example, economists seem to prefer the word 'labour' and psychologists 'work'. The two words are difficult to define but they often refer to the same subject matter. Im my view, therefore, when we are talking of problems of labour and labour relations we also speak of problems of work and work relations although the word selected by a particular writer may be judged by him (or her) to be more appropriate in a particular context.

This element of judgement was applied to the selection of the title for this book. The word labour was chosen because of the connection between labour problems and the problems of the economic phenomenon of inflation - a link discussed in a number of the chapters, particularly in 11 to 14. However, I would describe the research enquiries which I carried out in factories (which provided the base for chapters 5 to 10) as studies of work and work behaviour; and I examine problems of work relations, using the more customary title of industrial relations, in chapters 2 to 4.

The book brings together in one volume my major contributions in this area. Chapters 2 and 3 are

Introduction

scene-setters concerned with the identification of various fields of enquiry. They provide a map of topics and represent analytical evaluations of what is happening in the field of industrial relations. Chapter 4 takes this further by a more detailed assessment of the problem of strikes.

By contrast chapters 5 to 14 cover findings and insights from empirical enquiries and present them (with the exception of chapter 6) in the order in which the research was carried out. They thus provide a picture of the continuities and discontinuities in research; they illustrate how one investigation can lead to another and to extensions into new fields.

A few points about my background, and that for the enquiries which I carried out, are relevant. My qualification for entering academic life five years after graduation was a degree in economics, with economic theory as special subject, and eleven years of different work experience in a number of organisations. For instance, while studying, I held a full time teaching job in the first year and later a part-time post as shorthand typist at the London School of Economics which gave me free access to lectures.

The jobs I held had aroused my interest in problems of work relations, work organisation and monotony. The offer of a research assistantship at Birmingham University in 1949 to join a team which was investigating problems of labour efficiency therefore appeared attractive. The appointment started me off on a career in which I became involved in three major research programmes. I may briefly label them as absence, incentives, and attitudes to inflation enquiries.

The first two of these three programmes were sponsored by the Research Board of the University of Birmingham's Faculty of Commerce and Social Science. The team, under the chairmanship of Professor P Sargant Florence, was concerned with investigating industrial incentives and measures of the efficiency of labour. My first brief was to collect information on absence and labour turnover from the personnel records of a number of firms represented on the Midland Advisory Council on Productivity, to prepare reports on both topics for the managers of each of the firms, and to bring the absence evidence together in a monograph that would be of interest to both managers and academics. (See Behrend, 1951).

The Birmingham absence enquiry was carried out in 1949-51 during a period of full employment. As labour had become scarce, the need to use it efficiently had come to the fore and gave rise to growing concern about absenteeism and its effects on productivity not only in Britain but also abroad. This found expression in an invitation I received from the editor of the International Labour Review in 1958 to prepare an article on this problem (see chapter 5). Ten years later, I returned to a study of this topic. The two field enquiries were carried out in 1969 and 1975 in a Scottish factory, which was experiencing an absence problem, and covered a one-year and a six-year period. The main findings are outlined in chapter 6.

When I began to analyse the size of the absence and turnover problems among different groups of workers in the Midlands in 1950, I discovered that the evidence I collected was not amenable to economic demand and supply analysis, although it did throw light on the problems of the efficient use of labour as a resource. Instead, stimulating discussions with my senior colleague, Dr Baldamus, introduced a sociological dimension into my studies. My horizon was extended further when the Medical Research Council Research Unit directed by Wyatt and Marriott began to carry out a study of attitudes to factory work in a plant in which I was also collecting data (see Wyatt and Marriott, 1956). The question of whether we could help each other arose and they offered to let me have access to questionnaires on attitudes to work, together with absence data, for a tentative analysis which is briefly discussed in my monograph. This initiated my interest in attitude studies and the examination of psychological variables.

Having once crossed the inter-disciplinary boundary lines, I began to ignore them. I started new enqiries by formulating questions to which I sought answers which would throw light on a particular problem rather than on a particular theory. I would then choose an appropriate research method.

This interdisciplinary outlook was furthered by my appointment as a research lecturer to the University of Edinburgh Social Science Research Centre in 1954. The Centre had been set up by the Arts Faculty and was run by the Committee on Co-operation in the Social Sciences. The teaching department to which I was attached, and in which I was expected to lecture is now called the Department of Business Studies. In 1964, shortly after the Faculty of Social Science came into being, the Social Science Research Centre was changed into a facilities centre and the academic staff were

transferred to their teaching departments as full-
time lecturers, in my case to the Department of
Business Studies.

During my last year at Birmingham University I
had become involved in an interview-based empirical
investigation, initiated by Professor Sargant
Florence, into the use of payment by results. We
had some stimulating discussions and I arrived in
Edinburgh with plans for the continuation of the
incentives study with a further round of interviews.
The publications which resulted from this research
analyse the wage-work bargain from different points
of view (see chapters 7 to 10). The focus shifts
from looking at payment by results as a managerial
tool of production control and an economic
incentive, to an analysis of belief systems, and an
examination of employee reactions to the controls,
ie output behaviour and the incentives and
disincentives which affect it, including bargaining
and social norms. I hope that a comparison of the
different ways of looking at these problems is of
special interest to readers.

At a Social Science Research Centre Seminar in
1957, I presented a discussion paper on social norms
and economic decisions. This was criticised by the
then Professor of Economics as of no interest to
economists - which was discouraging. A joint
research programme in this area had been proposed by
Centre members and this attack foreshadowed its
abandonment. I still hold that social norms
represent an important variable in economic
behaviour.

Continuing on my own, I began to examine
managerial aspects of company wage problems and
policies and the influence of the external
environment on these; in particular, the
interrelation between payment by result schemes and
inflation and how much room for manoeuvre
managements have in the wages field. While I was
engaged in these analyses, ideas for a new project
began to take shape. A growing conviction developed
that it was important to know more about conceptions
of earnings and notions of fairness with regard to
pay, and also to look more closely at the relations
between beliefs and facts, in order to get a better
understanding of wage problems. At the same time,
some practical difficulties which the Research
Centre encountered when recruiting secretarial
staff, pointed to some investigable problems that
appeared worth following up. In addition, the
perusal of the literature in this subject area and
the study of current events gave rise to my growing

interest in problems of inflation and incomes policy.

Among other books, Sherif's account of frames of reference in unstructured situations struck a chord. Sherif (1948, chapter 7) argued that 'a vague and ill-defined situation becomes a plastic canvas on which our pre-occupations, motives and stereotyped attitudes block in the picture'. It struck me that inflation presented a related type of situation. Furthermore, my curiosity was aroused when I read the final sentence of the Fourth Report of the Council on Prices, Productivity and Incomes (1961) which read: 'At the heart of the problem of inflation under full employment is a frame of mind'. I wanted to find out the characteristics of this frame of mind.

Having concluded that inflation was a key variable which must be included in studies of attitudes to pay, I proceeded to work out a strategy for pilot studies. In an article in 1964 I outlined the thought processes that led to the formulation of this venture and presented the first results, and in 1966 in a second paper I described the findings from the pilot studies.

Once the project got under way, this research acquired a momentum of its own. In April 1965 I obtained financial support from the Foundation for Management Education for taking on a research assistant for six months and in October 1965 I was awarded funds by the Department of Social and Industrial Research for a project (later taken over by the Social Science Research Council) entitled Frames of Reference for Judging Incomes (Behrend, 1971). This enabled me to build up a small research team and to conduct our first national sample survey into attitudes to inflation. Supplementary grants led to further sample surveys and a new grant for 1971-75 for a project entitled The Impact of Inflation on Conceptions of Earnings and Attitudes to Work (Behrend, 1976). In addition, the research attracted two outside commissions, one from the Economic and Social Research Institute in Dublin for conducting a sample survey of male employees into Attitudes to Pay Increases and Pay Differentials in 1969 and the other from the National Economic Development Office to conduct a national sample survey into Attitudes to Price Increases and Pay Claims in 1973. Chapters 11 to 14 describe the major findings from the inflation enquiries.

Finally, chapter 15 discusses some of the implications of my research and the insights which I have gained from it.

Introduction

REFERENCES

H Behrend, Absence under Full Employment, Monograph A3, University of Birmingham Studies in Economics and Society, 1951

H Behrend, Price and Income Images and Inflation, Scottish Journal of Political Economy, Vol XIII, No 3, November 1966

H Behrend, Price Images, Inflation and National Incomes Policy, Scottish Journal of Political Economy, Vol XIII, No 3, November 1966

H Behrend, Frames of Reference for Judging Incomes, Final Report to SSRC, July 1971, British Library Lending Division, Reference B/H/172

H Behrend, The Impact of Inflation on Conceptions of Earnings and Attitudes to Work, Final Report to SSRC, March, 1976. British Library Lending Division, reference BLLD HR 1305

Council on Prices, Productivity and Incomes, Fourth Report, HMSO, London, July 1961

M Sherif, An Outline of Social Psychology, Harper and Bros. 1948

S Wyatt and R Marriott, A Study of Attitudes to Factory Work, Medical Research Council Special Report Series No 292, HMSO, London 1956

2 Problems in the Field of Industrial Relations

First published under the title 'The Field of Industrial Relations' in British Journal of Industrial Relations, Vol. 1, No. 3, October 1963.

I

The term industrial relations is used in two different senses: it is sometimes used as an all-inclusive term and sometimes as a term restricted to collective relations.

In the all-inclusive sense industrial relations are defined as 'all the relationships between management and employees in the community'. This is the sense in which they are defined in the syllabuses of many university courses on industrial relations. In this sense, the field of industrial relations covers relations between individuals such as the individual employer and employee, and between organised groups such as trade unions and employers. It also covers unorganised or informal relations, and organised or formal relations.

In the restricted sense, the term industrial relations is used to denote only collective relations between trade unions and employers. This usage is illustrated by the following extract from an I.L.O. organised Meeting of Experts on Industrial and Human Relations (Geneva, July, 1956):

> 'Labour-management relations include all the relations between workers and management or employers, and between workers' organisations or representatives and the representatives of the employers or their associations or federations ...a deficiency in the conduct or spirit of either personal relationships, which we may call human relations, or of group or collective relationships, sometimes referred to as industrial relations, can each have a detrimental effect on labour management relations'.

7

Problems in the Field of Industrial Relations

It is doubtful, however, whether the different types of relations can easily be separated from each other, for interpersonal human relations take place against the background of group and collective relations and the borderline between formal and informal, collective and personal, relations is not clear-cut - there is constant interaction between them.

It would seem more correct to view the relations as a wide range of different mixtures of the formal and informal. In the least organised form of relations we have practically no verbal communication. In the most organised form, the relations are defined in legal contracts and in government legislation. Formal rules for regulating relations and behaviour may be strictly enforced, but they may also be ignored. Gouldner (1955, p52), for instance, related that the 'no smoking' rule was enforced only when inspectors from the insurance company made their infrequent tours of the plant. To understand industrial relations, therefore, it is not enough to study merely formal relations. Nor is it enough to study the relations only at the level of the firm or only at the level beyond the firm, for again these relations interact upon each other.

In present-day Britain, many questions of labour-management relations are not settled within the individual firm; they are settled by national agreements between trade unions and employers' federations. This applies particularly to agreements on working conditions and wage rates; only their detailed application is settled within the firm. Thus, wage disputes may develop at the level beyond the firm where the trade unions are bargaining about wage rates with the employers' federations, or at the level of the firm where they may argue about additional bonuses or piece rates. Conflict may arise within or outside the firm.

Ideally, therefore, any study of industrial relations should be all-inclusive, taking account of the whole situation within and outside the firm. In practice, the teacher of industrial relations cannot present at any moment of time a complete picture of the industrial relations scene; he must isolate specific aspects and discuss them in turn. This means that often the same issues reappear in different contexts, and the whole picture is put together piecemeal. This is of necessity unsatisfactory but unavoidable. It has led to the practice of separating industrial relations courses into two parts - one dealing with problems within

8

the firm, and the other with the wider issues, with the so-called framework of industrial relations and the development of collective agreements - but it must never be forgotten that the two aspects of industrial relations are interconnected.

II

In spite of the growing attention which has been focused on industrial human relations as a problem-area in recent years, little attempt is made in the literature to define basic problems. Most writers confine themselves to the study of one or other aspect of industrial relations. As a result, we get at least as many different approaches and emphases as there are disciplines in this field. Nevertheless, it is possible to see how one set of problems leads to another.

There is general agreement that the human problems of industrial organisation differ in nature from the technical problems. From this realisation spring the widely used clichés that 'men are not machines'; 'workers are human beings'. The essential difference is that the behaviour of machines is more or less predictable; the behaviour of men cannot necessarily be predicted. Men may respond favourably to an appeal for co-operation; on the other hand, they may not respond at all. While machines don't answer back, men do. Men cannot be assumed to be indifferent to being organised and manipulated; their co-operation has to be sought and won.

These considerations have led to the study of the so-called 'human factor' in industry. As a result, some students of the field focus their main attention on problems of 'human efficiency'. These are viewed as problems of the worker's capacity to work on the one hand, and of his willingness to work on the other. The capacity to work is seen as a problem of fatigue and training; hence it involves the study of questions of optimum working-hours, of the effect of rest-pauses, and of physical conditions of work; and questions of recruitment, selection and training. Capacity to work, however, would not appear to be the key variable; for capacity alone does not ensure efficient production; it needs to be supported by willingness to make use of one's capacity. Viewed in this light the problem becomes one of motivation and incentives. For willingness to work is not a constant - it fluctuates; it depends on the balance between inducements and sacrifices. In the study of inducements attention must be paid to questions of wages and financial incentives, but non-financial factors also need to be taken into account; questions of promotion, of job-security and job-satisfaction need to be studied. The disincentives also must be considered, such as effort, unpleasantness of work, monotony, and loss of freedom. The focus on problems of 'human efficiency' is a focus on the individual worker and his adaptation to work and to the work-group. This, however, is only one approach to problems of industrial relations.

Another approach considers that co-operation is the central factor that needs to be studied.

Co-operation in an industrial enterprise may be said to fulfil two main functions; that of the production of goods and services and that of the provision of incomes from the sale of these goods and services. The production advantages gained from co-operation need not be elaborated in detail here. They are described in many other contexts. The arguments briefly are these: co-operation makes possible the optimum use of resources; it enables a firm to take advantage of the division of labour, of specialisation and of large-scale economies; its main function is to enable people to produce more than they would produce individually, and as a result, to earn larger incomes than they would earn if they worked on their own. Thus it makes possible the production of a bigger national income which in turn means that more goods are available for consumption.

National income statistics show that the national income of Great Britain has risen steadily since the industrial revolution. All sections of the community have shared in this increase, and the standard of living has steadily improved. Some writers claim that statistical evidence indicates that labour's (proportionate) share in the national income has remained constant (1).

This means that each increase in the national income has been shared between labour and other income groups in fairly fixed proportions. Such proportions, however, are not sacrosanct, and they may be changing.

In theory, the gains from co-operation are shared by all the members of a co-operative enterprise. In practice, however, there is no guarantee that the gains from co-operation accrue to all; nor that they all share equally in the gains. The benefit that each individual derives from co-operation depends on the division of the total income between the members of the organisation. The question as to how the total income of an organisation should be divided among its members is an ethical one, but the solution to the problem of the division of shares may not depend on ethics. There are no accepted rules with regard to their division. Sharing out the income of an organisation appears to be largely a question of power; it is a question of bargaining, of a type of warfare where each side tries to improve its position vis-a-vis the other. If one side is much more powerful than the other, then the latter may benefit very little from co-operation. This, in turn, may give rise to a struggle to alter the situation. Thus we have here a problem area from which much conflict can spring.

Co-operation cannot proceed without some friction or conflict. And conflict is stressed by many writers as the basic problem of industrial relations, on which we should centre our attention. Concurrently, the achievement of industrial peace and harmony is often held out as a goal, as the ideal state of affairs which we must strive to reach. This idealistic goal is attacked as unrealistic by some who consider that conflict is necessary for progress and that the best that can be accomplished in a complex society is to reduce friction to an 'area of tolerated conflict' (Moore, 1951, p356). They argue that there will always be hostility side by side with mutuality, a kind of 'antagonistic co-operation' (Miller and Form, 1951, p468). The aim is to contain conflict.

If we consider industrial relations as a kind of warfare, of antagonistic co-operation, then,

'the study of industrial relations as a day-to-day problem is an examination of the tactics used by both sides to improve their situation'.

(Stagner, 1956, p291). It is a study of management's attempts to control and manipulate labour, of its development of specific managerial techniques to control and raise labour efficiency, of worker resistance to managerial control, and of trade union attempts to obtain improvements for labour by collective bargaining or other trials of strength.

III

The problem of containing industrial conflict

11

(and also of containing the demands made by both sides) is a problem not merely for the parties concerned but for the society to which they belong.

Industrial conflict may affect persons not directly involved in the disputes; it may affect other workers, bystanders and consumers. For instance, a strike by 55 electricians at a key component factory of the British Motor Corporation in 1960 resulted in the laying-off of 24,000 employees, and halted car production at the Austin works at Longbridge (2). According to the Ministry of Labour Gazette (June 1962, p1), 99,000 workers were laid off in Britain in 1961 through disputes in which they took no part but which happened to take place at their factories. Such repercussions cannot be ignored. They raise questions of public policy, such as: Within what limits may conflict occur? When should the government intervene? What legislation is required to contain industrial conflict? What measures, if any, should be adopted to limit strikes? What measures, if any, should be adopted to limit wage demands? What sort of wage-policy is required? These questions illustrate the need to study the institutional framework of our industrial relations and its adequacy. They also lead to an examination of problems of economic policy, particularly with regard to inflation and wages.

Research, however, cannot answer questions of policy. Answers to these questions depend, as Moore (1951, p356) pointed out, on the ideals and norms of the society in which we live. They depend on our traditions and on the laws which embody our values. They are shaped by such ideals as that of personal freedom, the belief in the right to strike, in the right to bargain for wages, and the right to choose one's own job - beliefs which are embodied in our institutions and legislation. A knowledge of the institutional and economic framework within which industrial co-operation and conflict take place is therefore essential for understanding the problems of industrial relations, and many writers in the field have focused their main attention on these aspects.

The institutional framework of a society may be described as the system of formal and informal controls by which order is maintained in the society. In the context of this discussion, it is the system of controls which regulates industrial relations. Institutional controls may be formal or informal; they range from legal enactments, enforceable in courts of law, to verbal reproofs.

Problems in the Field of Industrial Relations

The rules of conduct which form the institutional structure of a particular society determine the rights of the various interest-groups; for instance, in industrial society, the rights of management and workers. The development of an institutional framework for industrial relations implies the development of adequate rules of conduct by the state or by the parties concerned.

Conflict tends to arise where the institutional system is inadequate in defining the rights of the different groups or where these groups do not accept the existing institutional system. It arises where power-relations are unstable or changing. This starting-point thus also leads us to a study of power-groups, of organisations such as trade unions and employers' associations, and to the study of conflict and conflict-resolution.

IV

The emphasis given to the study of co-operation, on the one hand, and of conflict, on the other, must not be taken to imply that these are distinct phenomena. Co-operation and conflict represent different aspects of the same problem, for any industrial undertaking involving more than one person represents a co-operative enterprise, but the effectiveness of co-operation in the enterprise depends on the amount, quality and degree of conflict within it. It depends on how well or badly management and workers get on together and on how much hostility exists between them.

Usually a considerable amount of friction arises in the process of co-operation, but the amount varies in different plants. In some plants conflicts resulting in strikes are frequent, in others they are rare. For example, at Briggs' motor bodies factory a Court of Inquiry (3) reported that 234 strikes had taken place in the eighteen months period from August 1955 to March 1957; at Vauxhall's there had been none.

The causes of industrial conflicts are highly complex. There is no one single cause. The importance of different causative factors, however, varies.

Important elements in the situation are interests and goals which cannot be reconciled, for one person's achievement of his objective may make it impossible for someone else to reach his goal. For instance, if Mr Brown is promoted to works manager, this may thwart Mr Smith's ambitions for

Problems in the Field of Industrial Relations

that post. Analysing this problem, Kornhauser (1954, p62) argued:

> 'Industrial conflict is human conflict. At its core are people with certain interests and motives opposing other people with divergent interests and motives. The opposition, the warfare - 'hot' or 'cold' - stems from conflicting desires, incompatible objectives, goal values that are not shared by the two groups. Each perceives the achievement of its goals as interfered with by the efforts of the other. The understanding of these opposed 'goal strivings' is the central problem in this field ....A search for the roots of industrial conflict ..... calls for an inquiry into the wants and frustrations of 20th century "industrial man". What are the directions and dimensions of working people's desires, and to what extent do they feel that their needs are being satisfied?'

This line of thought points up the need to study motivation. It shows how the school of thought that studies industrial conflict converges with the school of thought that studies human efficiency; both consider the problem of motivation a basic one that needs to be studied. Some of the fundamental questions that need to be answered are: What are the motives, goals and attitudes of management? What are the motives, goals and attitudes of employees? Which of these provide a basis for co-operation and which are likely to cause conflict?

Most writers in this field are agreed that management and workers have both common and divergent motives and goals. Common goals, however, do not of necessity mean that there are no clashes of interest, nor do divergent goals necessarily mean conflict. What matters for co-operation is whether the goals are complementary or competitive, whether they are compatible or incompatible, whether they can be shared or not. Thus, common goals can have completely different effects on industrial relations in different situations. In some cases they may unite people; in others they may divide them. Some common ground is essential; without some common interest there can be neither conflict nor co-operation, for there is nothing to fight about or to work for (4).

A community of interests exists where participants in co-operation have a common goal

14

which can be shared or where they pursue complementary goals.

An example of a common goal which helps co-operation is that of survival. In war-time where survival becomes the chief objective, most people go all out in their productive effort. In a period of depression when a firm may be threatened with bankruptcy, management and workers may sink their disputes in a concerted effort to save the firm. For example, during a recession in the British hosiery industry, workers agreed to a cut in wage rates to enable the industry to meet a difficult trading position. Thus some people hold that the fear of loss is more uniting than the hope of profits. Chester Barnard (1949, p16) for instance, argued:

> 'Fear of loss, not profit, dominates the business complex....As a practical force affecting personal relations in all kinds of employment, industrial or otherwise, I should think effort to prevent loss is many times as important as the effort to secure profit. If this is true, it is exceedingly important to recognise it, because it is easily demonstrated that all interests coincide on the question of losses. Men cannot be paid, cannot even be employed, if outgo exceeds income'.

And Katz (1954,p87) expressed a similar view when he wrote:

> 'The area of co-operation is basically on the side of production at a sufficient level for the company to remain in business and pay wages'.

Examples of complementary goals which can help co-operation are the employer's desire to secure a dependable product market and the employee's desire to secure a steady job.

Clashes of interest arise when managers and workers compete for the same goal and when the chances for achieving this goal are limited. They also arise when managers and workers strive for different goals which conflict rather than complement each other. An example of a goal which it is difficult for all to achieve at once is that of higher incomes; and competition for larger shares in the income of a co-operative enterprise often leads to bitter and protracted struggles which hamper effective co-operation. This clash is considered by Katz (1954, p86) to be the root of industrial conflict. He reported:

'Industrial conflict is basically a struggle between two organised groups which are competing for their share of a joint product'. And he continued (p87) 'The major conflict (between management and workers) develops ...on the side of the distribution of rewards.....It is possible that increasing co-operaton on the production side may open the way for more conflict on the side of the distribution of rewards. The percentage of the return to the owners and workers is more flexible the greater the margin of profit and hence subject to more argument and more struggle'.

A similar view was expressed by Moore (1951, p399):

'the like interests of management and labour may be incompatible because the means for satisfying these interests are scarce. Thus, managers and labourers alike may be intensely interested in increasing their incomes, but since money is not inexhaustible this may become a point of conflict. In this sense the interests of management and labour may be "basically the same" and yet the relations between the two groups be anything but harmonious'.

Co-operation must always involve this problem of the distribution of rewards, of the division of the income of the organisation. But at times, and in certain situations, participants may acquiesce and accept the share allotted to them; at other times, and in other situations, they may attack their share as unfair and press for higher returns with resulting conflict over the desire for 'more'. Thus, the post-war period in Britain has witnessed continuous conflict over the division of shares; continuous demands for revisions of wage rates followed by concessions.

Another example of a common goal which cannot be shared is power. Participants in an organisation often compete for power. By combining in trade unions, workers increase their powers of bargaining; through their collective strength they are able to challenge management power and infringe upon management prerogatives. Trade union authority competes with management authority for worker loyalty. Power is important in the struggle over the distribution of rewards for work. Thus the goals of power and income are closely connected, for power means wealth and, conversely, wealth means power.

As has been pointed out, conflicts of interest also arise where managers and workers strive for divergent goals which conflict rather than complement each other. For example, workers may strive for certain satisfactions in work such as craftsmanship or status, while management may strive for technical efficiency which involves standardisation and mass production, with the consequent creation of unskilled jobs. Workers may strive for recognition, and participation, while mnagement wishes to preserve its power and authority. Workers want secure employment while management may want a flexible work-force to adjust to fluctuating markets.

From the foregoing arguments two general propositions may be formulated:

1. Co-operation between management and workers is facilitated if both sides seek the same goal and if this goal can be shared. It is made easier if both sides seek complementary rather than divergent goals.
2. Co-operation is handicapped if management and workers seek the same goal and if this goal cannot be shared. It is also made difficult if conflicting goals are considered as important (5).

Stagner very aptly points out that 'a bigger income to be shared' is a goal that can be sought by co-operative techniques; for instance, if both sides strive for higher productivity. But a 'bigger share of present income' cannot usually be achieved by co-operation; it can usually only be won by a tug-of-war. A further proposition may be added:

3. That an increase in the number of common goals which can be shared and a decrease in the number of conflicting goals will lead to better co-operation.

The limitations of such a hypothesis however, must be realised. To be useful, the statement needs to be translated into a principle for action. As it stands it is too general and too abstract a statement to be a guide to action.

Problems in the Field of Industrial Relations

Conflicts of interests may be questions of fact or belief. This distinction is highly important for industrial relations, for what matters for co-operation are the opinions and beliefs of the people involved and not the facts which they may ignore. It is perceived interests rather than actual interests which determine whether the parties adopt co-operative or antagonostic attitudes. One may say that it is often not the facts, but the attitudes of the parties to the facts, which are important. For this reason Miller and Form (1951, p468) argued:

'When two parties fail to build good relations, it is not because of irreconcilable interests so much as (because of) the presence of irreconcilable attitudes'.

And the editors of Industrial Conflict wrote (p145):

'The reality of opposed interests as seen by the parties is, of course, the decisive fact. And the perceived relationship obviously depends not only on the "economic facts of life" but also on the social interpretations current among the people involved. It is possible that, at least for limited periods of time, workers and managers may falsely believe that they have conflicting interests, when, in fact, no objective basis for such beliefs exists. Conversely, they may accept a doctrine of complete harmony even though genuine grounds for conflict are present'.

In Britain, an example of the clash between perceived and actual interests is represented by the clash between wage demands (the perceived interest) and wage restraint to combat rising prices (the real interest in a period of inflation). As pointed out in the Fourth Report of the Council on Prices, Productivity and Incomes (July, 1961, pp14-15):

'The amount of goods and services available to us has been rising, taking one year with another, at the rate of about 6d. in the £ each year; but year by year we have helped ourselves to more money income at the rate of 1s. 4d in the £: and prices have had to rise to take up the excess 10d. If we had not grasped at the illusory 10d, the genuine gain would have been more than 6d'.

The authors of the report further claim (p29) that oppositon to a national incomes policy

'does not stem from real self-interest. The sources of opposition are, rather, a strong attachment to principles learned the hard way in a world very different from the one we live in; failure to realise that we should gain if we were able to avoid inflation; and the fear that self-discipline will only leave the way open to others. At the heart of the problem of inflation under full employment is a frame of mind'.

In other words, people cling to perceived interests and this impedes progress in dealing with the problem of inflation. What is required is a change in outlook. It follows that people need to be better informed in order to be able to judge things more adequately - they need to see the relation between beliefs and facts. It is here that the different disciplines that have studied industrial relations may have to meet and examine how their contributions can complement each other. It is not enough to say that people's perceptions determine their actions, nor that the situations created by their actions are the result of a frame of mind; we need to know also how perceptions can be changed and brought into line with economic realities. In my view, industrial relations, specialists may find it worth their while to consider this, too, as a basic problem.

VI

It has been shown that the field of industrial relations covers a wide range of human behaviour. Different schools of thought have approached it from different angles, and have stressed as basic problems for study such elements as human efficiency, co-operation and conflict, and the wider repercussions on society and public policy. From different starting-points they have often arrived at similar statements of problems that arise, such as the need to study motivation, the need to study tactics of the power struggle between management and labour, and the importance of understanding the

19

institutional and economic background and of examining questions of public policy.

Many different branches of the social sciences have staked a claim in these problem areas, including such diverse disciplines as economics, psychology, sociology and anthropology. Each separate discipline has approached the subject with its own emphasis and bias, using its specific tools, methods and jargon. In my view this has resulted in poor communication across boundaries and has often hidden considerable overlaps in the problems studied.

Yet, as I have shown, the problems in this area are interconnected and held together by a particular logic. The field of industrial relations has not so far been considered a discipline in its own right. However, the need to bring together accumulated and developing knowledge in it can hardly be disputed.

NOTES

1. Keynes, for instance, wrote in 1939 that 'the stability of the proportion of the national dividend accruing to labour is one of the most surprising, yet best-established, facts in the whole range of economic statistics, both for Great Britain and for the United States'. See Keynes, Economic Journal, 1939, 'Relative Movement of Real Wages and Output', pp 78-9. Evidence presented in the Fourth Report of the Council of Prices, Productivity and Incomes (HMSO, London, July 1961) shows that in Britain during the period 1950 to 1960 'from one year to another pay and profits have very generally gone up together, and in much the same proportion. In the United Kingdom, for example, the total wages and salaries paid out by companies was very nearly doubled in only nine years, from 1950 to 1959, but meanwhile those companies' gross profits likewise very nearly doubled. This constancy of proportions is the general rule .... other western countries have experienced it too'. (p 16).
2. See the report in the Times, 2 February, 1960.
3. See Report of a Court of Inquiry into the Causes and Circumstances of a Dispute at Briggs Motor Bodies Limited, Dagenham, existing between the Ford Motor Company Limited and Members of the Trade Unions represented on the Trade Union Side of the Ford National Joint Negotiating Committee, Cmnd. 131, 1957, p.11, paragraph 32.
4. Compare Moore (1951, p 399) 'In a complete absence of like interest there can be no conflict;

20

there is nothing to fight about'. And F J Roethlisberger, Management and Morale, 1949 edition, p 119: people 'have been brought up to share certain common values, to have common hopes, faiths and standards of living ....Without some such common feelings and sentiments, effective co-operation is impossible'.
5.   Compare Stagner, (1956, p 472).

REFERENCES

Chester I Barnard, Organisation and Management, Harvard University Press, 1949
A Gouldner, Patterns of Industrial Bureaucracy, Routledge and Kegan Paul, London, 1955
Daniel Katz in Industrial Conflict (ed A Kornhauser, see below)
A Kornhauser, R Dubin and A M Ross (eds), Industrial Conflict, McGraw-Hill Book Co., New York, 1954
D C Miller and W H Form, Industrial Sociology, Harper Brs., New York, 1951
Wilbert E Moore, Industrial Relations and the Social Order, Macmillen, New York, revised edition 1951
R Stagner, Psychology of Industrial Conflict, John Wiley and Sons, New York, 1956

3 Why so much Fuss about Industrial Relations?

Adapted from paper first published in Industrial Relations Journal, Vol. 8, No. 4, Winter 1977/1978.

This paper which deals with matters of concern in industrial relations was written in response to an invitation to give the Sixth Shirley Lerner Memorial Lecture at the University of Manchester in 1977. The subject is one to which Shirley Lerner herself made some major contributions in the 1950s and 1960s and a scrutiny of her publications shows that they provide insights into contemporary problems of industrial relations (even in the early 1980's) in spite of changes which have taken place in the intervening period in the British economic and industrial relations scene. Shirley Lerner, for instance, drew attention to issues such as the right of not belonging to a trade union, or only to a trade union of your own choice; and the question of the wisdom of closed shop legislation and of inflexible rules of trade union membership. She examined problems of wage drift and inflation and of the lack of a close relationship between increased earnings and productivity which are still with us (1).

The lecture provided me with an opportunity to examine where we stand as regards the state and status of the subject of industrial relations. Why do people make a fuss about them? It would appear that much of it is based on images of industrial relations which may or may not be borne out by facts. The picture which is often projected is one which depicts industrial relations as a kind of British disease. Our industrial relations are terrible, we are told, there is something drastically wrong with them; they are at the root of the country's problems. Such critical attitudes are frequently associated with a tendency to make industrial relations a scapegoat for the country's problems and to blame trade unions and strikes for our industrial troubles. However, sweeping generalisations are not helpful for understanding the very complex problems of industrial relations. In order to understand them, we must be more specific and more cautious.

An important point to stress in this context is that the term industrial relations is used as a general label for a mixed set of phenomena. Another is that the term is a misleading label, a misnomer. The application of the term does not cover only relations in industry and relations between individuals or groups of individuals. Logically it has to include the origins of the relations and the results and effects of the relations. Correcting the label we may define industrial relations briefly for the purpose of this paper as work relations and everything that affects work relations; that is, work where there is more than one party.

The relations we speak about are based on work and the division of labour because work provides goods and services and incomes; the wherewithal for living. The development of industrial relations involves the development of rules of work behaviour, formal or informal, and of institutions which try to formulate and regulate work behaviour and the shape of the wage-work bargain.

The study of industrial relations has been, and is, to a large extent, problem-based and problem-oriented. If one accepts this argument, progress in thinking about the problems depends on the formulation of the relevant questions to which answers are required rather than on the development of abstract theories. We need to understand the nature of the problems (and the subject matter) and we need to be realistic about the possibility of finding easy solutions; about the dangers of the search for panaceas for industrial relations troubles.

Why then are we concerned about industrial relations? It seems that we are concerned about industrial relations for quite disparate reasons. For instance, we may be concerned about work and the quality of working life, that is, the quality of the work environment and of the work itself; also about the effectiveness of work and about actions which hamper effectiveness such as restriction of output, absence, turnover and strikes. We may be concerned about the human relations at work and the frictions which arise; and about what we may consider to be undesirable organisational, institutional and economic effects which have resulted from certain industrial relations situations.

THE MAJOR AREAS OF CONCERN

If we look at the problems and anxieties we can divide them broadly into three major areas of concern:

1. The quality of industrial relations, that is of the human relationships, particularly at the place of work, and linked to this, the quality of work performance.
2. The adequacy of the rules and institutions of industrial relations.
3. The interrelations between the quality of industial relations and the working of the economy.

However, before looking at each of these in turn (a discussion in which the first area will be taken last) some thought needs to be given to the relationships between them.

Overall, we can say that industrial relations news is topical and given prominence in discussions because industrial relations are concerned with problems of interdependence; the interdependence between what happens at the place of work and what happens in the world at large. This means that the problems in the major areas of concern which I have just outlined are interrelated; there is constant interaction between them; and there are spill-over and ripple effects from one set of problems to another.

As an intellectual exercise in thinking about these interrelations, it can be useful to do some arcmchair doodling, spelling out consequential interactions, a kind of potential 'logic of events'. Two illustrations of this method of stimulating awareness of the interdependence and repercussion effects are presented next.

EXAMPLE 1 We are worried about the quality of human relations:

Whether the human relations are good or bad, they affect output, productivity, profitability and economic viability. If good, they may help to raise productivity and economic prosperity and may help to raise standards of living. If bad, they may find expression in conflict and may lead to restriction of output and through this, affect the economy adversely and hinder

24

improvements in the standard of living. Conversely, what happens to the economic variables affects the quality of human relations.

EXAMPLE 2 We are interested in the effect of the law on industrial relations:

If the law permits the formation of trade unions, and gives them the right to bargain and to call strikes, then trade unions can operate and recruit members and take collective action regarding work relations and conditions of employment, etc. This affects management action and management power. It also affects society, public policy, and the type of legislation which is introduced. The public in turn may demand protection against the consequences of employer and trade union power and against the effects of industrial action.

However, we must not get carried away too far by doodling enthusiasm. We may have to check whether the postulated relationships are real or imaginary.

CONCERN ABOUT THE ADEQUACY OF THE RULES AND INSTITUTIONS OF INDUSTRIAL RELATIONS

Turning to the three separate areas of concern (taking the second one first) The question of the adequacy of the rules and institutions of industrial relations leads into the problem area which has perhaps received the greatest public (as well as industrial relations specialist) attention in this country because it is closely linked to the question of possible reforms. Do we need more legislation or less? Do we need better rules, better institutions? A major illustration of the pre-occupation with the question of reform in Britain was the setting up of the Royal Commission on Trade Unions and Employers' Associations which produced the Donovan Report (1968). Another illustration is Allan Flanders' book (1965): 'Industrial Relations: What is wrong with the System?' that is, with the system of rules? The literature which has examined various aspects of this topic since the 60s is vast. New legislation has been passed (should one say experimented with?) and altered.
The controversy over questions of reform is

likely to continue in Britain. So will the controversy over better rules for industrial relations, over the role of the state and over the law in industrial relations, and over the conflict between the tradition of free collective bargaining and voluntary and statutory incomes policies.

CONCERN ABOUT THE INTERRELATION OF INDUSTRIAL RELATIONS AND THE WORKING OF THE ECONOMY

This brings us to the question of concern about the interrelation of industrial relations and the working of the economy. The continuing controversy as regards anti-inflation policies, pay restraints and the question of a more permanent incomes policy which has been going on for several decades is clearly important in this context. Inflation, I need hardly stress, has been one of the major economic problems in the western world in the post second world war period. Rising prices, the fall in the purchasing power of money and associated balance of payments problems have produced recurrent economic crises. So far we have managed to survive. But are not many of us worried about the future and about the effects on the economy if we cannot contain the rate of inflation?

In the fight against inflation we get clear examples of the importance of good industrial relations and of the interrelations between industrial relations and the working of the economy. For instance, if we look at the influence of economic factors on industrial relations, we can see that the rate of inflation affects the size of pay claims and the determination to pursue them; also it can have a detrimental effect on work contribution and thus industrial performance; it can generate bitter conflicts and can worsen the whole climate of industrial relations in the country; and, ironically, anti-inflation measures can have similar effects on industrial relations.

If we look at the effects of industrial relations on the economy, we can see that high pay settlements affect costs and prices, and feed the rate of inflation. Moreover, increased costs can make exports less competitive, can lead to balance of payments crises and affect exchange rates. Increased conflict over pay can affect economic profitability and may reduce or halt economic growth. Non co-operation in incomes policies can lead to the use of more drastic monetary and fiscal measures, and in turn, to an economic downturn and unemployment.

I would hold that the attitudes and expectations of the government, of employers, employees and individuals as consumers are very important variables in these interactions and will continue to influence the course of inflation. They will determine the outcome of pay negotiations, and in turn affect both our economy and our climate of industrial relations. In turn, again, the climate of industrial relations may affect the attainment of the economic goals of governments and of the population favourably or adversely.

CONCERN ABOUT THE QUALITY OF INDUSTRIAL RELATIONS

If we accept that attitudes and frames of mind, human relationships and the industrial relations climate are important for economic viability, it follows that the area for action, for improvement, cannot be confined solely to the most visible areas; for instance, to the conclusion of 'reasonable' pay-increase settlements in an incomes policy. What we must look at is the question of improvements in the quality of human relations at plant level. This means far more attention may have to be given to what happens in the individual firm. In evaluating industrial relations problems in the context of individual organisations, we need to look (among other things) at available information about the frequency and severity of frictions and of other symptoms of malaise; at the explanations and diagnoses which have been put forward and at suggestions for remedial action.

As mentioned earlier, industrial relations are often perceived as suffering from a kind of cancer which threatens the economy and the country: the 'British' disease. From this perspective, the state of our industrial relations is seen as a 'condition with symptoms' - a term used by Walker (1961, p57) in his discussion of morale. The symptoms of low morale he argued, were often considered to be such phenomena as high absenteeism, high labour turnover, low productivity. The parallel adjective for describing the condition of industrial relations is bad or poor. Thus, the anxiety about the state of industrial relations relates to the perceived poor quality of human relations which exists in certain situations.

What questions are raised by introducing the concept of the quality of industrial relations? First of all we must recognise that we are not dealing here with an either/or state of affairs but with one of variable qualities covering a potential range from very good to very bad. We must also be more specific as regards the aspect of industrial relations which we are looking at and the type of quality we are interested in. For instance, we may want to distinguish qualities of behaviour which range from relatively democratic to relatively autocratic; or from relatively co-operative to relatively hostile.

In thinking about assessing differences in the quality of industrial relations, we are faced with further questions; for instance, in the light of the fact that industrial relations are so multi-dimensional, are we in a position to measure the differences? If we make the attempt, what criteria should we apply? Which symptoms of bad relations should we look at: grumbling, absenteeism, restriction of output, labour turnover or strikes?

Having chosen a symptom for study, we may want to look at such questions as: How 'typical' is the absenteeism of an individual employee of the behaviour of the whole work-force? How 'typical' is inapt handling of employees by a manager of all managers? How 'typical' is the strike record in one plant of all plants? Evidence relating to these questions tends to indicate that behaviour patterns are distributed unevenly.

Frequency distributions of absence from work, for instance, have revealed very skew distributions in which far more individuals have low records than high records. Thus, my enquiry in a West of Scotland engineering company revealed that 70 per cent of all the working days lost through absence in the year ending 31st May 1969 were lost by the quarter of the men with the highest absence days records; and also that 58 per cent of the total absence spells were incurred by the quarter of the men with the highest spells records. Again, in our six-year enquiry (covering 1969 to 1974) the absence records of three-quarters of the men lay between 0 and 28 spells in six years (that is an average record of 4 absence spells or less per year). This can be considered a reasonable record. Ten per cent had as low a record as 5 absence spells or less in six years. By contrast - the top ten per cent of the men in the frequency distribution - the critical group requiring remedial attention - had each incurred 40 or more absence spells in six years (2). Poor attendance, as shown in other absence studies, is apparently a problem which is mainly found among small sections of the work-force.

Why so much Fuss about Industrial Relations

What about strikes? Is the British record as bad as often made out? An article in the Employment Gazette (1976, pp1219ff) reported that on average, during any one year of the period 1971 to 1973, 98 per cent of manufacturing plants in Britain were free of strikes, and 81 per cent of the employees in the manufacturing industry worked in plants where no strikes occurred. Strikes, thus, are also a problem of minority rather than majority behaviour.

Strike statistics indicate that it is quite wrong to assume that the whole British population is strike-prone. This does not, however, mean that concern abut strikes is misplaced and that there are no grounds for anxiety. It would seem that concern about the effects of strikes on the economy and its citizens can be justified when industrial action takes place in strategic industries and occupations. For example, the 1974 miners' strike had wide-ranging effects which were quite traumatic. Not only did it affect the economy and ordinary people but it led to a change of government. In addition, uncertainty about impending strikes and fear of the potential effects of what might happen if they do take place can be a source of great anxiety.

How important then is minority behaviour in the industrial relations sphere? It would seem that minorities can wield considerable power and can further or hamper industrial performance. Furthermore, in using their power, small numbers of employees can cause considerable disruption which can spread to the whole factory or industry and which can affect other factories and industries. It would seem that there exists an 'a-symmetry' between the effect of minority and majority behaviour in the sense that the actions of a minority can produce serious economic effects which cannot be offset by the work contribution of the majority; in other words, a small number of employees may have the power to undermine the achievements of the rest of the workforce because of our economic interdependence. They can produce effects which bear no relation to their number. For instance, one grumbler can sometimes sow seeds of discontent which it may take months of patient effort to alleviate or cure.

THE QUESTION OF DIAGNOSIS

These arguments raise some interesting questions: Which kind of anxieties are most justified? Is the fuss that is being made about industrial relations necessarily about the 'right' issues? How do we define the 'right', most important, issues? Are they the ones that do the greatest damage to the economy? or the ones where there is the greatest scope for remedial action and where yet little action is taken?

Finding the 'right' issues brings us to the problems of diagnosis. For instance, what causes strikes? This seems to be a topic on which the literature both causes confusion and is itself confused. From an analytical point of view, this confusion seems to stem from, what one might call, an umbrella use of the word cause whereby it is made to cover too many different meanings. For one thing, we should not equate the causes of conflict with the causes of strikes because more factors give rise to conflict than to strikes. What we need to identify are the specific factors which lead to specific strikes.

Two initial questions suggest themselves. What are strikes about? and why do they take place? The first question helps us to identify what the disagreement was about; the second why no agreement has been reached. With these questions in mind, examine the following quotation: 'Most disputes (in 1966 to 1974) were about pay, accounting for four-fifths of working days lost. But only just half the number of stoppages were caused by disputes over pay'. Does it make the same distinction as the two questions? At first glance I thought it did; but in reality I was taken in! The juxtaposition was meant to be between two dimensions of strikes, namely days lost and number of stoppages (3).

Yet the distinction between the two questions is an important one, and one on which my division of industrial relations into three areas of concern can throw some light. For strikes may be about a disagreement in one of the three areas and may be brought about by factors in one of the other areas. Moreover, there may be a whole series of factors which combine and culminate in a strike. Further questions need to be considered, for instance, what kind of factors are likely to have led to the non-agreement in this case? Also, what kind of strike was this? Was it official or unofficial?

One cannot stress enough the importance of the existence of different types of strike, so well put by Ross and Hartman (1960, p9), when they stated that it is 'most unlikely that a strike of eighty days could have the same causes and consequences as a strike of two days'. In this context, official national strikes about unconceded pay-increase demands have provided some of the clearest situations for identifying the major causal factors. For, while the strikes were about the size of pay-increases, they were often sparked off by government anti-inflation policies and by attempts by employers to stand firm, which led to breakdowns in negotiations.

Another source of confusion stems from the psychological literature which does not ask why collective action takes place but why individual workers are motivated to go on strike, and this is a different issue.

These considerations indicate that there is a need in discussions of industrial relations problems to watch out for, and identify, wrong diagnoses and misplaced analogies, missing questions and semantic confusion.

CONCLUDING COMMENT

To conclude, let me return to the question of why there is so much fuss about industrial relations. I have argued in this paper that there are three major anxieties: we are concerned about defects in the quality of work relations and work performance; about inadequacies in the rules and institutions of industrial relations; and about the adverse effects of poor industrial relations on the working of the economy. Although, on the face of it, these problems would appear to be very disparate, they are closely interrelated and must be seen in the wider perspective of continuous interactions. From the point of view of the nation as a whole, the interactions between the working of the economy and the climate of industrial relations would appear to be the most important. What we need to learn as citizens therefore is to recognise and keep in mind this wider perspective.

It is also very important to investigate in more detail the implications of these arguments for our understanding of industrial relations and for policy and decision-making. In this context it is pertinent to stress that there is apparently often an 'a-symmetry' in industrial relations phenomena. For instance, the actions of a particular person or group, or the impact of a particular rule, law or policy, if ill-advised or hostile, can have an immediate detrimental effect on the climate of industrial relations which may last for a long time, whereas the building up of good industrial relations depends on continuous effort and goodwill. The

31

reactions to the Industrial Relations Act of 1971 illustrated this point.

In general, a better understanding of economic realities by all concerned would seem particularly important for good industrial relations.

As regards the objective of improving industrial relations I would hold that (in spite of external constraints) the scope for positive action is probably greatest at the level of the firm. Progress in this area may tend to be slow but we should not forget or belittle the tremendous progress which has been made during the last hundred and fifty years. One major focus of attention at the present time is the problem which is often referred to as 'the humanisation of work'. In this context what is often required is greater sensitivity in employer-employee relationships; an ability to appreciate another person's point of view and to respect the other person as an individual in his or her own right. Management and trade union training could be helpful in this. Also important is the question of direct employee involvement in making decisions which affect them in their work, a need which has been stressed by industrial psychologists for several decades.

On the question of the work itself what can be useful is an examination of the specific features of jobs which are suspected of causing stress, to see whether the elements which cause it can be identified and altered or eliminated. For instance, one could carry out strain assessments, similar to the ones which were pioneered by Baldamus (1951, pp65-69) in the early 1950s. Then one could examine whether more traction could be introduced, that is, elements which make it easier to keep going on a repetitive task. Non-financial 'dissatisfaction compensations' (Baldamus pp36-41) in the work situation are also worth further study; among them that of 'leisure at work'; the chance to relax and talk to others, because often perhaps only work-relations can be 'humanised' and not the work itself.

NOTES

1. See S Lerner. The TUC Jurisdictional Dispute Settlement, 1924-57, (The Manchester School, September 1958), and Workshop Bargaining, Wage Drift and Productivity in the British Engineering Industry (The Manchester School, January 1962). In her 1958 article, Shirley Lerner concluded that 'Many workers

still believe in the principle of freedom of choice and are unwilling to have their exercise of this right sacrificed to the ideal of orderly inter-union relations; as a result, some members become non-unionists or apathetic while others revolt against their union. The prevalence of these problems which harm the trade union movement raises the question whether it is possible to establish orderly inter-union relations without violating the rights of members to join the union of their choice. If not, it is still arguable that the trade union movement has gone too far in pursuit of the goal of orderly inter-union relations, and that more freedom of competition between unions would restrain bureaucracy and act as a healthy stimulus to recruitment'.

2. This subject is discussed in more detail (and with references) in Chapter 6.

3. The quotation was taken from Employment News 30, Department of Employment, HMSO, London, March 1976, p.71. In both cases the wording in the quotation referred to the formal issue, as a cross-check with the Employment Gazette revealed. (See 'The incidence of industrial stoppages in the United Kingdom', p115, February 1976).

REFERENCES

W Baldamus, Incentives and Work Analysis, Monograph A1, University of Birmingham Studies in Economics and Society, 1951

Donovan Report see Royal Commission

Employment Gazette: Distribution and concentration of industrial stoppages in Great Britain, November 1976

A Flanders, Industrial Relations: What is wrong with the System? Faber and Faber Ltd. in association with the Institute of Personnel Management, London, 1965

A M Ross and P T Hartman, Changing Patterns of Industrial Conflict, Wiley, New York, 1960

Royal Commission on Trade Unions and Employers' Associations: Cmnd 3623, HMSO, London, 1968

Nigel Walker, Morale in the Civil Service; a study of the desk worker, Edinburgh University Publications, Edinburgh, 1961

4   Reflections on the Incidence of Strikes

Written for private circulation, January 1982.

The purpose of this paper is to look more closely at questions relating to the incidence of strikes (raised briefly in Chapter 3). To do so is important because strikes do not only affect labour productivity and the industrial relations climate within a firm but they can also influence and be influenced by inflation and anti-inflation policies, all of them topics which fall within the scope of this book.

The content is based on many years of reflection, the preparation of material for lectures and the analysis of ongoing events. In trying to make students understand the difficulties which are encountered in studying strikes I set certain questions for group discussions and found that each of these raised new questions and perspectives; questions which one must keep in mind when thinking and reading about the problem. The paper thus is not a literature survey but reflects my own view as to the points which are important in analysing strikes.

ASCERTAINING THE CAUSES OF STRIKES

It is hardly ever possible to get first-hand impartial evidence from direct on the spot observation of the whole course of a strike. The main providers of information are the news media, government collectors of statistics and, at times, enquiries by conciliators, mediators, arbitrators or courts of inquiry who obtain as much information as they can for their tasks from the participants.

The mass media represent the most immediate providers of information when a strike is imminent or occurs and we have to base our initial (and often subsequent) judgements on the information which they provide. This can lead to over-reaction and one-sided judgements. Thus, an important psychological effect of the threat of an impending strike can be anxiety, or even fear, about its potential impact, about what it will do to our economy and our everyday life. This in turn can lead to the purchase of industrial peace by hasty concessions - and one price which we have often paid for this in the post-war period has been the acceptance of inflationary pay demands. Thus, the strikes themselves, the publicity given to them and the public discussion that they arouse, affect the attitudes to, and perceptions of, strikes and add to the problems of studying them.

As a starting point, when a strike breaks out, an analyst must try to find answers to two questions, namely what the strike is about and why it is taking place. The first question tries to identify the bones of contention and the second the reasons for not reaching agreement without recourse to a strike. However the label 'causes' is frequently applied to both issues.

The literature on strikes often makes a distinction between two categories of causes. The first category is referred to as overt, immediate or ostensible causes, i.e. the formal issue or issues; the substance of what the trade unions or employees say they are striking about. It usually takes the form of a demand or demands addressed to the management. This is a category referred to by Stagner as necessary (but not sufficient) for the occurrence of a strike (1).

The formal and verbalised demands or issues provide an answer to the question of what the strike is about but not to the question of why it occurs. What needs to be explained is why the dispute was not settled by collective bargaining or by the use of normal disputes procedures. Hence the breakdown in disputes settlement must be attributed to something other than the formal issue. Nevertheless official statistics of strikes have tended to use the label 'causes' or 'principal causes' of strikes when providing information relating to the formal issues in the dispute. To avoid confusion it would appear preferable to use the label 'formal issues'.

The second category is referred to in the literature as the underlying, hidden, psychological causes of strikes. Knowles for instance, suggested in 1952 that strikes 'are to a large extent an expression of the unconscious of the labour movement. Their causes are not always clear even to the strikers themselves'. Knowles suggested that underlying causes may be grouped under three general headings: 'bad social conditions, fatigue and frustration in industrial work and the inferiority of the workers position' (Knowles, 1952 Chapter 4, pp212ff).

One implication of references to hidden psychological causes is that these forces are not necessarily verbalised; their existence and operation is inferred and put forward as an interpretation of the occurrence of strikes, often without supporting evidence. Another snag is that the statements about them are often vague and too generalised to be useful. They pinpoint potential sources of conflict but do not explain why hidden frustrations should lead to a strike rather than to other forms of unrest and discontent. Thus to avoid confusion it is important to make a distinction between the causes of conflict and the causes of strikes. One must find out why a particular conflict has taken the form of a strike.

With regard to conflict as a potential source of strikes two questions appear important, namely how often a conflict over a particular issue culminates in a strike and why it does so. As regards the question of how often, we can state quite briefly: only in a minority of cases. The majority of disagreements and conflicts between management and employees are settled by informal discussion or formal disputes procedures. It is mainly when these channels fail - or are disregarded or perceived to have failed - that we get recourse to a strike.

The question as to why some conflicts take the form of a strike is a complicated one. It would seem, however, that some precipitating force is required such as a strike call from a union or from an unofficial leader, or a strong outburst of emotion. In this context it must be remembered that strikes are not necessarily an expression of the discontents of individual employees. Some employees may be in favour of a strike or may support it out of solidarity; others may be reluctant strikers and may disapprove of the aims of the strike or of the use of the strike weapon. Thus, it is important to stress that the individual's reasons for joining a strike do not by themselves explain why the strike takes place. It may simply be that the striker has accepted union orders as part of the membership rules by which he must abide.

It is a curious point that the literature on

strikes seldom mentions the words goal or objective. Yet one can postulate that there must be some kind of aim, if only to voice a protest or highlight a grievance. Insofar as a strike is a protest against conditions or situations which the employer is unwilling to change one can argue that the main aim of a strike is change and that, broadly, two types of change are fought for by employees and their representatives:

> 1. To affect a change in the conditions of employment, ie to get a better bargain from management than is on offer.
> 2. To set a perceived wrong between the parties right, for example, in cases of what employees call victimisation.

However resistance to management proposals for change can also take the form of a strike. Thus the prevention of change can be a trade union aim as has been demonstrated in some of the printing and railway industry strikes.

The strike weapon may therefore be used both to affect a change and as a speedy response to changes proposed by management, in addition to putting pressure on management and making a show of determination and power. It may also be chosen to try to win public support.

The question of the bone of contention in a strike is closely allied to the question of what a strike is intended to achieve but not synonymous with it. However, in quite a number of cases, the settlement of formal issues represents the major aim of the strike.

We may conclude that a strike must be 'about something': an official demand for a change in the conditions of employment, a disagreement, a conflict of opinion, a grudge, a desire to lodge a protest. Where the bone of contention can be identified the label formal issue or issues would appear to be the most appropriate. However there seem to be some strikes where it may not be possible to identify what it is really about, or indeed whether there is or was a formal issue.

The important point to remember is that the identification of the formal issues or bones of contention does not by itself explain why there has been a decision to use the strike weapon. We need an answer to the question of why the dispute has not been settled by other means.

Reflections on the Incidence of Strikes

DIFFERENT TYPES OF STRIKES

In thinking about strike problems it is also important to make a distinction between different types of strikes. As Ross and Hartmann reported in 1960 (p9): 'It is most unlikely that a strike of 80 days could have the same causes and consequences as a strike of two days. To consider all strikes as homogeneous occurrences stands in the way of enlightenment'.

Strikes can be official or unofficial, long or short; they can involve thousands of employees or just a few; they can affect workers in particular organisations, occupations or industries or all unionised employees in a general strike. Strikes can originate at local or national level, within or outside the organisation (or organisations) which are affected. Occasionally they can represent political protests.

The difference between official and unofficial strikes is the one that has perhaps received most attention in Britain; partly because it was highlighted in the Donovan Report (1968) in which the Commission stated (para 4 and 5) that they had no hesitation in saying that 'the prevalence of unofficial strikes, and their tendency (outside coalmining) to increase, have such serious economic implications that measures to deal with them are urgently necessary'.

Briefly, an official strike may be described as a strike supported by the trade union (or unions) in accordance with union rules. In other words, it is a strike which is called or ratified by the trade union (usually by its national executive) according to the union's rules. The unofficial strike by contrast does not have official trade union support; it tends to flare up suddenly and is sometimes described as a 'spontaneous' strike. It is usually bound up with local issues, fears and discontent. The boundary line between the two types of strike, however, often becomes blurred.

The official strike which is used as a tool in collective bargaining represents in my view a particularly important category of strike. The threat of the trade union negotiators to call their workers out on strike is used to put pressure on management; to convey their determination to pursue the demands and their belief in the union's power. The threat, thus, represents a weapon in the struggle between organised labour and organised management; refusals to go to arbitration reinforce such a threat.

Reflections on the Incidence of Strikes

Sometimes, while negotiating, the threat of an intention to strike may be enough to achieve the union's goal or goals. Indeed, it may at times be more effective than a strike. On the other hand, in using the threat, the trade union must be prepared to implement it, should management stand firm. This means that in this sort of political warfare, the trade union leaders need to assess: Will it be worthwhile to use the strike weapon? Can we get a better offer? Have we sufficient power and member support to win? Have we enough funds? Are the conditions favourable or unfavourable for success?

Miscalculations can have serious consequences for the union members and the trade union and its officials. Two early examples of miscalculations of a union's ability to succeed, referred to by Ross (1961, p64), were connected with an under-estimate of management's ability to carry on production without the workforce. Thus in 1959 in an American oil refinery, management discovered that by the tenth month of a strike by 1250 employees, 300 supervisors on their own were achieving 75 per cent of normal output. The unions had to abandon the strike for fear of making the workers permanently redundant. An important factor in this outcome was automation. It was equally important in the outcome of a telephone strike in 1955 in which the ten-week stoppage by about 50,000 employees caused little in the way of noticeable disruption to the service because a high percentage of the telephones were dial-operated. The union had to give in because the cost of the strike pay was developing into a financial 'near disaster'.

The 1971 British post office workers'·strike for an improved pay offer contained some similar features. The hope that a short all-out strike would exert enough pressure to get a major concession was mistaken. The strike stopped postal services for 47 days but could not disrupt telephones. Thus, here too, automation reduced the impact of the strike. Another important factor was an under-estimate of the Government's determination to pursue its pay-increase de-escalation policy which aimed to reduce pay claims in the public sector.

In 1980, in the three months long British steel strike for an improved pay offer, the unions similarly seem to have miscalculated the ability of the employers to resist their pressures. With the worldwide recession in the steel industry there were apparently sufficient stocks of steel in hand to meet the reduced demand.

Reflections on the Incidence of Strikes

Similar to the trade unions, the employers have to assess their chances of success in resisting strike threats as well as weigh up the pros and cons of concessions to avoid the strike. They must ask themselves: Can we carry on production, and, if yes, how will output be affected? Have we enough stocks to meet important orders? Will we lose many customers? What are the likely short and long-term costs and effects of resisting as opposed to giving in? In this context, it seems, employers have many reasons for desiring a speedy settlement in a period of economic prosperity, and this puts unions in a strong position. During a recession, however, an employer may see no necessity to obtain a speedy settlement especially if he has large stocks and overcapacity as was shown in the long drawn-out British Steel strike of 1980 referred to above.

In Britain, the use of official strikes as a tool in collective bargaining has increased since 1968, and in particular its use to obtain larger-sized pay increases than are on offer. In these wage-round strikes, particularly in the national ones where collective bargaining negotiations have broken down, it should be recognised that the principal formal issue (but by no means the only bone of contention) can be and often is a straightforward one - a demand for a higher pay-increase than the employer or employers are willing to grant or are permitted to grant. Other formal demands may be linked to the pay dispute as additional or substitute benefits.

However the trade union pressure for large pay increases and the employers' refusals to concede them have to be interpreted in the wider perspective of the economic situation and of government policies. Pay increase demands are often linked to the cost of living and employers' concessions to their ability to pay and thus to inflation and economic circumstances. They are also affected by government economic policies, such as pay and price restraints and cash limits on expenditure. These can lead to attempts by employers (in both the public and private sectors) to stand firm and resist pay claims - hence to breakdowns in negotiations; also, at the end of periods of restraint, to trade union attempts to catch up again.

In this context the official wage-round strike, especially the national one, can be said to originate from factors without the firm or organisation and illustrates the interaction between the quality of industrial relations and the working of the economy. Thus, the incidence of official

40

strikes may be considered as a measure of the adequacy and effectiveness of collective bargaining and existing disputes machinery and of the appropriateness of particular economic policies.

THE CONCEPTS OF STRIKE-PRONENESS, CENTRES OF STRIKES, STRIKE CYCLES, STRIKE WAVES AND CONTAGION

The word causes is not the only one that presents semantic difficulties in discussions of strikes. The use of the word strike-proneness as a casual factor in strikes can also be a source of confusion. In 1969, Turner raised an interesting question when he published the book Is Britain really strike-prone? It made a good title for the book. However, he did not define the term; instead he used the words of 'Comparative Strike-Propensity' as a chapter heading. He argued that the frequency and incidence of strikes in Britain compared with other countries was no cause for grave anxiety.

However, if we are concerned with comparisons of strike activity, the use of the word strike-prone when we encounter it can be misleading. The notion of proneness implies that a particular kind of behaviour or condition occurs considerably more frequently than normal or than due to chance. It represents repetitive behaviour, a state of affairs which is manifest over a number of years not just one.

Another difficulty is the problem of defining who or what is strike-prone; whether proneness is a characteristic of the behaviour of particular types of workers, or of specific conditions associated with a location, such as particular firms, industries, geographical regions or countries.

Knowles, in his pioneering and scholarly book on strikes, applied the term strike-proneness to a measure which he developed for comparing strike activity in different regions and industries. It is clear that he had reservations about the choice of the word because he introduced it as follows:

'The tables which follow give an indication of what, for want of a better term, may be called the "strike-proneness" of the workers in each region relative to that of the workers in other regions or the country as a whole .... It must be strongly emphasised that the term "strike-proneness" is intended to be quite colourless. The "strike-proneness ratio" simply indicates the extent to which workers in one region have

41

been involved in strikes - regardless of why they have been so involved - as compared with workers in other regions; it is a measure which in itself carries no implications' (2).

However, in everyday life, the word is not seen as a neutral term. It has critical overtones, implying that strikes represent undesirable behaviour, a kind of malady which afflicts employee behaviour; an outlook which is difficult to reconcile with the concept of the right to strike.

In Knowles' formulation, the number of workers involved in strikes in particular periods, regions and industries provides the basis for comparison. In his tables for the period 1911 to June 1945 the highest 'strike-proneness ratio' was found among miners followed by textile, metal and transport workers. In his discussion he made the point that the inclusion of big strikes in the calculations of the ratio can give a misleading picture and documented that the 'exclusion of great national strikes reduced the relative "strike-proneness ratio"' of miners considerably' (pp 201 and 203) - an observation which is relevant for interpreting recent and current strike statistics. The problem is that counts of numbers of workers involved in strikes do not throw light on the question of whether the strikers downed tools frequently or just once.

Two other measures of strike-proneness, which have been put forward use different bases, namely the number of working days lost by strikes per 1000 employees or the number of strikes in different regions, industries or occupations per 100,000 employees (3). We must therefore examine whether these can be said to represent repetitive behaviour.

When considering the first of these measures it is difficult to see how it could be a measure of repetitive behaviour. Days lost by strikes represent a composite variable; the number varies with the duration of the strike, the number of workers involved as well as the total number of incidents. A long strike for instance involving a million or more employees can make a dramatic contribution to the measure. However, while such a long strike can demonstrate the determination of a particular trade union to win the particular dispute, this does not mean if it happens just once that the employees are strike-prone.

There are also problems with the second measure, namely with the ratio of number of strikes per 100,000 workers. A country, region or industry can

Reflections on the Incidence of Strikes

cover millions of workers employed in very different geographical locations and occupations; in large and small units and in public or private enterprises. This means that the strike figures may cover many separate and unrelated strikes. A considerable amount of extra information therefore is needed if one wants to find out whether a significant number of the strikes was due to repetitive strike action in some black spot within these large geographical or industrial units. This consideration suggests that the local factory, farm, shop or office provides the most appropriate basis for assessing the repetitive incidence of strikes. If this is so, a comparison with national figures is not required; it is up to management to judge whether the incidence of strikes within its organisation is unacceptably high or not.

Thus, when Sir Michael Edwardes, the former Chairman of British Leyland, reported in 1983 (Back from the Brink, p 209) that the 'disputes and wildcat strikes multiplied until in 1977 British Leyland and Ford were clocking up 300 disputes apiece every six months', it is clear that the firms had bad records. It is merely an additional interesting point that the total number of reported strikes in Britain for the whole of 1977 was 2703. To use the word 'strike-prone' in such a situation seems unnecessary and not helpful because it is defeatist. Instead the problem should be considered as a challenge which could and should be tackled with determination and patience by attempts to create a better industrial relations climate, better disputes procedures and perhaps yet unknown other improvements. That it is possible to change such strike patterns was borne out by the very marked reduction in the number of strikes since 1977 at British Leyland, which enabled Sir Michael Edwardes to state, at a meeting with unions in November 1980: 'we were free of disputes for 98.2 per cent of working days' (Back from the Brink p 138).

Alternative concepts to that of strike-proneness were put forward by Ross in 1961. He argued (pp66-73) that strike patterns change over time and introduced three concepts as a frame of reference for analysis: centres of strikes, cycles of strikes and the residual level of strikes. He considered that centres of strikes can shift when cycles of strikes come to an end and concluded that '...the termination of strike cycles throws doubt on the proposition that certain industries are inevitably strike-prone because of economic and sociological factors peculiar to them'.

Reflections on the Incidence of Strikes

In addition it can be argued that there can be cycles of strikes without centres; for instance, the wage-round strikes which are connected with national collective bargaining may be described as cyclical but in their case it is trade unions in separate industrial and occupational groups who organise the strikes, which follow each other, and many of these groups do not strike again in subsequent wage-rounds. It is perhaps better, therefore, to refer to them as 'strike waves' which come and go with different economic tides and policies. These waves can take the form of periods of 'contagion' where one successful wage-round strike encourages the adoption of the strike weapon by other trade unions in the pursuit of their pay claim, based on the assumption that a similar hard line approach would pay off or on the belief that they have an especially good case. The reports on the mass media, particularly television, can contribute to such emulation.

WHAT CAN WE LEARN FROM STRIKE STATISTICS?

Although, as I have argued, existing strike statistics cannot provide us with useful information about repetitive behaviour, we can examine whether they tell us something about centres of strikes and cycles or waves of strikes. It is therefore appropriate to assess what we can and cannot learn from studying strike statistics.

In Britain the Department of Employment provides annual (and monthly) counts of three dimensions of strike activity: the number of stoppages; the number of people involved; and the number of working days lost, for the country as a whole and for different regions and industries. By relating these counts to each other and/or the working populaton different measures of strike activity can be calculated such as the number of working days lost per 1000 workers mentioned earlier.

It should be noted that there are many problems connected with the collection of such statistics, especially differences in the types of records published by different countries. However there is not room in this book to examine these in detail (4).

In spite of the compilation snags it would seem that strike statistics can fulfil two functions. They can tell us something about the size of the problem and thus provide a base for getting strikes into perspective, and they can help us to examine the question of trends and discontinuities in the incidence of strikes in a particular country. For assessing trends it can be argued that the information on number of stoppages, people involved and working days lost can be used, without relating them to the size of the employed working population, as long as this population has not changed rapidly and the base for data collection has not been altered.

What sort of picture do these national time series provide? An analysis of the British data shows very clearly that the figures for number of strikes, number of workers involved and the number of working days lost have changed from year to year, occasionally just a little but sometimes very dramatically. For the 26 years 1955 to 1980, for instance, the figures for the number of recorded strikes reveal marked fluctuations round a level of about two and a half thousand without revealing any long term upward (or downward) trend.

One possible explanation for this observation is that reductions in strike activity in one location may be offset by increases in others. Applying Ross's concepts this would mean that there was a residual level of strikes as well as cycles of strikes in certain centres which came to an end while others started. Evidence illustrating such an offsetting effect from increases and decreases in the incidence of strikes in different industries was presented in the Donovan Report (1968 para 366). It showed that in the period 1957 to 1967 the number of stoppages due to industrial disputes in coal mining decreased from 2224 to 391 whereas the number of stoppages in all other industries increased from 635 to 1694. For the total number of stoppages, the Donovan Report concluded that no clear trend up or down was discernible.

However there are many factors that need to be taken into account if one wants to explain the size of the fluctuations in strike activity which took place. To provide a picture of the size of the fluctuation in the number of strikes between 1959 and 1980 the following percentages were worked out by me for those who like figures. The period started off in 1955 with a 22 per cent increase in the number of recorded strikes over the previous year and ended with a 36 per cent decrease from 1979 to 1980 which brought the number of recorded strikes for 1980 down to the lowest figure for the 26 year period. The largest upward change following two years of decrease was a 35 per cent increase from

Reflections on the Incidence of Strikes

1959 to 1960, when 739 more strikes took place. The most dramatic downswing following three years of rising figures was a 43 per cent decrease from 1970 to 1971 when there were 1678 fewer recorded strikes.

These percentages were calculated from evidence which I collated from the relevant annual reports in Ministry of Labour and Department of Employment Gazettes (5). The fluctuations in the number of strikes (on which the percentages are based) are illustrated in the graph which accompanies this text. This drawing also illustrates the annual records for number of workers involved and for the number of working days lost. While the numbers of strikes run into thousands, the number of the other two series add up to millions. The three graphs, using a comparable scale, illustrate the size of the fluctuations for the three sets of figures and show that the upward and downward fluctuations in strike activity were even more marked with regard to the number of workers involved and particularly conspicuous with regard to the number of working days lost. In the case of both these series the level of participaton in strikes rose. Thus in 1955 to 1967 the number of workers involved in strikes was above 1 million in only two of the thirteen years but in 1968 to 1980 in ten out of thirteen. In 1955 to 1967 the number of working days lost was above 4 million in only three out of thirteen years but in 1968 to 1980 it had risen to twelve out of thirteen.

To explain these trends we must look at the type of strikes which represent the most likely candidates to have contributed significantly to the number of strikers and days lost in a particular year; that is, at official national strikes and not at unofficial strikes. Even if the latter constitute the majority of strikes they tend to represent what Ross called the residual level, local disputes and sporadic outbreaks of discontent, usually involving small groups of workers and not lasting very long. Their incidence is reflected predominantly in the number of strikes. A single official national strike by contrast can involve very large numbers of employees and of working days lost.

Perhaps one of the most interesting examples of the impact of one official national strike is the British Steel strike of 1980, the first one of its kind in the industry, which took place in the year in which the number of reported strikes reached its lowest point for the last 25 years. The formal issue was a rejected pay offer of 2 per cent and

46

Reflections on the Incidence of Strikes

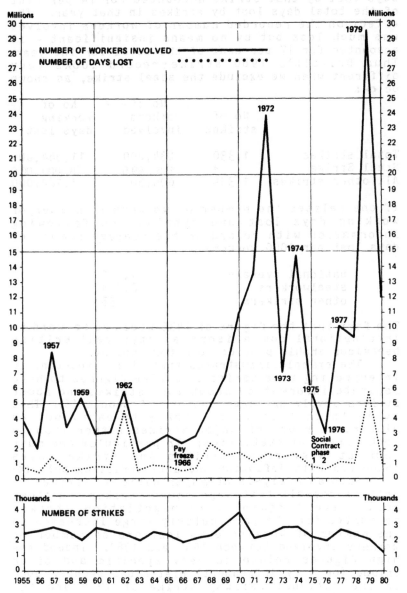

Industrial Disputes in the United Kingdom 1955-1980*

*Graphs based on figures published in the relevant annual reports in Ministry of Labour and Employment Gazettes, HMSO, London.

Reflections on the Incidence of Strikes

after 13 weeks the strikers accepted a Committee of
Inquiry award of 16 per cent overall. The impact of
days lost by that strike accounted for 74 per cent
of the total days lost by strikes in that year. The
effect on the recorded number of workers involved
was much less but by no means insignificant - it
accounted for 17 per cent of the total for the year.
Thus Britain's 1980 strike record looks very
different when we exclude the steel strike, as shown
below:

	No of strikes	No of workers involved	No of working days lost
Total strikes	1,330	834,000	11,964,000
Steel Strike	1	138,495	8,800,000
All other strikes	1,329	695,505	3,164,000

If one relates the number of workers to number of
working days lost one obtains the following
information with regard to the average number of
days lost per 1000 workers:

national average	1,435
steelworkers	6,354
other strikers	455

The fact that the figure of 1435 would go forward to
international comparisons as 'typical' British
behaviour should provide food for thought.
    The example illustrates that it is important in
interpreting time series of strike figures to have
separate information about long strikes and about
strikes involving large numbers of people (6). This
suggests that it is necessary to carry out an
historical study of major strikes rather than to
look merely at statistics. In particular one must
look at wage-round strikes and strike waves
connected with inflation and anti-inflation policies.
    Such an analysis of major national strikes in
Britain reveals that wage-round strikes and other
collective bargaining re-negotiation strikes
accounted for the particularly large increases in
the number of working days lost and of number of
workers involved between 1955 and 1980. Indeed the
high figures relate to very specific and often
unique (or very infrequent) historical events, such
as the national railway strike of 1955 and the
national engineering and shipbuilding workers'
strikes of 1957 and 1962 in which the employers
refused to meet the pay claims put forward by the
unions. The uniqueness of this type of strike in

48

those days is underlined by the return to lower figures in subsequent years. However, after the 1966 pay freeze followed by three more periods of pay restraint, wage-round strikes connected with inflation and incomes policy began to increase again in 1968 and the pay explosion which began in 1969 was accompanied by a 'wave of strikes' for higher pay awards in which days lost reached a peak in 1972. After the introduction of a statutory pay freeze in November 1972 followed by a second stage of incomes policy, days lost by strikes decreased dramatically in 1973. However, a further period of conflict and strike waves over pay claims led to the 1974 peak in number of days lost which included the miners' strike which led to the fall of Mr Heath's Conservative Government.

This type of strike activity declined during the 1975 and 1976 stage of the social contract between Mr Wilson's Labour Government and the trade unions but a new pay explosion and strike wave reached a peak as regards days lost in 1979.

The existence of such large fluctuations in the number of working days lost by strikes and the number of workers involved due to major strikes which has been documented here points to a dilemma which faces people who try to make international strike comparisons or who try to build economic models of strike activity for the purpose of prediction. Unique events cannot be predicted nor can they be interpreted as representing habitual behaviour. Moreover if they are a response to economic and political events they cannot be understood without information about the specific circumstances which prevailed at the time.

If one takes single years as a base for international comparisons of strikes, large fluctuations can mean that countries change rank from one year to the next. To obviate this the International Labour Office statistics present five or ten-year averages which spread the impact of exceptionally high figures over longer time periods. The places in the rank order in such a ten-year comparison for the United Kingdom for 1969-1978 came out as follows in Table 2, p1176, in the article, referred to earlier, by Stephen Creigh et al (see note (4)):

For number of days lost per 1,000 employees 12th out of 20 countries

For number of strikers per 1,000 employees 13th out of 20 countries

Reflections on the Incidence of Strikes

For number of stoppages per 100,000 employees 10th out of 18 countries.

UK TEN-YEAR AVERAGE STRIKE FIGURES

Days lost per 1,000 employees	472
Strikers per 1,000 employees	60
Stoppages per 100,000 employees	12

These ranks indicate that the United Kingdom appeared in the middle region in the 'strikes league' - enough to feel reassured, proud or despondent about the record! However, I am still not convinced that these measures of strike activity are appropriate measures for assessing the size of a country's strike problem and for comparisons with others. Normally, only a small percentage of the population is involved in strikes which means that they represent minority behaviour. In addition, frequency distributions for the duration of strikes and for numbers of employees involved are very skew. As shown in the case of the British Steel strike, a single strike can distort the representativeness of a figure based on an arithmetic average. Whether it is possible to ascertain the medians and quartiles for working days lost and striker participation is doubtful.

These considerations suggest that it may be more appropriate to use quite a different type of comparison for assessing the size of a country's strike problem. This is to compare the record of strikers with non strikers - a comparison which provides a new and different perspective. In this context, the British Department of Employment has from time to time used strike statistics which it compiles to estimate the percentage of workers who have been reported as involved in strikes during a particular year (7). The series shows for the 17 years for which figures were provided for the years 1958 to 1975 that the percentage of workers who were reported to have gone on strike represented a very small minority of the total workforce. In two of the years it was as low as 1.9 per cent. The highest figure of 10.6 per cent for 1962 is accounted for by the involvement of three and a half million shipbuilding and engineering workers in two one day token strikes for an increase in wages and a reduction in working hours. This means that even in this exceptional year just under 90 per cent of the workforce had not been involved in recorded strikes, and in 11 of the 17 years 95 per cent or fewer of the workforce went on strike. These statistics therefore underline the point that it is quite wrong to assume that the whole British population is strike-prone.

As regards individual firms a special article in the November 1976 Employment Gazette (p1219) reported that, on average, during any one year in the period 1971 to 1973, 98 per cent of manufacturing plants in Britain were free of strikes, and 81 per cent of the employees in manufacturing industry worked in places where no strikes had occurred. Even if there has been under-reporting of strike incidents this evidence suggests that although there are some strike-prone plants these are the exception rather than the rule.

Finally, we can compare the number of working days lost by strikes and by absences. This shows that far more working days are lost through absences. For instance, the exceptionaly high figure for days lost by strikes in 1979 of just under 29.5 million (which compares very badly with other years) compares very favourably with the figure of 371 million working days lost through certificated sickness in 1979 (8). In addition there is the time lost through voluntary absence and accidents. If the days lost by strikes were distributed evenly over the population the loss in all but very exceptional years would amount to less than half a day. Thus, an extra one day national holiday involves a greater loss of working time.

We may conclude then that in any one year (if we exclude very exceptional circumstances) only a very small minority of the working population tends to go on strike and only a comparatively small number of work establishments experiences a high incidence of strikes and also that strikes are not a very major contributor to the country's annual loss of working days. This does not however mean that the effects of strikes are unimportant - a topic which will be examined next.

THE UNEQUAL EFFECT OF STRIKES

Strikes about the same issue and possibly associated with similar reasons for breakdowns in negotiations do not necessarily have the same consequences. One strike may clear the air and lead to a speedy settlement and better relations; another may be long drawn out and costly for both sides and may lead to a settlement with a heritage of bitter feelings.

Reflections on the Incidence of Strikes

This consideration suggests that the impact of strikes depends on a combination of many different factors. It is, for instance, only partly a question of what type of strike is taking place; the occupation of the strikers, the industry they work in and the strategy adopted to highlight the issues about which the strikers say they are striking matter at least as much and probably more.

Similarly, although a strike may last a long time, the loss of working days and even the loss of output may not be as important as the terms of the settlement and the effect on the long term viability of the organisations affected by the strike (9). In this context the state of the country's economy is also important. Thus, in the 1950s and early 1960s some firms in the British motor car industry seemed to show considerable resilience in recovering from strikes. In the course of the 1970s and 1980s, however, car firms have become vulnerable because of oil price crises, the economic depression and the emergence of strong foreign competition which has captured a large share of the British domestic market.

Another facet of strikes which must be considered here is that of the population which is affected. Often it is not only the participants who are affected, i.e. the managers and owners of the firms and organisations concerned and the strikers and their trade unions; other firms and organisations may also be affected, as may individual citizens in their role as consumers. Furthermore, strikes in key occupations or key industries can affect the whole country and its economy, highlighting our problems of interdependence. These considerations indicate how difficult it is to assess the consequences of a strike for the whole population.

In theory, what is required for such an assessment, is a kind of balance sheet which shows the adverse and beneficial effects for the different participants and the rest of the population in the short and in the long run. In practice it is unlikely that we can obtain enough information for drawing up comprehensive balance sheets. Most of the assessments which have been made have focused on the wider economic and psychological effects.

Many writers on strikes, certainly up to 1960, have argued that the economic consequences of strikes in the western industrialised countries were not serious, that the loss of output and lost production was negligible compared with that caused by other types of industrial action. Kornhauser and his co-editiors (1954), for instance, stated (p8):

> 'Among the various sources of economic loss strikes must be regarded as relatively minor. Certainly there are more important reasons why work is not performed and output not produced ...The judgement of most specialists is that the economic consequences are overrated'.

They then pointed out that it is the psychological effect, 'the overtness of the strike' - Knowles has called it the shock effect - which creates the impression that strikes are the most damaging form of industrial action.

However, it is unwise to underestimate the potential damage which can be inflicted by a major strike in an industry or occupation on which the whole economy depends. The 1974 British miners' strike over a pay claim was a dramatic reminder that anxieties about strikes can sometimes be justified. The miners' strike affected all of us at work and at home. It led to the rationing of electricity by electricity cuts and the three day working week which the Government introduced as an emergency measure; as well as to a general election and a change of government and of government pay policy. It also led to the award of a large pay increse for the miners which marked the beginning of another pay explosion.

The national strike in the coal industry has thus demonstrated that a major strike can have very wide-ranging repercussions and not just economic ones but also psychological and political ones. It is difficult nevertheless to judge the long-term effects. Looking back to the early 1980s it would seem that the industrial relations climate in the industry benefited from the favourable pay settlement which initiated a period of co-operation and of considerable growth in productivity. So far there has been no repetition of an all out strike, which, one suspects, is partly because the Conservative Government, afraid of a repetition of the 1974 confrontation, made concessions on the issue of fifty pit closures and financial aid in the February 1981 coal dispute. The long-term effect on inflation and labour costs in the country is more difficult to judge but should not be underestimated.

How much of this could have been predicted? In my view one could not foresee that the outcome would be a lost general election followed by a victory for the National Union of Mineworkers. The critical decision of holding an election may well have misjudged the mood of the public which had put up with the electricity cuts and three day week; many members of the public may have felt let down by that decision and cast their vote accordingly.

The example illustrates the uncertainty which surrounds the potential repercussions of a strike; they can look very different before the strike takes place than after the event. This means that past judgements of specialists which concluded that the economic consequences of strikes were overrated may not be borne out in current or future strikes. We must accept that certain types of strike, if they are fully supported and go on for a long time, can seroiusly affect the country and its economy and can disrupt the life of the ordinary citizen.

It is in this area of the effects of strikes (or as the trade unions may see it, their effectiveness) that we as a society have to face what may be described as an 'a-symmetry of power'. For, although strikes represent minority behaviour, strikes in key industries or occupations can cause widespread disruptions of production which may give rise to serious economic repercussions and can affect millions of people. In some cases, trade unions have found that a strike by a few key workers can be enough to produce considerable disruption and that such a strategy reduces strike costs and enables the union to engage in a long trial of strength. Other trade unions have discovered that they can increase their 'muscle' by different methods of picketing; for instance, by stopping transport in and out of their place of work and by picketing the employer's customers and suppliers (the practice referred to as secondary picketing). As a counter-measure to this practice, the Conservative Government's Employment Act 1980 narrowed the scope of legal immunities with regard to picketing.

The changes in trade union tactics which have taken place suggest that we have been witnessing a learning process in which certain lessons were learned by the unions about the conduct of strikes and the reduction of strike costs, based on strategies which proved (or did not prove) successful. In this learning process, which could be said to be promoted by media coverage, success seems to breed success and also imitation; the kind of contagion referred to earlier.

Reflections on the Incidence of Strikes

SOME FINAL OBSERVATIONS

As I have shown in this paper, strikes represent a very heterogeneous species of events. As a letting off of steam a one day strike can clear the air and consequently be beneficial to production. As a long drawn out battle, where neither side is willing to make concessions, a strike based on stubborness can do serious harm well beyond the work organisation in which it takes place. Thus strikes are part of, and illustrate, our problems of economic interdependence which is one important reason why the topic deserves attention.

Strikes can originate in any one of the three areas of concern in industrial relations which I described in Chapter 3 and they can also be about any one of the three. This means that they can originate from within or without the plant. For tackling any particular strike it is important to diagnose which dimensions are involved.

For instance, a strike in a plant may be about the application of a particular disputes procedure but caused by tensions between an employee and his or her superior. In such a case, management must not only tackle the human relations problems which have arisen but also the question of the meaning or adequacy of the procedure (which is the bone of contention) and this issue may have to be cleared up with national trade union officials. A very different situation arises in a national wage-round strike where the dispute is not with a particular firm but with the employers' organisation which represents it. There the firm can, perhaps, only plead that their representatives should develop better negotiating skills and procedures.

There is no panacea for preventing strikes or dealing with strikes. An individual firm cannot insulate itself against them either by handing over major bones of contention such as pay and conditions of employment to national negotiators nor by doing all the negotiations itself.

Insofar as bad human and industrial relations enter into strikes, however, there would appear to be considerable room for improvement but this requires patience and skill, sensitivity and everyday attention. Regular scrutiny of plant rules and the functioning and adequacy of disputes procedures could pay off in firms which have a strike problem. So could the improvement of channels of communication and consultation between management and employees. An analytical study and evaluation of each strike by asking appropriate questions and perhaps drawing up profiles of strikes could also be helpful in the process of learning how to improve relations.

Insofar as it may be possible to learn from other people's experiences and mistakes, published reports of enquiries into individual strikes would appear to be particularly useful, such as reports published by ACAS and earlier Court of Inquiry reports.

NOTES

1. See R Stagner, Psychology of Industrial Conflict, 1956, p423. 'It would be desirable if we could specify the necessary and sufficient factors for determining the occurrence of a strike'.
2. Knowles, (1951), Chapter 4, p195. The middle sentence in the paragraph just quoted describes the method used for calculating his strike-proneness ratio: 'If the percentage of strikers in the region is divided by the percentage of industrial population in that region, a ratio is obtained which can be compared with 1.0 (the figure for the UK as a whole, which contains 100 per cent of the strikers and 100 per cent of the population)'. The higher the ratio the worse the record. His more complicated standardised strike-proneness ratio is described on p207.
3. See, for instance, Richard Hyman, Strikes, Fontana, reprinted 1972, p29: 'The "strike-proneness" of an industrial or occupational group can be calculated by relating the number of stoppages or striker-days recorded to the size of the labour force'.
4. The recording and methodological problems connected with strike statistics have received wide coverage in the literature. The following article gives a good account as well as useful references. Stephen Creigh, Nigel Donaldson and Eric Hawthorn, Stoppage activity in OECD countries, Employment Gazette, November 1980, pp 1174-1181.
5. A summary of the 1960 to 1980 figures can be found in the special features article, Stoppages caused by industrial disputes in 1980, Employment Gazette, July 1981, Table 9, p294.
6. For an interesting article examining industrial stoppages involving the loss of 200,000 working days or more, see Large industrial stoppages 1960-1979, Employment Gazette, September 1980, pp 994-999.
7. Estimates of the percentage of workers involved

in strikes from 1956 to 1967 were based on the net number of individuals involved, corrected for double-counting. No estimates were provided in 1969 and 1970. For 1971 to 1975 the estimates were not corrected for double-counting (ie people striking twice) which means these figures are more liable to represent over-estimates than the corrected ones. On the other hand there can be under-reporting of strikes but such omissions cannot alter the conclusion that the percentage of workers who go on strike in any one year represent a very small minority of the total workforce.

8. Figures quoted in Employment Brief: OHE report on absence, Employment Gazette, September 1981, p379.

9. Compare J W Durcan and W E J McCarthy, What is happening to strikes? New Society, 2 November 1972, p269. 'What is important to discover is not so much what is happening to strike statistics, but how far the strikes that do take place are either productive or counter productive. One will want to know whether a given strike has prevented, or promoted, a more realistic appraisal of the long-term interests of both sides; whether it has led to increased bitterness and intransigence, or a more workable and viable solution of common problems'.

REFERENCES

Donovan Report, see Royal Commission below

M Edwardes, Back from the Brink, Collins, London, 1983

K Knowles, Strikes - A Study in Industrial Conflict, Oxford University Institute of Statistics Monograph, 1952

A W Kornhauser, R Dubin and A M Ross Eds., Industrial Conflict, New York, 1954

A M Ross, Prospects for Industrial Conflict, Industrial Relations (University of California) Vol 1 No 1, October 1961

A M Ross and P T Hartman, Changing Patterns of Industrial Conflict, Wiley, New York and London, 1960

Royal Commission on Trade Unions and Employers' Associations 1965-1968 Report, Cmnd 3623, HMSO, London, 1968

H A Turner, Is Britain really strike-prone? A review of the incidence, character and costs of industrial conflict, Cambridge University Press, 1969

5   Voluntary Absence from Work

First published in International Labour Review,
Vol. LXXXIS, No. 2, February 1959.

AUTHOR'S PREFACE 1983

In the course of my career I carried out two
absence enquiries, one in the Midlands in the early
post-war period before the computer age had begun
and another in Scotland when the computer age was
well under way. A monograph based on the first set
of factory field studies was published in 1951 by
the University of Birmingham. The findings from the
second enquiry were published in two articles and a
monograph and will be discussed in Chapter 6.

The article to be reproduced here was
commissioned in 1958 by the editor of the
International Labour Review who was particularly
interested in the question of the economic effects
of absenteeism. However the scope of the paper had
to be widened and the result was a literature based
stock-taking exercise of our state of knowledge as
regards the incidence, effects and possible control
of voluntary absence from work.

This chapter reproduces the survey of research
findings and discusses the insights which may be
gained from them including cautionary comments about
unfounded beliefs and pointers for action. In my
view these insights have remained relevant and
important.

Voluntary absence has been described as 'the
practice of workers failing to report for work on
some slight excuse or other or none at all'. (Moore
1947, p254). Absenteeism, an ambiguous term in
everyday language, is used in this paper as
synonymous with voluntary absence, that is, its
meaning is restricted to the above definition.
Attempts to measure its incidence try to exclude
sickness absence from available absence counts.
However this task raises major difficulties; for

instance, that of locating organisations which keep suitable individual absence records and that of identifyng which of the recorded absences are voluntary and not due to sickness.

In 1958 many researchers reported that few organisations kept absence records and most of those that were kept were group records. The three measures which were used by researchers at that time for measuring voluntary absences were make-shift ones. They tried to minimise the sickness bias in total absence counts. Thus:

> The Other Reasons Absence Rate was used to measure the number of days lost through absences other than certified sickness; this means it measured uncertificated absences of which some may have been due to sickness. The rate expresses the number of days lost as a percentage of the number of days scheduled to be worked.

> The Absence Frequency Rate was used to measure the average number of absences per worker over a given period (and not the days lost) thus reducing the sickness bias. (Fox and Scott, 1943).

> The Blue Monday Index used the difference between Monday's and Friday's absence rates as a measure of voluntary absence.

This last measure (developed in my Birmingham studies) was based on the discovery of regular variations in the incidence of absences on different days of the week (1), far more days being lost on Mondays than on Fridays, suggesting that this surplus represented voluntary absences. My 1951 monograph presented supporting evidence for this interpretation. When I examined the relationship of the three measures of absence described above the comparison of the evidence showed a close correspondence, indicating that they were measuring the same phenomenon.

This evidence, and the specialist problems of the identification and measurement of voluntary absence, were described in greater detail in the 1959 version of this paper of which the first section has been replaced by this preface.

Chapter 6 uses a different method of analysis and illustrates it with examples.

Another topic dealt with in more detail in 1959 was that of beliefs about absenteeism. Managers

often expressed, and still do, beliefs about
absenteeism without being able to provide evidence
to substantiate them. In assessing their firm's
record, for instance, some of the managers I talked
to expressed the view that absenteeism was
negligible in their plant and yet, when I looked at
their figures, they turned out to be quite high. As
regards causes, managerial beliefs were often based
on hearsay, on fleeting impressions and hunches but
not on factual evidence. In this area therefore
researchers as well as managers were and still often
are faced with what I would like to call a 'beliefs
or facts? dilemma'.

This dilemma pointed to the need to examine
which of these notions were based on facts, a
central objective of my survey of factors in
absenteeism of which the results are presened
below.

FACTORS IN ABSENTEEISM

The Level of Employment

Unfortunately, little infomation exists on this
topic apart from the indirect evidence of public
concern with the problem of absenteeism in several
countries during the Second World War and the post-
war period of full employment.
The writer (1953) studied the effect on absenteeism
of a local rise in unemployment. Thirteen out of
fourteen factories of a Birmingham engineering
company revealed an Other Reasons Absence Rate of
more than 1 per cent during the period of full
employment. During the first half of 1952, a period
of less-full employment, absence rates were lower,
although the factories themselves experienced no
redundancy. The reduction in the level of the Other
Reasons Absence Rates in this firm's factories was
statistically significant. Another engineering
concern which worked a normal working-week, although
dismissing men for redundancy, showed a similar
significant fall in Monday absenteeism from the
period of full employment to that of less full
employment. Reductions in the level of labour
turnover in firms not hit by the trade recession
were also found to be statistically significant.

It seems plausible that the level of employment
is an important factor in the level of absenteeism,
and that this is quite apart from the effect it has
on hours worked. Under full employment a worker is
not afraid of taking a day off. He assumes that he

60

will not be dismissed for irregular attendance, and, whatever happens, other jobs are always open to him. When unemployment afflicts an industry, workers fear dismissal and this may prevent the expression of dissatisfaction through absenteeism. Thus improvements in attendance due to a recession may not represent an improvement in motivation. More research is needed on this topic.

Wages

The connection between wages and absenteeism is problematic. Some believe that high earnings stimulate good attendance, while others think it leads to absenteeism. The belief that a worker's main interest in work is money - the foundation of the advocacy of financial incentives - conflicts with the absentee's willingness to forgo earnings. Some authors (2), to explain this disregard, have argued that the worker has a fixed standard of living and is content when his earnings are enough to maintain it; thus absenteeism increases with earnings. Similarly, Mayo (1952 p78) and others argued 'that larger earnings induce workers to take unjustifiable week-end holidays'.

It is hard to prove the existence of an association between wages and absenteeism, especially for workers on payment by results. But the problem may be studied in two ways. One can search for a fluctuation of absenteeism when there is a change in wage rates or average earnings. No reliable evidence based on this method came to light (3). Alternatively the records of workers with different earnings or wage rates can be searched for different absence rates. The writer's 1951 inquiry used this second approach; it showed that among workers on eight different engineering jobs in factories the four occupations with the highest and lowest Monday absenteeism had similar average earnings. From this evidence it could be argued that these groups - all of them on piece rates - had adjusted their attendances and output to reach the same wage target. The middle groups as regards absenteeism, however, had both higher and lower earnings. The facts of this survey seem to yield no conclusive argument. Liddell (1954, p81) found among miners a connection between higher earnings per shift and increased voluntary absence only for underground daywagemen, and for them in only one of the two areas studied.

Shepherd and Walker (1958, pp53ff), examining

hourly wage rates for workers in an iron and steel plant divided into six different wage-level groups, found that 'absence without permission varies with wage level, although the association appears to break down in the highest and lowest wage groups', and that 'apart from the lowest-paid group, the number of single-shift absences increased steadily as wage level increased'. In another study Shepherd and Walker (1957, p271) showed that 'the men on heavy work received higher pay than those in the other groups' but that 'the relation was not systematic, and there was also no correlation between the absence rates of the groups (eg men with differing heaviness and continuity of working), and their average earnings'.

This topic demands more research. Inquiries into the effect of changes in wage rates on absenteeism in a given job would be particularly valuable, as the comparison of the absenteeism records of workers with different wage rates has one serious drawback. Workers in different wage rate groups are usually engaged on different jobs so that the wage factor is difficult to isolate. Comparisons of the earnings and absenteeism records of individual workers engaged on the same job would avoid this difficulty of isolation. The whole subject of the influence of wages is highly complex, and it is likely that conceptions of earnings rather than actual earnings matter most. And these differ for people of different status and in different situations.

Sex and Family Responsibilities

Studies in Britain, America and Australia revealed variations in absenteeism among different types of workers. For instance, women usually had higher rates of absenteeism as well as of labour turnover than men, particularly in factory work (4). These variations may have resulted partly from the type of work, since women in factories usually hold unskilled jobs. For professional and clerical work the position is often different. The writer's study of women teachers showed that they had incurred no voluntary absences.

Again, family responsibilities may have a part to play. Among male workers they may tend to reduce absenteeism, but among women the effect may be exactly the opposite.

Liddell found that single men in the Durham coalfield lost more time voluntarily than married

men, but in the Cannock Chase coalfield no such
relationship could be discerned. Kahne and his
fellow reseachers (1957, p191), found that younger
married men in an American food-processing plant had
a lower Absence Frequency Rate than single, widowed,
or divorced men. The Absence Frequency Rate
decreased among married men as the number of
dependants increased. There was no clear pattern
among men over 45. Shepherd and Walker (1958, pp
56-57) found that absence without permission was
highest for single men and fell to a minimum for
those with two dependants, again increasing
progressively for men with more than two dependants.

Little material existed on the connection
between absences and family responsibilities among
women. 'Firm Z', a food-processing plant, found in
1955 that for the factory as a whole married women
had a higher Other Reasons Absence Rate and higher
Monday absenteeism than single women, but in
approximately one-third of the departments they had
a better record. More evidence on this topic would
be useful.

Age

On the question of the connection between
absenteeism and age the evidence is conflicting.
Kossoris's data (1948, p17) showed a consistent
downward trend with age for the Other Reasons
Absence Rate for men but no regular trend for women.
The writer's 1951 enquiry revealed no relation
between age and Monday absenteeism for men. Monday
absences occurred at all ages, but it seemed that
sometimes beyond a certain age discontent found
expression in absenteeism rather than labour
turnover. Liddell (p.83) noticed in one coalfield
that the youngest men lost more time voluntarily
than their elders. 'Firm Z' found in 1955 that the
Other Reasons Absence Rate and the Blue Monday Index
were highest for men below 30. For both married and
single women the Other Reasons Absence Rate was
highest below 40, while the Blue Monday Index was
highest in the 30 to 39 age group. From another
piece of research in a food-processing factory Kahne
and his colleagues produced similar evidence. They
found that for both men and women the Absence
Frequency Rate decreased with age. These findings
suggested that the reluctance often shown by
employers to recruit older workers can be mistaken.

Voluntary Absence from Work

Length of Service

The relationship between absenteeism and length of service is hard to study because many newcomers leave before an absence record can be compiled, and workers with a long enough record are no longer really new. Fox and Scott (pp 7-8) found that during three months in a casting shop and sheet-mill absences were slightly higher among 'new' employees (ie those engaged within the year preceeding the observations) than among 'veterans' who had been with the company for more than a year. The present writer (1951, p 95), using records for engineering workers who had been with the firm for at least the whole of the survey period of nine months, found that men with no absences in this period had almost double the length of service of men with a Monday absenteeism pattern, while the average age of the two groups was approximately the same. 'Firm Z' found in 1955 that the Other Reasons Absence Rate was high for men with less than one year's service no matter what age, and low for workers with more than ten years' service for all possible age-groups. Among married women the Other Reasons Absence Rate was highest in the first two years of service. The data were inconclusive for single women. Kahne and his colleagues reported that with one exception the Absence Frequency Rates declined as length of service increased. However, they confessed that they could not eliminate the age factor and that this might have affected the results.

Type of Work

Considerable evidence is available on the incidence of absenteeism in different occupations. Fox and Scott, for instance (section II), noticed that in three American metal-working plants casters were absent more often than workers in sheet-mills and manufacturing. Logan (in a private communication 1950) reported from Manchester that in a light engineering plant draughtsmen had higher Other Reasons Absence Rates than male clerks. The present writer (1955) studied over a period of four years a group of women teachers in a Birmingham grammar school. Their records displayed no voluntary absenteeism. Again a survey of Midland engineering workers showed that skilled men had a lower Blue Monday Index than unskilled men; fitters and floormoulders had a low Blue Monday Index while foundry labourers, press operators and drillers had

64

a high one. Walker and Guest (1952 pp 120ff) in an
American study and using a rating type of method
found a statistically significant correlation
'between absenteeism and mass production
characteristics' in a car assembly plant. Their
study revealed that workers on highly repetitive
jobs were absent more often than men whose jobs
showed few mass production features. Again in
America Metzner and Mann (1953, p 472) found in an
electric light and power plant that 'blue collar'
men had significantly higher Absence Frequency Rates
than 'white collar' men. Liddell in his survey of
two British coalfields noticed that faceworkers had
more voluntary absences than other underground
workers, and that surface workers were the most
regular. Shepherd and Walker (1957, pp 266ff) used
a carefully devised rating scale for judging
heaviness of work in their study of an engineering
firm and two iron and steel plants in Britain. They
found a statistically significant relationship
between heaviness of work and absenteeism as
measured by the percentage of workers with more than
six and less than three absences in the year and by
the Other Reasons Absence Rate. The Absence
Frequency Rate per 100 workers also suggested an
association with heaviness of work. The authors
observed 'an interaction between the heaviness and
continuity of working such that the men on
continuous heavy work had high absence rates'.
Kahne and his colleagues (pp 140-141) found that
'the absence frequency rate for salaried male
workers under 45 was less than that for hourly rated
employees under 45. Among hourly rated employees
the rates declined as occupational status
increased'. It was highest for unskilled and
service workers and lowest for skilled workers.

All the available evidence suggested that there
was a strong association between absenteeism and
type of work. This conclusion corresponded to
findings about labour turnover where a close
association with type of work was also discovered.
This raised the question of whether jobs rather than
people are prone to absenteeism and rapid turnover.

Conditions of Work

Baldamus (March 1951, pp44ff) made a
distinction between 'type of work' - a term which
refers to the specific characteristics of a job,
describing it by its activity - and 'conditions of
work' - a term which refers to the physical

environment in which a job takes place, eg
conditions of heat, cold, noise, dirt, lighting and
so on. He argued that reactions to job
characteristics are not 'subject to the wearing-off
effects of adaptation' but crystallise into
consistent likes and dislikes while 'conditions of
work do not produce any definite emotional
attitudes' and workers get used to them in time. A
newcomer may be affected by the environment of his
job, but not the seasoned worker.

If this hypothesis is true, no close association
is likely between absenteeism and working
conditions, except for newcomers. This has found
support in a number of research studies. For
instance, Fox and Scott (p 5) discovered that better
physical conditions of work in one of three casting
shops did not give rise to much higher regular
attendances. Mayo, discussing these results (p 91),
concluded that improved working conditions may be a
necessary basis for better teamwork but 'they do not
of themselves lead inevitably to it'. The writer
(1951, p91) found that floormoulders had a much
lower Blue Monday Index than foundry labourers,
although they worked under the same working
conditions. Their labour turnover rates were also
markedly lower. Liddell (p 79) found no sign in his
colliery study that attendance was 'affected by the
availability of pithead baths or by the extent of
the service in pit canteens'. Again Shepherd and
Walker's inquiry (1957, pp 268-269) revealed no
evidence of increased absence frequency in metal
working plants where workers were exposed to high
temperatures, nor of a consistent link between
absence frequency and exposure to dust or fumes.

The evidence therefore suggestdd that high
absenteeism does not follow of necessity from poor
working conditions.

Size of Industrial Units

It has often been said that large factories or
departments have a higher rate of absenteeism than
small industrial units. For instance, Hewitt and
Parfit's inquiry (1953, pp 38ff) in a hosiery firm
showed statistically significant differences in the
Other Reasons Absence Rates and in the Absence
Frequency Rates of large, medium and small groups,
absence being lower the smaller the workroom. The
rates were standardised as far as possible and there
were no important differences in type of work and
average age. The authors thought that the risk of

contact with poor morale was greater in the larger
shop. Liddell too (1959 p 80) found a marked
association between the labour force of a colliery
and its voluntary absenteeism rate, the large pits
having the higher rates. Investigators of the Acton
Society Trust (1953, 1957) studying cases in
different industries postulated a 'size effect'.
They reported that 'workers go absent for one reason
or another proportionally more frequently in large
concerns than they do in small concerns'. Uris
(1956, p 52), in a popular article, gave figures for
one firm from four different sizes of department.
They found that the larger departments had a higher
proportion of employees with one or more absences
per month.

   While the evidence quoted above supported the
hypothesis of a 'size-effect', not all pointed in
this direction. Buzzard remarked that one needed to
be cautious because there might be a tendency for
less able workers to go to the larger factory, which
might also be less efficient in removing long
absentees from its records. Furthermore, as the
Acton Society Trust investigators remarked, it was
not size but other factors 'behind it' such as the
quality of management and supervision which
mattered. These, however, are not of necessity
better in smaller departments or firms. The
relationship of size and absenteeism seems to be a
complex subject and needs to be viewed with caution.

Incidence of Pay-Day

   It is often said that absenteeism is lowest on
pay-day. However, this belief requires close
investigation. For the fact that in British
industry pay-day generally falls on Friday, which
tended also to be the day of lowest absenteeism,
could be a coincidence. Loveday (see note 1)
described a case where pay-day was not the day of
lowest absenteeism. In his investigation pay-day
was a Tuesday, and he reported a regular decline in
lost 'morning quarters' from Monday to Saturday,
broken only by a slight rise in lost time from
Tuesday to Wednesday. In 1956 the writer obtained
evidence from a motor manufacturing company with a
pay-roll of about 16,000. Wage-payments were spread
over Tuesdays, Wednesdays and Thursdays. During a
period of five months an average of 733 persons per
day were absent on the three pay-days (769 on
Tuesdays, 737 on Wednesdays, 691 on Thursdays). But
on the 19 Fridays that were non-pay-days an average

67

of 653 persons were absent. In this instance, Friday, a non-pay-day, was the day of best attendance.

By contrast, Wyatt and Marriott (1947) found that for night-shift workers who were paid during the Thursday night-shift absenteeism was lowest on that night and it rose sharply on Friday. Here the pay-shift coincided with the moment of lowest absenteeism. This could be explained by the operation of two forces: the 'pay-day effect' and the unsettling influence of the approaching week-end. With his pay in his pocket the worker feels he can relax his efforts for a time. Furthermore, he finds it hard to settle down on Friday nights if the day-workers have finished their week's labour when he has to go on duty. The night-worker's experience resembles that of the man who has to work on Saturday mornings and finds it hard to capture the working mood for a half day. He looks forward to his leisure time activities and the journey to work seems hardly worth while (5). The fact that these workers have received their pay on the previous day strengthens the week-end feeling. The high incidence of absenteeism on Friday nights and Saturday mornings has important implications for the organisation of working hours. More research on this subject could yield much of interest, especially in cases where pay-day is at the beginning of the week.

External Factors

Climate has been suggested as an external factor affecting absenteeism. Liddell, in his study of coalmining, mentions that attendance at the pithead is affected by the weather. But on the other hand the writer was unable to distinguish weather as a factor in daily variations in absence in the investigation of one company over a period of six years. Here, the seasonal fluctuations were clearly due to sickness.

Again it is contended that absenteeism is influenced by the length of the journey to work, especially on Saturdays. Only two of the enquiries surveyed provided evidence on this. Vernon and Bedford (p 32) found that voluntary absence was related to distance of miners' homes from the colliery, and Liddell (p 80) reported for a coalfield in a rural area that 'attendance is better at those pits where the men have less distance to travel on average'.

Psychological Factors

There is much statistical evidence to show that
the bulk of absenteeism is due to a few people
losing time repeatedly and this has given rise to
the view that absenteeism is a problem of the
minority. 'Chronic' absentees and good attenders
often work side by side in the same department. For
instance, the writer found that in a small machine
shop, employing 34 men, 14 had a 'Blue Monday
absence pattern', while 10 had no absences at all.
This agrees with Liddell's suggestion (pp 83ff) that
there may well be 'habits of absence'.

The focusing of attention on the habitual
absentee has given rise to the view that there may
be absence-prone workers. By applying statistical
tests to the records of employees for two successive
periods of six months, Arbous and Sichel (1954 pp
77ff) claimed they had proof of the existence of
absence-proneness. Again Liddell (p 84) found that
miners repeated their voluntary absence patterns in
three successive years, and Holt (1956) found a
statisically significant relationship between
absence-patterns for bank employees for two
consecutive years.

The workers who were found to repeat high
absenteeism patterns over as short a period as a
year (or two or three years respectively) might be
called 'absence-prone'. Whether one uses the term
or not seems a matter of definition. In my view,
the term gives rise to misconceptions because it
conveys the impression that an individual is
absence-prone whatever his job, age, or length of
service. It seems important to test what happens to
habits of absence when a worker is transferred from
a 'bad' job to a 'good' one, and when he grows older
and acquires family responsibilities. Most studies
cover too short a period of time to establish the
existence of absence-proneness.

The concentration of interest on the regular
attender and the habitual absentee has led to the
neglect of the 'occasional' absentee; yet his or her
record may be just as important. Casual absenteeism
does not necesarily show up in individual records.
For instance, Wyatt (pp 4 and 11) found that the
majority of women workers in two factories were
absent during a period of six weeks but that only a
few were absent regularly. Again, in the
investigation of a department of 80 employees the
writer was unable to trace the high departmental

Voluntary Absence from Work

Blue Monday Index to particular individuals. Yet the absenteeism record was exceptionally poor for a department employing skilled workers and this demanded some explanation. Thus a bad departmental record may be due to a few habitual absentees or to many occasional absentees, and in either case it requires attention.

* * * *

To sum up, this survey of the data on absenteeism found that comparatively little can be said with certainty about the subject. Many opinions had not yet received the essential test of research. Evidence was patchy, and mainly in the form of case-studies relating to specific situations. On the other hand, several of the case-studies revealed the same themes and arrived at similar results. This has made it possible therefore, to advance the following tentative conclusions with regard to factory workers:

1. Absenteeism is liable to occur after a break, like the week-end, after pay-day and on half-days.

2. It is likely to be influenced by type of work; occupations with certain characteristics, for instance, mass production characteristics, seem prone to it; more varied work and higher status jobs are often free from it.

3. Women are more liable to irregular attendance than men.

4. Single men are more likely to stay away without excuse than married men, especially married men with several children.

5. Newcomers are more liable to absenteeism than seasoned workers.

6. Unskilled workers are more likely to stay away without excuse than skilled workers.

7. Casual unexplained absences are not confined to habitual absentees.

By themselves these conclusions do not tell us much about the causes of absenteeism. Any explanation is inferred from the behaviour we observe and from the situations in which it arises. For instance, absentees themselves may not be aware of the actual causes of their behaviour, especially when their absence borders on sickness. There are probably both immediate and underlying causes. A football match may provide the immediate stimulus for taking an afternoon off, but it does not explain why one worker gives in to the temptation while another resists it. Deeper motivational factors of outlook and occupational adjustment must be investigated to explain this, and these tend to be many and varied.

Many writers have argued that absenteeism reflects an unfavourable attitude to work, and a number of studies have shown that in certain types of job high absenteeism is associated with expressions of low job satisfaction (6). Good attendance, on the other hand, is not necessarily connected with high job satisfaction; it may be due to economic or moral pressures.

Willingness to work changes with time of day and the day of the week. After a break in the routine of factory work, such as is provided by a week-end or holiday, it is difficult to start work again. The return to work on Mondays thus requires a special effort. Where the job is disliked the reluctance to return to work may be so great that it leads to absenteeism. Once the absentee returns - be it because his desire for leisure has decreased or because economic necessity dictates - he becomes used to the work again, and the dislike of his job decreases as the week-end approaches, while the need to earn money becomes more urgent. Thus attendance improves towards Friday. Variations in daily attendance not only reflect changes in the worker's attitude to work from day to day but also that he rejects any obligation to maintain a regular attendance, while a conscientious worker returns to work on Mondays whether he likes it or not.

Variations in attendance not only reflect differences in willingness to work and job satisfaction but in outlook, in accepted standards of work conduct. Some social settings inculcate good attendance norms into individuals in childhood and later life. Here it is 'not done' to absent oneself from work for no reason. Such standards of conduct were particularly marked in the case of teachers studied by the writer (1955). They may also account for the non-occurrence of absenteeism in 1951 in two German factories, studied by the writer. In other social settings absenteeism is not condemned but permitted; the workers consider themselves entitled to stay away when they choose. In my view, this question of what are the accepted standards of conduct of an employee is of crucial importance for understanding absenteeism.

Any attempts to reduce absenteeism must take account of these deeper motivational factors which cannot be changed by disciplinary measures but can only be tackled by changes in the factors which make for low job satisfaction, by changes in attitudes and in accepted standards of conduct.

Before discussing the implications of these conclusions for managerial action it seems appropriate to consider the effects of absenteeism. Only this can provide a true perspective. For it is important that decisions for action neither overestimate nor underestimate the problem of absenteeism and its consequences. Otherwise an attempt to limit absenteeism may produce unexpected or disappointing results.

EFFECTS OF ABSENTEEISM

Unfortunately, factual evidence about the influence of absenteeism on production and costs is scarce. Measurement of all the effects of absenteeism appears impossible, and most assessments seem to contain a subjective element. Nevertheless it is perhaps safe to assert that absenteeism makes itself known in at least two ways that in practice are inseparable:

1. it may interfere with the productive efficiency of a plant and of the workers who turn up for work;
2. it may involve loss of potential output from the absentees.

The disruption of production through absenteeism may be serious or negligible, depending on the type and organisation of work. When expensive machinery stands idle there may be needless waste. Teamwork could be disrupted and bottlenecks created, reducing the rhythm of work in the plant or factory. Tempers may be frayed and the morale of the remaining workforce sapped when absenteeism increases the load of work for regular emloyees. The Harvard studies showed that 'the behaviour of the regular attendants in Companies A and B was affected by the general deterioration' (Mayo, p86) in attendance and morale. If the speed of work declines and output diminishes management may face difficulties in meeting production schedules. There may be recourse to overtime and consequent rises in the cost of production. On the other hand management may allow for absenteeism in its staffing policy and the planning of production; it often carries a pool of reserve labour to overcome these difficulties. Overmanning, however raises production costs and represents an uneconomic use of manpower in a full employment economy.

Absenteeism can create considerable disorganisation; of this there is little doubt. Court provided some evidence of this (1951, p113). Describing the history of coalmining during the Second World War he reported that avoidable absenteeism -

> 'took place at week-ends on Mondays and Saturdays, particularly before or after a holiday. The importance of this kind of absenteeism and the anger it caused both among mine managers and miners on the shift was due to disorganisation of underground work. This was based on a minimum strength for each gang or team. Where the mine was mechanised and where persistent absenteeism took place the effect was to throw out the carefully built up cycle of mining operations, because preparatory shifts could not accomplish their job. The loss of production in such a case was out of all proportion to the number of manshifts lost' (7).

The degree of disorganisation, however, as Buzzard (p 245) pointed out, depends on conditions in the individual pit. In pits working to their maximum capacity for bringing coal to the surface an increase in average attendance would not yield more coal. This would only be possible if the increased labour were sufficient to allow the development of new coal faces and other technical changes. Again, it should be remembered that a few absences in strategic jobs may create far more dislocation than many absences in less vital positions. Buzzard concluded that there are two extremes:

> 'places with high absence rates where improvement might have no effect on production and places with low rates where improvement could have a great effect. In between are a diversity of particular problems, in most of which the relationship between average lost time rates and production is singularly obscure'.

73

Voluntary Absence from Work

Of course, complex conditions prevail in the coalmining industry but problems connected with plant capacity and unreliability in strategic jobs apply also in other industries. Absenteeism can cause disorganisation; but the degree of disruption cannot be certain and the effect of absences on productivity is a problem that still needs thorough investigation.

The loss of potential output from absentees and its measurement presents an even more complicated problem. The effects of absenteeism on actual work can be observed, making investigation possible even if little research has been carried out as yet. But estimates of potential output lost by absentees must, of necessity, be speculative. Such calculations are inevitably based on arbitrary assumptions about what the productivity of the absentees would have been if they had worked. Most figures which have been published are based on the assumption that absentees would work at the same speed at which the average employees normally work. Such estimates are not difficult to arrive at. For instance if one knows the average output per manshift in the coalmines, a multiplication by the number of shifts lost and the number of men employed supplies a figure (8).

Another series of assumptions becomes necessary to translate the potential loss of physical output into financial terms. Two Australian studies (9) developed a technique for this purpose which entails

'the calculation of the amount by which a firm's net profit for a certain period would have been increased if there had been no absences during that period. This is done by calculating what, if there had been no absences, would have been the increase in sales value of production and the consequent increase or decrease in certain costs and expenses. The basic assumptions underlying the method are that there is a direct relationship between man-hours worked and the volume of output, that raw materials would have been available at the prices paid during the period to enable the extra output to be manufactured, and that this extra output could have been sold at the prices which were obtained for the goods actually produced.'

The first case study which covered a light engineering factory employing just under 1,000 employees calculated that the net profit forgone for

74

each lost man-hour ranged from 3s 6d (Australian currency) to 21s 6d in different departments. The factory average was 13s 2d. The second case study dealing with a small engineering firm of 130 employees estimated that the net profit forgone for each lost man-hour was 10s 5d. The total net profit forgone in the six months period which was studied was estimated to be £18,006 in the first factory and £3,912 (or 2.3 per cent of the actual value of production) in the second factory.

It must be stressed that these estimates are purely hypothetical and based on highly simplified assumptions. But two functions, among others, may be foreseen for such calculations. First, the practical one of guiding management towards a decision on the economics of employing an attendance officer as well as special staff to replace absentees, and the general one of attracting managers' attention to the problem of absenteeism, of making management 'absence-cost-conscious'. The underlying assumptions are that absenteeism is undesirable, that management ought to do something about it, and that the need for action can best be demonstrated by translating the problem into financial terms. The estimates then become an educational tool - as dramatic as newspaper accounts of strikes; but they may be equally misleading with regard to the true economic significance of the phenomena they describe. In my view they overestimate the loss because the assumptions on which they are based are unrealistic. In certain situations it is quite possible that a reduction in absenteeism does not increase the volume of output. This does not mean that management can neglect an investigation of absenteeism. Much can be learnt from such studies, but in my view the aim of reducing absenteeism does not require a knowledge of the cost of absence. It may well be that the immediate economic effects of absence are not so very great and that it is the effect on morale (and the possible long-term repercussions of this on the efficiency of the undertaking) that matters.

Many people try to visualise absenteeism in terms of the physical or financial loss of output in a desire to understand the problem. Mayo (p 79) describes this as the 'inevitable tendency' of people to assume that the total man-hours lost in a given week are capable of translation into pounds of metal. His discussion shows up the pitfalls of this approach.

'If a worker misses his eight-hour shift,

75

eight man-hours of production have been lost -
sometimes this was translated into an agreed
equivalent of pounds of metal. This last
figure was not wholly reliable; we found
instances in which equal losses of man-hours
in a casting shop had been followed by a
considerable loss of poundage in one case and,
in another, by no loss at all. In the former
event, several furnaces were 'down'; in the
latter, no furnace scheduled for work had been
forced to shut down.'

Thus the loss of potential output from the
absentees is controlled by the many complex factors
of factory organisation, factors entirely beyond the
limited field of personnel management.

While organisational and technical factors
determine the productive potentialities of a job or
factory department, the actual rate of performance,
and therefore the rate of output (ie actual
productivity), depends also on the worker's capacity
and willingness to work. It depends on the worker's
motives and attitudes to the task. Daily variations
in attendance are not the only signs of fluctuations
in willingness to work. Changes in the rate of
performance provide another indicator. There is no
guarantee that a worker who stays away from work
would work at his normal pace if he were persuaded
to attend. Moreover, it is often argued that
workers on payment by results make up for earnings
lost through absenteeism by working faster when they
return to work so that little - possibly no -
potential output is lost through their absence.
This conflicts with the claim that wage-incentives
reduce absenteeism. In fact they may well encourage
it by enabling the worker to make up for lost
earnings.

It is important in this discussion to discover
whether the low or the high producer stays away from
work. Beaumont (1945 p17) contended that 'it is a
mistake to assume that absence is characteristic of
low producers ...... It is not at all uncommon among
the better workers who may feel entitled to take a
day off just because their record compares
favourably with that of others'. Mayo, by contrast,
reported (p95) that a small group of workers with
practically no absences had a reputation for
'working like beavers'.

The interrelation between absenteeism and
labour productivity is more complex than would at
first seem. Where there is restriction of output
absenteeism may increase the worker's willingness to

work, and thus his rate of performance on the days
on which he attends. Again it is possible that
restriction of output is an alternative channel to
absenteeism for discontent, so that some workers may
show dissatisfaction by taking a day off but working
hard for the rest of the time while others vent
their feelings by going slow and loafing. Research
into these questions is needed and ought to be
fruitful.

In this context it must not be forgotten that
discontent expresses itself in many different ways.
Knowles (1952, p225) put forward the hypothesis
that 'strikes and absenteeism in coalmining are to
some extent "interchangeable"', and gave figures
which indicated that 'if strikes losses are high
absenteeism losses tend to be low and vice versa'.

Dockworkers, described by Knowles as strike-
prone, were said to show low absenteeism in a piece
of research on the Port of Manchester (10).

Other writers have suggested that absenteeism
is an alternative to labour turnover. However it is
difficult to obtain evidence on this. Firm Z,
mentioned earlier, examined the records of
individual workers and found that the absence rates
of workers who handed in their notice during the
survey period were far greater than those of workers
who were still with the firm at the end of the
period. If one accepts the contention that
absenteeism is an alternative to other expressions
of discontent - and this is plausible - then a
decline in absenteeism does not necessarily mean an
improvement in morale; it may merely mean that
employees express their discontent in a different
way. One must keep this possibility in mind when
tackling the problem of absenteeism. It may well be
that absenteeism is a safety-valve for discontent,
and that its rigorous suppression may give rise to
worse expressions of unrest.

The effects of absenteeism are not the same for
all concerned. Normally, absenteeism represents a
loss to the employer and also to the national
economy; it is not a loss to the worker. The
employee who chooses to take a day off gets what he
wants - relief from unbearable conditions, the
opportunity to devote time to his hobbies or to
engage in better-liked or better-paid part-time
employment, or the time for a change, perhaps
watching a football match.

It is usually held that the main area of
conflict between management and workers is on the
question of the distribution of rewards. There
would appear, however, to be another debated region

here which deserves consideration. Co-operation
does not only involve sharing out the product of
working together, it also involves agreement on
one's title to leisure and holidays. As Greenwood
(1951, p168) pointed out, it is interesting that the
workers most criticised for absenteeism get least
holidays.   This raises the question of what is
'reasonable' leisure, what is a 'reasonable' working
day, a 'reasonable' holiday?   Answers to these
questions deserve careful evaluation. The planning
of working hours and the distribution of free time
may well be one key to the control of absenteeism.
As Wilbert Moore (p 254) pointed out, absenteeism is
a sign that the working week is too long in terms of
the worker's personal evaluation of the situation.
It means the intrusion of values other than maximum
productivity, such as increased leisure or the
expenditure and enjoyment of earnings. It is not
wise to ignore these other values.

MANAGERIAL ACTION AND THE PROBLEM OF ABSENTEEISM

        In dealing with absenteeism the evaluations of
what is a reasonable level of attendance and a
reasonable working week as well as the right length
of holidays need to be considered. There is no
scientific formula to help and the answers rest on
subjective judgments. Management assessments may be
greatly influenced by the economic situation, while
the worker's judgments may not introduce this
criterion. On these issues it is important to reach
formal agreement with the firm's employees, for
divergent ideas about leisure may give rise to
absenteeism or other forms of go-slow.
        A study of the extent and incidence of
absenteeism in a plant may help management to make
their assessment. Other things, too, may be learned
from such a study, for example, about pockets of
dissatisfaction, about the possible better
deployment of labour, and about the effectiveness of
selection and supervision. The deeper understanding
that emerges from such an analysis may be worthwhile
in itself without any specific action being taken
about absenteeism. It might even seem better to
live with the problem rather than face some more
serious unrest. On the other hand the examination
may indicate certain possible courses of action.
Action, if it is deemed necessary, should not be
confined to the application of superficial
techniques which have the lure of facile solutions
but are at best palliatives that fail to reach the

root of the trouble.

An examination of the use of attendance bonuses suggests the importance of this distinction between the superficial method and an approach based on a deeper understanding of the problem derived from detailed study of the total situation. Frequently an attendance bonus is paid only once a year and the amount is insufficient to act as an incentive. Yet financial incentives only seem to work if they are immediate, visible, and sufficiently large. Misconceptions about the functioning of attendance bonuses may well account for the apparent high 'mortality' rate of these schemes. An American survey (11) of 17 different bonus schemes showed that six of them were abandoned and four more were described as ineffective by company officials.

First and foremost a bonus should act as a reward. In practice, however, an attendance bonus may become part of the expected wage - a payment the worker considers himself entitled to, especially if it is paid weekly. In 1958, for instance, it seemed to have acquired this role in the British coalmines (12). In such a situation any withdrawal of the bonus for non-attendance becomes a penalty. Payment of the bonus ceases to be a reward; its non-payment acts as a punishment, a discplinary measure giving rise to resentment. Moreover, a moral problem attaches to rewards for good attendance. As Greenwood (p 168) pointed out 'it ought not to be necessary to offer people rewards for doing what they agreed to do without them'.

Again, purely punitive measures must be regarded with caution. The American Research Council for Economic Security (13) pointed out that plans aiming at the elimination of absence-prone workers or of applying discipline miss the mark and accomplish neither the prevention nor the control of absenteeism. Moos (1951, pp106-107) quoting a National Coal Board report showed that in 1948 and 1949 respectively 4,900 men and 8,000 men were dismissed for bad attendance in British coalmines but that this did not improve attendance.

The chief weakness of reward and punishment systems is that they fail to reach the underlying difficulties. They do not alter job factors and they are not likely to change basic attitudes. If absenteeism is an attempt to escape from a disliked situation, one must alter the situation which gives rise to the discontent. If it is an expression of poor morale, one must try to improve morale. A more far-reaching and comprehensive policy is required if it is to have any permanent impact on worker

Voluntary Absence from Work

behaviour and morale.

Two complementary approaches commend themselves for such a policy; a person-centred and a condition-centred approach. The person-centred approach assumes that a certain proportion of individual workers have a high absenteeism rate and that this is connected with low morale. It tries to uproot ingrained habits of absence and concentrates its efforts on the individual and on personal relationships. Attention is centred on the quality of supervision and on the core of good attenders in order to build up group morale and to establish high standards of work conduct. The condition-centred approach assumes that specific circumstances cause high absenteeism and tries to modify conditions which give rise to it or to adjust the organisation of work to them.

Both approaches demand an adequate recording system, and one record can serve both purposes. An individual absence record is recommended for this task.

The person-centred approach uses individual absence records to identify 'chronic' absentees and to begin the investigation of unexplained absences. The attendance officer may investigate unexplained absences by home-visits and may be able to resolve difficulties which have given rise to them. Habitual absentees can be dealt with by letter or interview. Often they are threatened with dismissal if their record does not improve. Like other disciplinary measures such warnings touch only the surface of the problem and could give rise to feelings of victimisation. Nevertheless, regular scrutiny of absence records by an attendance officer is essential. It has been said that better attendance among small groups is due to the conspicuousness of the absentee. Conversely, it is true that in large plants and departments a bad attendance record may remain undetected for a long while, especially where there is poor supervision; knowledge that one can get away with it is likely to encourage would-be absentees, while knowledge that management attaches great importance to good attendance may prevent a worker from giving in to the impulse to stay away. It also affects the attitude of the supervisor, and through this the effectiveness of supervision.

Handyside (1953 pp43ff) showed that the Blue Monday Index provided a fair measure of supervisor efficiency, and the writer's study (1951 p 89) also, showed that Monday absenteeism was lower where there was more careful supervision. The foreman, as Uris

80

(1956) reported can make the absentee run out of excuses by talking to him after each absence. Again, employee attitudes to the supervisor are of importance. Metzner and Mann (pp 475ff) found that far fewer of the white-collar men with high Absence Frequency Rates than with low ones felt that they could talk freely to their supervisors. Lax supervision clearly makes bad attendance possible; it does not follow, however, that good supervision can of itself cure absenteeism. In certain circumstances it may merely act as a brake. Again, more evidence on this topic is desirable. An experiment by Mann and Sparling (1956) to reduce absence rates revealed the need for collaboration between supervisors in a factory and for awareness among them of the problem. This introduced regular supervisor conferences and new computation procedures. As a result absenteeism was reduced among both men and women. Similar experiments should prove worthwhile.

Kahne (et al) found that when factors were operative which heightened an employee's sense of responsibility this was reflected in fewer voluntary absences, and many writers have stressed the need to foster a greater personal sense of responsibility. The problem lies in the embodiment of this concept in the everyday life of office, workshop and factory. One suggestion which is often made in this connection is the abolition of 'clocking-in'. Jacques (1951, pp41-42) claimed that this reform met with great success at the Glacier Metal Company. Another suggestion places the organisation of free time into the hands of the work-group, and thus takes advantage of the social controls exercised by the group. Such a system, for instance, was found to be effective in one of the companies studied by Fox and Scott, and also in the Hawthorne Investigations (Roethlisberger and Dickson, 1939, pp83ff).

The need to develop a team-spirit and group cohesion has been stressed by many writers, but few studies actually show up an interrelation. One of these, by Metzner and Mann (op cit p 478), showed that blue-collar men and accountancy clerks had lower absence rates where they felt they belonged to a group. But one must always remember that in many industrial situations the type and organisation of work is hostile to group formation. A further suggestion is the establishment of absentee committees. These were partially successful during the Second World War, but as a result of difficulties in recruiting workers to committees that seem to pass judgement on their fellows they have now largely disappeared.

An absence policy that focuses all its attention on people and personal relationships is obviously one-sided. It neglects important knowledge on other aspects of absenteeism which so far has received little attention. It would be valuable to supplement an absence policy with facts and ideas from this other field. This may be achieved through the condition-centred approach to absenteeism. Its primary assumption is that high absenteeism occurs in specific circumstances where it is diffused among a large number of workers.

In order to recognise the conditions in a factory that are associated with high absenteeism it is necessary to prepare summaries from individual absence records describing the absenteeism records of different groups of workers according to department, occupation, sex, age, marital status, number of dependants, length of service and different days of the week. An analysis of these summaries will reveal where action is particularly urgent and where reorganisation may be necessary.

If the analysis uncovers a department that is prone to absenteeism it may be possible to effect an improvement by reorganising work and supervision. Where absenteeism is high among newcomers an attempt may be made to combat this by improving employee selection, induction and training. With married women management may have to examine the possibility of providing shopping facilities or half-days. Inadequate transport facilities, too, may be among conditions giving rise to high absenteeism, and it may be possible to improve them.

Since, in the writer's view, type of work is one of the chief causes of high absenteeism, a detailed study of absenteeism-prone jobs seems particularly important. It would be profitable to investigate whether the jobs can be changed and irritating characteristics which give rise to absenteeism eliminated. It may even be worthwhile in extreme cases to investigate whether a particular job can be eliminated.

It is also important to study the distribution of absences and to discover whether work can be reorganised to make the best use of prevailing patterns of attendance. For example, if particular shifts or days of the week are liable to absenteeism management may be able to eliminate these shifts. Saturday morning, a time notorious for absenteeism, could be abolished by spreading the working hours over the remaining five days. In 1947 many British factories made this change and a fall in the average level of absence followed. Most factories redistributed the working hours through the five-day week, but a few were content with shorter working time.

Holt compared the leave policies of two Australian banks and found that the branch which authorised leave on Saturday mornings lost less time from casual absences between Monday and Friday than the branch which compelled Saturday morning attendances. He remarked that work was slack on Saturdays so that branches could afford to give time off while time lost on other days of the week, when work was at full pressure, caused disorganisation. An intelligent policy of authorised leave in slack periods of working can be very profitable. When there are forseeable fluctuations in the workload, it may be preferable to give time off to people in rotation rather than have the whole labour force underemployed. This may be a useful concept in the organisation of clerical work where underemployment often leads to restlessness and dissatisfaction. The interim report of the Health of Munition Workers Committee also mentioned faulty organisation which leaves employees without work as a cause of absenteeism. Again the success claimed for 'leisure-bonuses' may be bound up with this.

Buzzard (1954 p 245) pointed out that what is often needed is not so much an improvement in total attendance as a more even distribution of attendances throughout the week. Obviously uneven distribution means working below capacity on certain days, and to full capacity on others. One colliery manager, he reported, 'told his men that he was not particularly concerned about their total attendance but asked them to arrange among themselves a more even attendance throughout the week. The result was satisfactory'.

Shepherd and Walker (1956, pp105ff) uncovered another valuable idea. They found that single shift absences in an iron and steel plant were concentrated on the morning shifts and were largely unpremeditated. They suggested that this was due to the early morning start and might be avoided by a reconsideration of shift-times. With day-workers, too, examination of starting and finishing times in relation to transport, shopping facilities, and other needs may be fruitful. It might be helpful to pursue research on the optimum length of the working day.

Again the planning of overtime requires thoughtful treatment by managers. It is often said that some workers work overtime at week-ends to get extra pay at higher rates, absenting themselves on other days of the week. In one firm the writer (1951, p 63) found evidence that workers doing overtime tended to be absent on other occasions. By contrast, in another factory the workers on overtime had a lower absence rate than the factory average. A re-check for a four-week period in 1958 showed that only 3 per cent of the 2,300 odd workers with the highest overtime figures also had higher absence rates. Nevertheless their overall attendance record was as good as that of others if one included their overtime. It must be remembered that week-end work is sometimes essential to meet urgent orders and that managements do not always mind if their workers take a day off later when work is slack. In other cases it may be useful to examine whether week-end overtime is economic, especially if it encourages absence during the week. More research could be pursued on the relations between absenteeism and overtime.

All these organisational factors require careful managerial attention. For instance, the introduction of a new product might require extra productive effort. With sufficient foresight advantage might be taken of the declining weekly absence curve by concentrating extra production on Thursdays and Fridays.

The organisational problem of carrying an adequate absentee cover, it is often said, can be mitigated by making workers interchangeable, with transference to other jobs when necessary. 'Firm Z', however, found that transferees showed much worse Monday absenteeism than established workers due to the impossibility of building up a group spirit among men who were constantly moved from one department to another. Other firms reported similar experiences. One solution of this problem is to operate a special team under a separate supervisor, to supply labour for urgent work and to replace absentees. To secure efficiency such a team needs to be given higher rates of pay and superior status.

It has been argued in this paper that the study of absenteeism may be valuable because of the insights which may be gained from it as well as the pointers for action. An absence programme, if it is deemed necessary, should not rest content with superficial techniques. It is essential to survey the whole field, to consider the total situation. In designing such a programme management should consider carefully any repercussions that might be created through the diversion of discontent to other outlets. Above all perspective must not be lost in any scheme of this kind. Despite the published estimates of the economic waste and financial losses from absenteeism it is possible that the economic consequences of absenteeism are not so great; perhaps the most troublesome aspect of absenteeism is the 'nuisance' element, the disturbances caused to supervisors and managers in running the plant when employees do not turn up for work. But absenteeism can have a deeper meaning as a symptom of unrest, of lack of identification with the work, and of an unfavourable attitude to it. To alter these, one must try to change the accepted attitudes and standards of conduct in relation to work, above all through an elimination of the factors that make for low job satisfaction. A one-sided approach should be avoided. In the past, many absence policies have focused attention only on changing people's attitudes and behaviour, not on changing jobs and the organisation of work. This seems a mistaken approach. It could happen that more can be gained from job-improvements and work-reorganisation than from attempts to change people. Both approaches, however, are complementary and must be joined in a comprehensive absence programme.

NOTES

1. The phenomenon of a recurrent weekly absence pattern was observed by many investigators in Britain, for instance T Loveday 'The Causes and Conditions of Lost Time' in Health of Munition Workers Committee Interim Report: Industrial Efficiency and Fatigue, London, HMSO, 1917; S Wyatt, R Marriott and D E R Hughes, A Study of Absenteeism among Women, Industrial Health Research Board, Emergency Report No 4, London, HMSO, 1943. The phenomenon has been noticed in other countries, for instance, in America and Sweden. See The Problem of Absenteeism, NICB Studies in Personnel Policy, No. 53, New York, April 1943; and R Meidner, Svensk arbetsmarkmad wid full sysselsättning, Stockholm, Konjunkturinstitutet, 1954, p269.
2. See for instance P Sargant Florence: Labour (London, Hutchinson University Library, 1949). pp98ff and R B Buzzard, 1954, p249.
3. H M Vernon and T Bedford (1931) p 5 show for coalminers that a fall in wages was accompanied by a decline in absenteeism, but there was also a change in hours and a reduction in possible shifts.

Voluntary Absence from Work

4. See, for instance, the studies made by the Industrial Health Research Board and the British Institute of Management in Britain, by the Department of Labour and National Service in Australia, and American studies quoted by Dale Yoder: Handbook of Personnel Management and Labour Relations (New York, McGraw-Hill 1958), section 7.1.
5. Compare W Baldamus: (1951) p 26 'The ability to capture and maintain the working mood changes according to the day of the week. Monday appears to be least conducive to a steady working mood. Nor is it easy to settle down on Saturday morning ....' (See also pp 50-58).
6. See, for instance, E W Noland: 'Worker Attitudes and Industrial Absenteeism; a Statistical Appraisal', American Sociological Review (Albany, New York), Vol 10, 1945. W A Kerr, G J Koppelmeier and J J Sullivan: 'Absenteeism, Turnover and Morale in a Metals Fabrication Factory', in Occupational Psychology Vol 25, 1951, No 1, Metzner and Mann (1953).
7. Statistical evidence on this topic (published in the Ministry of Fuel and Power Statistical Digest, HMSO, London, 1946 and 1947), recording output per manshift and absenteeism on each shift for one week in 1946, showed an association between these two variables. The pooled correlation coefficient between output per manshift and absenteeism, eliminating the effect of time, for these figures was found to be -0.94 and highly significant, suggesting the existence of an inverse relationship between absenteeism and output per manshift. Studies of individual pits over longer periods are needed before any more definite conclusions can be drawn.
8. In 1950 for example voluntary absenteeism in British coalmines amounted to 13 manshifts annually per worker; output per manshift was 1.19 tons; the average number employed was 697,000 men. The estimate - assuming that output per manshift remains constant - would then demonstrate a loss of 10.8 million tons of potential output of coal. The shortcomings of this approach are discussed later.
9. See 'The Financial Effects of Absence from Work' Case Study No 1 by W J Byrt and L R Wall, in Bulletin of Industrial Psychology and Personnel Practice (Melbourne), Vol 7, No 4, Dec 1951: and Case Study No 2 by R Isherwood, ibid, Vol 8, No 2, June 1952.
10. See The Dock Worker: Analysis of Conditions of Employment in the Port of Manchester (Liverpool University Press, 1954), p197.

11. See Controls for Absenteeism, National Industrial Conference Board Studies in Personnel Policy, No 126, New York, 1952, p 42ff.
12. An attendance bonus was introduced in the British coalmines in 1947 under which miners who had attended five shifts during the week received an extra shift's pay. Agitation that this system discriminated against the sick miner led to alterations in the attendance bonus in June 1957. Under the new system the miner received a proportion of the attendance bonus for each day he attended, unless he had been away on strike during the week. Much publicity was given to an alleged increase in absenteeism after this change but it was difficult to judge the issue on the available data as the classification of voluntary and involuntary absences was changed simultaneously and Total Absence Rates were affected by an unusually high incidence of sicknes.
13. See report in The Controller (New York, Controller's Institute of America), Feb, 1956.

REFERENCES

Acton Society Trust, Size and Morale: A Preliminary Study of Attendance at Work in Large and Small Units (1953) and Part II: A Further Study of Attendance at Work in Large and Small Units, London, 1957

A G Arbous and H S Sichel, New Techniques for the Analysis of Absenteeism Data, National Institute for Personnel Research, South Africa: Biometrika, Vol 41, London, 1954

W Baldamus, Incentives and Work Analysis, Monograph A1, University of Birmingham Studies in Economics and Society, 1951

W Baldamus, Type of Work and Motivation, British Journal of Sociology, Vol II, No 1, March 1951

H Beaumont, The Psychology of Personnel, Longmans Green and Co., London, 1945

H Behrend, Absence under Full Employment, Monograph A3, University of Birmingham Studies in Economics and Society, 1951

H Behrend, Absence and Labour Turnover in a Changing Economic Climate, Occupational Psychology, Vol 27, No 2., April 1953

H Behrend, Normative Factors in the Supply of Labour, Manchester School of Economic and Social Studies, Vol XXIII, No 1, 1955

R B Buzzard, Attendance and Absence in Industry: The

Nature of the Evidence, British Journal of
Sociology, Vol V, No 3, Sept, 1954

W H B Court, Coal, History of the Second World War,
HMSO, London, 1951

J B Fox and Jerome F Scott, Absenteeism:
Management's Problem, Harvard Business School,
Research Studies, No 29, 1943

G B Greenwood, Is Absenteeism a Problem?, Journal of
the Institute of Personnel Management, Vol
XXXIII, No 316, London, 1951

J D Handyside, Supervision in a Cotton Spinning
Firm, Two Studies in Supervision, NIIP Report No
10, London, 1953

David Hewitt and Jessie Parfit, A Note on Working
Morale and Size of Group, Occupational
Psychology, Vol 27, No 1, 1953

N F Holt, Absence from Work in a Bank, Personnel
Practice Bulletin, Dept of Labour and National
Service, Vol XII, No 1, Melbourne, March 1956

E Jacques, The Changing Culture of a Factory,
Tavistock Publications Ltd, London, 1951

H R Kahne, C M Ryder, L S Snegireff and G Wyshak,
Age and Absenteeism, American Management
Association Archives of Industrial Health, Vol
15, No 2, Feb 1957

K G J C Knowles, Strikes: A Study in Industrial
Conflict, Basil Blackwell, Oxford, 1952

M D Kossoris, Absenteeism and Injury Experience of
Older Workers, Monthly Labour Review, Vol 67, No
1, Washington, 1948

F D K Liddell, Attendance in the Coal-Mining
Industry, British Journal of Sociology, Vol V,
No 1, March, 1954

F C Mann and J E Sparling, Changing Absence Rates:
An Application of Research Findings, Personnel,
American Management Association, New York, 1956

Elton Mayo, The Social Problems of an Industrial
Civilisation, Routledge and Kegan Paul, London,
1952

Helen Metzner and Floyd Mann, Employee Attitudes
and Absences, Personnel Psychology, Vol 6, No 4,
Baltimore, Winter 1953

Wilbert E Moore, Industrial Relations and the Social
Order, Macmillan Co., New York, 1947

S Moos, The Statistics of Absenteeism in the Coal
Mines, Manchester School of Economic and Social
Studies, Vol 19, No 1, 1951

F J Roethlisberger and W J Dickson, Management and
the Worker, Harvard University Press, 1939

R D Shepherd and J Walker, Three-Shift Working and
the Distribution of Absence, Occupational
Psychology, Vol 30, No 2, 1956

R D Shepherd and J Walker, Absence and the Physical
    Conditions of Work, British Journal of
    Industrial Medicine, Vol 14, London, 1957
R D Shepherd and J Walker, Absence from Work in
    Relation to Wage Level and Family
    Responsibility, British Journal of Industrial
    Medicine, Vol 15, London, 1958
A Uris, How to Increase Presenteeism, World Oil,
    Gulf Publishing Co., Houston, Feb. 1956
H M Vernon and T Bedford, The Absenteeism of Miners
    in Relation to Short Time and Other Conditions,
    Industrial Health Research Board, Report No 62,
    HMSO, London, 1931
C R Walker and R H Guest, The Man on the Assembly
    Line, Harvard University Press, 1952
S Wyatt and R Marriott, Absence during the War,
    Inudustrial Health Research Board Memorandum,
    MRC 47/168, IHRB 47/10, 1947

6   In-Company Criteria for Evaluating Absences

Written 1983.

THE SCOTTISH ENQUIRIES

In 1959, as described in Chapter 5, I recommended two complementary approaches for dealing with absence problems, a person-centred and a condition-centred approach. Ten years later an invitation to look at the absence problem at General Motors Scotland provided an opportunity to implement the recommendation. This chapter presents an account of the findings and insights derived from the enquries which covered sickness, as well as other absences, from work.

One objective in accepting the invitation was to find out what difference computerisation can make for absence studies and, in particular, whether the type of questionnaire analysis which we had used in national sample survey work (where information is collected in a form immediately transferable to punchcards and computers) can be applied to individual absence records and thus provide a basis for dividing the population, with the help of their records, into low to high absence groups - the approach which I had recommended in 1959.

The essence of the plan was that I would look at absence information the other way round. The groups to be examined would be those with similar absence records. Having established this similarity I would be able to find out what percentage of the population with certain personal characteristics had shown a particular type of absence behaviour. The analysis would provide frequency distributions to which statistical tests could be applied.

To execute the plan, information for two periods was provided by the Terex plant of General Motors Scotland, a heavy engineering factory in the West of Scotland. The mid 1968/69 enquiry covered a

one year period and a population of 762 male manual
workers employed throughout the year, and the
1969 to 1974 enquiry covered a six year period and a
population of 610 men continuously employed during
the six years, as well as men who had joined or left
the firm. For most of the time the factory was
operating a forty hour five day working week with a
rotating nightshift, dayshift system. Considerable
amounts of overtime were worked. Thus it emerged
that in spite of absences 90 per cent of the male
employees studied in 1968/69 had put in an average
of 39 hours per week which can be described as a
remarkably good overall record.

Very detailed evidence for the first enquiry
was provided by General Motors in computer-ready
form on a questionnaire which I designed. In the
second enquiry details of the personal particulars
of the employees were supplied in the form of a
computer print-out while the absence information had
to be extracted by us from the individual absence
records then in use at General Motors and added in
writing to the print-out, thus providing a new
computer-ready data bank.

While I undertook the one year study on my own,
the six year study was carried out jointly by Stuart
Pocock and myself. Hence the use of the word 'we'
in this paper. Dr Pocock was at that time a member
of the Medical Computing and Statistics Group of the
University of Edinburgh and had already made major
contributions to the study of sickness absences.
The one year enquiry is described in detail in
Behrend (1974/75) and the six year enquiry in
Behrend and Pocock (1976). The Monograph, How to
Monitor Absence from Work (Behrend, 1978), presents
evidence from both enquiries and additional evidence
not included in the articles.

In carrying out the two enquiries we included
all absence episodes whether they were covered by
sickness certificates or not. This contrasts with
the studies described in Chapter 5 which focused on
voluntary absence from work.

In addition we replaced the use of traditional
absence measures - absence rates and average number
of days or spells lost (all of them arithmetic
averages) - by the use of frequency measures such as
medians, quartiles and deciles. Since it had long
been established by research that the days lost
distributions of individual absence behaviour tend
to be highly skewed, these appeared to be more
appropriate measures for our study.

How unrepresentative the arithmetic mean can be
as regards individual behaviour is illustrated by

the following evidence from my first enquiry. In the year mid 1968/69 the average (mean) number of working days lost per male manual worker was 17.5 and yet 67 per cent of the men had lost fewer days than this. The median (the middle frequency in order of rank) was 8 days. Just over half of the men (51 per cent) had lost 8 days or less during the year.

The particular advantage of our approach is that it supplies criteria for evaluating absences which can be used as a base for action as well as for examining and identifying personal or other factors in absenteeism. A pre-requisite for applying this method, however, is the existence of a good individual absence record system.

The introduction of the Statutory Sick Pay Scheme (SSP), which came into force in Britain in April 1983, has made it imperative for British managers to keep individual sickness absence records and therefore the approach which we developed (and the record I have recommended) has become particularly relevant. An example of the record is reproduced at the end of this chapter.

THE DERIVATION OF IN-COMPANY CRITERIA

The Information Base

The following sections draw on our research evidence to illustrate the methods we used and to discuss the research findings and their implications.

The method we developed is simple. The only 'raw material' which is needed are counts of the number of working days lost and the number of absence spells incurred by each employee during the period; we also recommend a count of the number of one day absences. These counts are ranked in order of ascending size and summarised first as frequency distributions and then as cumulative frequency distributions. The latter make possible the identification of key reference points in the distribution, such as deciles, quartiles and medians which are required for the classification of the absences as well as for the division of the population into sub-groups with different levels of absence.

In-Company Criteria for Evaluating Absences

The Classification of the Absence Records

The products of the classification process are illustrated next by two examples from our enquiries.

Table 1
Classification of Individual Absence Records

mid 1968/69

Reference points*	No of Days Lost	No of Absence Spells	Label for Absence Level
Lower decile	1	1	very low
Lower quartile	2	2	low
Median	8	4	medium
Upper quartile	23	7	high
Upper decile	47	10	very high

N=762 N=762

*The lower decile, lower quartile, median, upper quartile and upper decile denote the amount of absence exceeded or equalled by 90, 75, 50, 25 or 10 per cent of the employees respectively.

Table 2
Division of Workforce into Absence Groups
by days lost

mid 1968/69

Classification		No in group	Percentage in group
Low	0-2 days	191	25
Fairly low	3-8 days	195	26
Fairly high	9-22 days	183	24
High	23 days or more	193	25

The classifications in Tables 1 and 2 can be used as reference frames for evaluating a particular individual absence record and thus provide in-company absence criteria. They can also be used for setting goals for the reduction of absences to the levels attained by the good attenders. In a small or medium sized organisation where the workforce is not very large these classifications can be carried out without using a computer.

Furthermore, the in-company criteria make it possible for managers to evaluate the absence records of their employees without reference to other factories. Up to now they have often tried to look at the records of other firms (where available) to assess whether their absences compared favourably or not. However, outside comparisons can be very misleading because of differences in the recording of absences and the defects in the traditional absence measures; and because the employee's job can affect the duration of absences, for instance, a clerk can come to work although he may have a broken ankle but a bus-driver cannot drive his bus.

THE USE OF CROSS-TABULATIONS

Age and Absence

The absence sub-groups in Table 3 provide the base for cross-tabulations with other variables. The first example examines the relation of absence and age by comparing the absence classifications for two age groups. The evidence selected comes from Factory B, a West of Scotland heavy engineering plant, and draws on evidence collected by King (1973) and made available to me. It was chosen because large and comparable numbers of male employees fell into the under 30, and 50 and over, age groups. It should be noted that the absence spells percentages provide an alternative measure to the Absence Frequency Rate (described in Chapter 5) which represents an arithmetic mean.

Table 3
Age and Absence
(Factory B 1968)

Absence Group	Percentage of men in absence group			
	Absence Spells Age Group		Days Lost Age Group	
	Under 30 230 men	50&over 203 men	Under 30 230 men	50&over 203 men
Low	12	36	14	32
Fairly low	20	30	25	23
Fairly high	25	19	33	19
High	43	15	28	26

Table 3 shows clearly that as far as absence spells were concerned the attendance records of the oldest age group in the plant were much better than those of the youngest. The more detailed table in my monograph included the 30-39 and 40-49 age groups and showed that the higher the age group, the higher was the percentage of men with good attendance records, and conversely the lower the age group the higher was the percentage with bad attendances.

Similarly, the figures relating to days lost showed that a higher percentage of the youngest age group had fairly high and high records than of the oldest age group although the difference was not so marked. It should be noted that almost a third of the men in the 50 and over age group were good attenders with a low absence classification.

The General Motors one year and six year studies provided similar evidence for days lost and absence spells (Behrend, 1974-75, pp 12-14); the percentage differences were most marked for one day absence spells (Behrend and Pocock, 1976, p 316).

Department and Absence

The next example presents evidence for two departments from the 1969 to 1974 General Motors Scotland enquiry. The classification of the absences is based on the whole six year period. It uses age standardised percentages.

Table 4
Department and Absence

Percentage of men in absence group
for days lost for the whole six year period
1969 to 1974

| Absence Group | Department | |
	Assembly 167 men	Welding 115 men
Low	26	14
Fairly low	29	22
Fairly high	22	28
High	24	36

As can be seen from Table 4, a noticeably higher percentage of the men in the welding department than in assembly had high absence records for days lost.

In-Company Criteria for Evaluating Absences

Days Lost and Absence Spells

The third example compares the employee absence group classifications for days lost and absence spells.

Table 5
Comparison of the Classification
of Days Lost and Absence Spells

Percentage of the 762 men in the different absence
groups
mid 1968/69 enquiry

Spells lost	Days lost			
	Low 0-2	Fairly low 3-8	Fairly high 9-22	High 23&over
Low 0-2	25	5	2	2
Fairly low 3-4	-	12	6	5
Fairly high 5-6	-	7	6	3
High 7&over	-	2	10	15

The totals for days lost are made up of absence spells of different duration; one must, therefore, expect an inequality in the relationship between the two variables, namely that the number of absence spells can never exceed the number of days lost. This is illustrated in Table 5 and accounts for the three empty cells. Similarly the table shows that a high days lost classification can occur together with a low number of spells; in this case just one or two long sickness episodes.

An examination of the degree of correspondence between the two types of behaviour shows that 57 per cent of the employees received the same classification for days lost and absence spells. One quarter, by far the largest sub-group, fell into the low absence classification for both dimensions while 15 per cent had high classifications for both.

This means, if time and resources are scarce, and action urgent, that attention can be given to this high absence group instead of studying the whole of the workforce. In such an investigation it can be helpful to work out multi-variable profiles for each individual and possibly to compare them with profiles of good attenders.

THE STUDY OF TRENDS OVER TIME

The in-company criteria can be used to find out whether the percentage of employees with high absence records is increasing or decreasing and also to monitor the effectiveness of an absence policy. The chosen base year would supply the low to high absence group classification for the trend comparisons. In the following example from our six year study, 1974 was chosen as base year because we were conducting a retrospective analysis.

Effect of Warning System

The example in Table 6 examines the effects of a disciplinary warning system related to lateness and one day absences with the ultimate agreed sanction of dismissal. Details for the low and high absence groups are reproduced below.

Table 6
Effect of Warning System Introduced in May 1970

Percentage of the 610 men who incurred
no one day absence spells in the year

1969	1970	1971	1972	1973	1974
20	18	34	38	29	33

Percentage of the 610 men who incurred three or
more one day absence spells in the year

1969	1970	1971	1972	1973	1974
41	44	24	20	29	24

Table 6 shows that the introduction of the scheme in May 1970 made a considerable impact in increasing the percentage of men who incurred no one day absence spells and in reducing the percentage of men who incurred three or more one day absence spells. Up to the end of 1974 no dismissal had become necessary.

In-Company Criteria for Evaluating Absences

SOME OTHER FINDINGS

Hours of Work, Overtime, Earnings and Absence

The one year General Motors study looked at the relation between hours of work, overtime, earnings and absence (Behrend 1974/75, pp 16-20). The year to which the enquiry related was one of prosperity, of full order books and expansion plans and consequently a considerable amount of overtime was worked on Tuesday and Thursday evenings and week-ends, in addition to the normal 40 hour working week. As a result, the average total weekly hours put in by the majority of workers was high: the median was 49 hours but some workers frequently put in as many as 60. The evidence revealed that for three-quarters of the employees the relationship between absence and hours and overtime was purely functional in the sense that an absence meant a loss of hours and a loss of overtime if it fell on an overtime day and similarly a loss in earnings. Thus the lower the average hours worked (that is, the greater the number of hours lost by absence) the greater was the percentage of employees in the lower earnings group and conversely, the higher the hours, the higher the percentage in the higher earnings group.

However, a few employees apparently managed to make up the loss of earnings from absences by working longer hours when they returned to work. There was no evidence of an abuse of overtime.

The Absence Records of New Entrants

In the period 1969 to 1974, the General Motors Terex Plant expanded its work-force twice by recruiting 242 male employees in 1969 to early 1970, and another 153 in late 1972 to 1973. It was possible to compare the absence records of the two groups of entrants with each other, and with the men who were with the firm throughout the six year period. The finding was that the attendance records of the two groups differed markedly. The first group of newcomers settled down well and showed as far back as 1970 a consistently lower level of absences than the men who were already there. The 1972-73 entrants, by contrast, had a worse record. 39 per cent of them, for example, had a high absence classification for absence spells, compared with 26 per cent of the men employed before 1969 and 18 per cent of the 1969-70 entrants. The findings thus indicate that there was a change in the behaviour of newcomers. As a possible explanation we were told that the morale in the factory had suffered during the winter of 1973-74 because of economic uncertainty and short-time working.

Absence and Labour Turnover

There has been much interest in the question of the relation between absence and labour turnover. The question which I looked at using our evidence was whether the men in the high absence group were more likely to leave than those in the low absence group. Evidence was available for Comapny B two years after the classification date for days lost. This showed that 25 per cent of the men in the high days absence group were no longer with the company compared with only 14 per cent of the men in the low days absence group. In the General Motors one year enquiry the interval we looked at was six years. Taking the 1968-69 absence spells classification as a base we found that 38 per cent of the high absence spells group had left compared with 22 per cent of the low spells group.

The Consistency of Absence Behaviour

In the six year study comparisons of individual absence records were made to examine the question of consistency in absence behaviour. These revealed a statistically significant positive association between the incidence of spells of absence in the two periods, in the sense that individuals with many absences in the first three years tended to behave in a similar fashion during the following three years. A significant positive association also existed for the numbers of one day spells and numbers of days absent.

Although these results established consistency of absence behaviour over a lengthy period there were exceptions: for example, one employee dropped from 12 spells to none whereas another went from 7 spells to 22. Such extreme reversals in behaviour were not very frequent but they do suggest that one must be cautious in using the concept of absence proneness.

Statistical Tests

I have just mentioned the existence of

statistically significant associations as regards
the consistency of absence behaviour. As pointed
out at the beginning of this chapter, one of the
advantages of our use of frequency distributions is
that it enables us to apply statistical tests. For
those interested, the final paragraph of his section
briefly summarises the results.

The tests revealed a number of statistically
significant associations, for instance, the finding
that the percentage of men who had incurred a high
number of absence spells was lower, the higher the
age group; that the percentage of men in the welding
department falling into the high days lost absence
group was higher than in the assembly department;
that the percentage of men in the high spells
absence group who left the firm was higher than the
percentage in the lower absence groups; also that
the percentage with high absence spells among the
most recent recruits was higher than among people
who had been with the firm for at least a year. The
reduction in the incidence of one day absence spells
after the introduction of the disciplinary warning
system was also statistically significant (for
details see Behrend and Pocock, 1976).

FINDINGS FROM THE ANALYSIS OF ABSENCE SPELLS

The amount of work involved in the analysis of
absence spells is far more time consuming, costly
and complicated than the work involved in the
analysis of individual absence records which has
been described. However, I was able to include a
section on this in the 1978 monograph which is based
on the evidence collected in the one year enquiry.
A brief account of the main findings follows.

To carry out this analysis I designed a record
sheet for the absence episodes incurred by each of
the male employees and a clerical assistant
transferred to this, from our questionnaires, a
detailed record of every absence spell which the
employee had incurred. This information was then
processed by computer.

Two different types of information were
obtained. Evidence about the duration of absence
spells, and the frequency with which absences of
different length had occurred, and information on
the days of the week on which absences of different
duration took place as regards starting day,
continuation and return to work.

In-Company Criteria for Evaluating Absences

The Duration of Absence Spells

This evidence made it possible to divide absences into different types; for instance into short and long, certificated and uncertificated. It thus provides a link with the topic of voluntary absence discussed in Chapter 5. Some of the major findings are summarised below.

The frequency distribution of absences of different length revealed that just under 80 per cent of the absence spells were short, lasting half a day to two days; only one in five absence spells was longer. One day spells which accounted for 63 per cent of all absences were by far the most frequent; the half day incidence was only 9 per cent and the two day incidence 8 per cent. The next percentage in descending order was 5 per cent for spells of a five day duration ie of one full working week.

The disturbances in the organisation of production caused by these short spells would thus appear to have warranted the attention which the General Motors Scotland management paid to the problem of uncertificated absences by introducing the warning system mentioned earlier. The half day absences (which were not included in the rest of our enquiries) may link up with the incidence of lateness which has rarely been studied in detail. On the six year records lateness appeared to have been a major problem.

What about longer absences? Their main impact related to working days lost. Just under 79 per cent of lost days were accounted for by absences lasting three days or more, that is, by absences which at that time were required to be accompanied by medical certificates. Furthermore it was found that 126 absences (out of 3472 spells) lasted longer than four weeks and accounted for 43 per cent of all days lost!

Differences in Daily Absence Patterns

Which were the days of the week on which absences of different duration took place? The investigation of this question revealed that uncertificated absence spells of one or two days gave rise to different weekly absence patterns than longer certificated absence spells of three days and more. These patterns are illustrated in the graphs which accompany this text.

The graphs (reproduced at the end of this chapter) compare variations in the daily absence

In-Company Criteria for Evaluating Absences

pattern of uncertificated and certificated absences
and of the combined total for two factories at
different points of time, namely for Factory H which
I studied in my Birmingham enquiries and for the
General Motors one year Scottish enquiry. The
illustration shows clearly that it was the impact of
the short (uncertificated) absences which dominated
the overall absence pattern at Factory H in 1950:
both showed a marked Blue Monday absence pattern.
At General Motors in 1968-69, by contrast, it was
the longer certificated absences which formed the
major component of total absences and determined the
overall absence pattern: both showed a sickness
absence pattern, that is, a slightly upward trend in
the incidence of absences in the course of the week.

Evidence from Company B for 1968 is also of
interest (see Behrend, 1978 p37). The High Absence
group of 221 men had a marked Blue Monday pattern as
regards the incidence of 1 plus 2 day absence spells
which dominated the men's overall record in spite of
a high incidence of certificated absences. For the
whole factory, however, the sickness absence pattern
predominated.

The evidence suggests that the trend in overall
absence rates can indicate the relative importance
of short and long absences. At the end of the 1940s
and early 1950s, it would seem, short absences
represented a much bigger proportion of total
absences than in the later period, and that,
therefore, the Blue Monday absence pattern
predominated, whereas at the end of the 1960s the
sicknes absence pattern emerged as dominant because
the incidence of certificated illness had increased.

The slightly upward trend in the incidence of
certificated absences in the course of the week was
found to be associated with the popularity of Monday
as a day of return after such spells. Thus 79 per
cent of the absences of three days or more ended
after the week-end. Indeed more people returned to
work on Mondays than started absences on that day.
Managers may thus be able to identify which
component of absences predominates in their plant by
examining whether the number of absences decreases
or increases from Friday to Monday.

Pocock (1973) commenting on this tendency in
his study introduced the concept of a 'delay factor'
in the return to work indicating that there may be
an interval between the return to fitness and the
resumption of work.

Night shifts can also contribute to an increase
in absences of the voluntary type on Friday which
would terminate on a Monday as was found in the one

year enquiry at General Motors. The General Motors
management dealt with this problem in the late 1970s
by abolishing Friday night shifts. This was
followed by a complete abolition of night shifts and
a re-organisation of the day shift pattern. I was
told that this led (in its early stages) to an
improvement in attendances and to a reduction in the
number of calls on the General Motors surgery.

SOME IMPLICATIONS

Long and Short Absences

The evidence with regard to the different
incidence pattern of long and short absence spells
which has just been described suggests that the two
types of episodes are different in nature and that
absences can be divided into two types using
duration as a factual base. Furthermore, the
finding that the certificated sickness component has
come to represent such a high proportion of days
lost suggests that more attention needs to be paid
to the medical aspects of absence studies by
managements and non-medical social science
researchers.

It has long been recognised, as discussed in
Chapter 5, that absence from work is a multi-
dimensional phenomenon and absence records have been
divided into categories, such as absences due to
sickness, accidents, authorised leave and voluntary
absences. The problem of classification, however,
is that the borderline between genuine sickness,
psychological malaise and disinclination to work is
blurred. Thus Taylor and Pocock (1982) have
suggested that sickness is difficult to define and
should more accurately be described as absence from
work attributed to incapacity because it does not
represent a reliable indicator of true morbidity.

The evidence presented in this chapter
indicates that we can replace the methods used to
identify voluntary absences described in Chapter 5
by a different approach, namely by focusing on one
day absences which have been shown to be the
predominant type of short absences.

Our suggestion is that one day absences should
be recorded as such by a special symbol on
individual absence records so that separate
frequency distributions and analyses of one day
absences can be carried out by use of the in-company
criteria method outlined earlier in this chapter.
This is a much simpler method than the absence

spells and duration analyses.

The evidence (reproduced earlier) illustrating
that the introduction of the early warning
disciplinary system was followed by a reduction in
one day spells among the low as well as the high
absence groups bears out the interpretation that
these represent voluntary absences. According to
information provided by management in 1975,
unauthorised one day absences had become infrequent
but an increase in certificated one day absences had
partially offset the reduction. Overall, the annual
numbers of employees with no one day absences of any
kind had inreased considerably.

This indicates that an analysis of one day
spells can help to identify the minority with a high
record of short absences which may require attention
whether disciplinary, medical or other. It also
shows that the in-company criteria method of
analysis can help to monitor the effect of remedial
policies or other events.

Type of Work and Absence - The Welders' Case

The vast majority of the men in the welding
department in the one year enquiry (95%) were
skilled men who had undergone a five year
apprenticeship and yet a high percentage of them had
poor attendance records for both days lost and
absence spells. This compared unfavourably with the
men in the assembly department who had only received
three months training. The welding department
therefore emerged from the analysis as a candidate
for managerial attention.

The personnel manager explained that the
departmental difference had something to do with the
selection of men for assembly (men wanted to be
moved to this work), and with the particular
background of the welders. It seemed that
management considered that it was an attitudinal
problem which could not easily be dealt with.
However, in the later six year enquiry the welders'
records only showed a significant statistical
association with days lost and not with absence
spells. This may have been due to the effect of the
warning system and to a reduction in the number of
welders.

The evidence thus suggested that to begin with
it was a dual problem involving both sickness and
voluntary absences and that the sickness incidence
had not changed. That this continued to be a
problem became apparent when I was approached in

October 1979 by the nursing officer in charge of the General Motors surgery about a problem that worried him. It turned out to be the high incidence of absence in the welding department. I mentioned that public concern had been expressed in certain quarters about respiratory complaints suffered by welders sometimes referred to as 'welder's lung' and he said that there might be something in this; they had a lot of respiratory trouble and he would look into it. Because of the takeover of the Terex plant by BSH Holding in January 1981 I did not hear the outcome. However, this case suggests that our in-company criteria approach can be used as an aid in the monitoring of occupational health hazards and that the discovery of an unusually high percentage of employees in the high absence group in a particular occupation warrants investigation.

The Person-Centred Approach

The General Motors evidence revealed that the minority of the employees with a high absence classification was widely dispersed among the workforce, although a sizeable number were located in the welding department. The scrutiny and analysis of the individual absence records therefore suggests that absences from work should be looked at as primarily an expression of individual behaviour or liability to sickness.

From the practical point of view the information which is required for assessing the problem and for taking action consists in a good individual absence record system and in appropriate in-company criteria for assessing what are reasonable absence records. This leads on to the identification of the employees with high absence classifications on whom managerial attention should be focused; and also to the question of remedial action, be it to improve the health or the motivation of individuals less well adapted to the work environment than fellow workers with good attendance records.

To do this it is desirable to study the records more closely with a view to gaining a better understanding of possible factors involved. If this anlysis pinpoints jobs or circumstances where absence is high among a sizeable number of employees, attention can be focused on the type of conditions which seem to give rise to this reaction and on the possibility of altering them. This would involve looking at the work itself and at its organisation as well as at the quality of the human relations in the workshops, the working climate, the interrelations of employees, supervisors and managers.

The climate of industrial relations has become more sensitive to these issues and more favourable to the application of 'conditions-changing' approaches than it was in the 1960s. Therefore our absence analysis method, in so far as it makes possible the identification of sources of dissatisfaction, stress and ill-health (which find expressions in reactions such as high absence) is of considerable potential importance as regards improving human relations and reforming jobs.

REFERENCES

H Behrend, A new approach to the analysis of absences from work, Industrial Relations Journal, Vol 5, No 4, Winter 1974/75

H Behrend and S Pocock, Absence and the individual: a six-year study in one organisation, International Labour Review, Vol 114, No 3, November-December 1976

H Behrend, How to Monitor Absence from Work, Institute of Personnel Management, London, 1978

H Behrend, Absence problems: are attendance bonus schemes the answer? Management Decision, Vol 18, No 4, 1980

M King, A Study of Absence among Shop-floor Workers, MPhil Thesis, University of Edinburgh, November 1973

S J Pocock, Daily variations in Sickness Absence, Journal of Royal Statistical Society Series C (Applied Statistics), Vol 22, No 3, 1973

P Taylor and S J Pocock, chapter in Occupational Practice, ed R S F Schilling, Butterworth, 2nd edition 1982

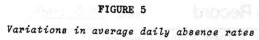

FIGURE 5

Variations in average daily absence rates

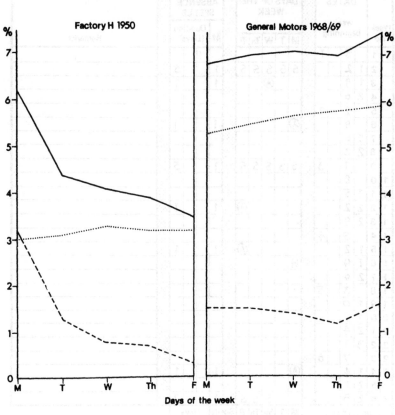

- - - - = uncertificated absences
.... = certificated absences
_____ = all absences

Absence Record   Name *R.B Smith*

Week No	week beginning			M	T	W	Th	F	No	Duration (Days)	Remarks
1	5	1									
2	1	2		S	S	S	S	S	1	5	
3	1	9				(A)			1	1	
4	2	6									
5		2	2								
6		9		(A)					1	1	
7	1	6									
8	2	3									
9	1	7	3	S	S	S	S	S	1	5	
10		8									
11	1	5									
12	2	2					(A)		1	1	
13	2	9									
14		5	4								
15	1	2					(A)		1	1	
16	1	9		H							
17	2	6									
18		3	5								
19	1	0									
20	1	7									
21	2	4									
22	3	1									
23		7	6								
24	1	4		(A)					1	1	
25	2	1									
26	2	8				S	S	S	1	3	
SUB-TOTALS weeks 1-26				M	T	W	Th	F	Spells	Days	
				4	2	4	3	5	8	18	

Surname 1-16	S M I T H					
Initials 17-19	A B		Starting Date 26-31	1	2 7 2	
Sex 20	1		Birth Date 32-37	2 4 1 0 5 0		
Clock No 21-25	1 2 3 4		Marital Status 38	2		
			Children 39			
			Home Location 40			
			Dept. 41-42			
			Occupation 45-47			
			Year 48-51			

In-Company Criteria for Evaluating Absences

Clock No. __1234__   Dept. _____

Week No	week beginning		M	T	W	Th	F	No	Duration (Days)	Remarks
27	5	7								
28	1	2								
29	1	9	HOLIDAY							
30	2	6	HOLIDAY							
31	2	8								
32	9			S	S	S	S			
33	1	6	S	S	S			1	7	
34	2	3								
35	3	0	Ⓐ					1	1	
36	6	9								
37	1	3								
38	2	0								
39	2	7	H							
40	4	1 0								
41	1	1	A	A			Ⓐ	2	2 + 1	
42	1	8								
43	2	5					S			
44	1	1 1	S	S				1	3	
45	8									
46	1	5								
47	2	2								
48	2	9								
49	6	1 2								
50	1	3	S	S	S	S	S			
51	2	0	S	S	S	S	S	1	1 0	
52	2	7								

SUB-TOTALS weeks 27-52	M	T	W	Th	F	Spells	Days
	6	6	4	3	5	6	2 4
TOTALS 1976	10	8	8	6	10	14	4 2

Absence Summaries

		sub-total 1			Sub-total 2			Total	
No of Spells	53-54	8		62-63	6		71-72	1 4	
No of days lost	55-57	1 8		64-66	2 4		73-75	4 2	
No of 1 day spells	58-59	5		67-68	2		76-77	7	
Employment record	60	1		69	1		78	1	

109

7 The Effort Bargain

First published in Industrial and Labour Relations Review,
Vol. 10, No. 4, July 1957.

ASSUMPTIONS UNDERLYING WAGE INCENTIVES

The use of payment by results rests on three assumptions: that effort intensity can be varied, that in work the financial motive is most important, and that the most effective or only way of harnessing this motive to increase effort is by the use of a system of payment by results. Only the first of these assumptions can be taken as factually established. The second is usually taken as self-evident, though on closer inspection certain qualifications are added to it. The third assumption, although it appears to follow from the other two, introduces a new element. If one assumes that effort intensity can be increased and that money is the most important motive for effort, then it seems logical that one should use money as an incentive to extra effort. But the mere payment of more money, the proponents of payment by results maintain, is not a sufficient condition for increasing effort; extra earnings act as an incentive to additional effort only if they are geared to effort by a system of payment by results. Under time rates, the proponents argue, effort intensity is determined independently of earnings, so that 'increased pay on day rates would not change effort' (1).

The problem of gearing effort to earnings is not as simple as it would appear. Most piece-rate systems fix the piece-rate price in relation to a weekly wage value. Total weekly earnings and the price per unit of output, when taken together,

110

represent an output target, because a given piece-rate price determines the amount of output that is required to make up the weekly wage value. The flaw is that effort intensity is defined only indirectly; there is no assurance that in practice it will coincide with that implied in the wage-value and piece-rate price, so that management has no guarantee that the worker will produce the output expected.

The latter consideration raises the question why proponents of payment by results should be so confident of the effectiveness of financial incentive schemes. It seemed useful, therefore, to conduct a series of interviews with management and union representatives (2) on the problem of effort standards and their determination.

The first point that emerged from these interviews was that it is practically impossible to obtain a definite answer to the seemingly straightforward question of whether the introduction of piece rates results in increased effort and thus raises output (3). This is due to the difficulty of isolating the effect of financial incentives from the effect of changes in methods of production and technical factors.

Although they could not provide factual proof, nearly all the management representatives interviewed expressed the opinion that payment by results is effective in raising labour productivity and that there are different standards of effort for time rates and for piece rates (4).

They attributed the difference to the system of payments, not to the level of earnings, and expressed the conviction that the standard of effort is lower on time rates, even if the level of earnings is the same as on piece rates. General wage increases were considered to have no effect on effort.

Lack of factual proof does not invalidate the proposition that output is usually greater under piece rates than under time rates. One can argue, moreover, that if the managerial system of beliefs with regard to the efficacy of financial incentive schemes endures, it must work reasonably well in practice; it will work as long as workers accept the proposition that standards of effort are, or ought to be, higher under financial incentive schemes and will act accordingly.

The critical factor is the worker's attitude to incentives and his willingness to increase his level of effort, and this must depend on the existence of mutual consultation and agreement. If one examines the situation closely, the question of agreement is, in fact, the key to the success of financial incentive schemes: for agreement, based on the acceptance of a norm that output should be increased, constitutes an effort bargain (5).

ELEMENTS OF THE EFFORT BARGAIN

If one analyses the situation it becomes clear that every employment contract (whatever the method of wage payment) consists of two elements:

1 an agreement on the wage rate (per unit of time or of output), i.e., a wage-rate bargain.

2 an agreement on the work to be done, i.e., an effort bargain.

The employment contract thus fixes the terms of exchange of work for money.

In normal market situations, no difficulty arises in defining the commodity that is being bought, but with labour the difficulty is that the 'article' that is being bought is not only difficult to define but impossible to measure. For what is being bought is a supply of effort for performing varying work assignments. Effort, however, is not a substance that can be measured (6). Only the effect of the application of effort - output - can be measured. Effort itself is a subjective experience, like utility. An individual can say whether the effort he expends in performing a particular operation in a fixed time is equal to, greater or smaller than, the effort he expends on another operation in the same amount of time, but he cannot quantitatively define the amount of the difference. In the absence of an agreement on the effort intensity per unit of time that is being purchased, effort intensity can vary between certain limits. Workers will have an upper limit to the amount of exertion they will put out and employers a lower limit to the level of exertion that they will tolerate without firing a worker. There is likely to be concealed bargaining about effort intensity, and the entrepreneur is likely to employ various devices of effort control such as supervision and machine pacing. If one postulates that more output means more effort, then it is possible to conlude an effort bargain, and this is essentially what a successful financial incentive scheme does. The worker agrees to raise his output in exchange for the guarantee of higher earnings (7).

British trade union agreements follow certain traditions in this matter. They lay down a rule that piece-rate earnings must be something like 25, 27.5, 30 or 33 per cent above day-rate earnings and agree that output should rise accordingly. If one views financial incentive schemes as a bargain, one can argue that they will tend to be effective so long as both sides keep their part of the bargain (8). If one concedes the possibility of effort bargaining it becomes possible to visualise alternative types of effort bargain. A wage increase on time rates, for instance, could be made into an effort bargain by linking it to an agreement on output targets.

When incentive schemes have been going for a long time, or when external circumstances change, some of the assumptions on which the original scheme was based may become invalid. There is evidence that there are limits to the effectiveness of money as a motive for additional effort or for the maintenance of a high level of effort. There may be workers who have a fixed standard of living and are not interested in earning more than a certain amount (9).

Under conditions where potential additional earnings no longer provide an incentive to a high level of effort, a system of payment by results provides opportunities for a relaxation of effort which may be absent under different types of effort control or effort bargain. This may be the reason why workers often prefer financial incentives to other types of effort bargaining. Only in exceptional cases or where the relaxation of standards of effort is extremely marked is there likely to be management action (10), especially when there is a shortage of labour. In such conditions, an all-or-nothing effort bargain, such as a bargain based on high day rates, using machine pacing or supervision as tools of effort control, may be more effective in ensuring a sustained supply of effort (11).

PRODUCTON STANDARDS AND EFFORT NORMS

The notion that effort intensity is greater under piece rates than under time rates implies a belief in the existence of stabilised standards of effort. For only if one believes that there are standards of effort which persist over time can one logically claim to be able to compare levels of effort (and their outward expression - productivity) and to estimate the difference between them (12). This also implies the existence of fixed, or at least fairly rigid, standards of effort, which can be raised only by strong stimuli, like a 30 percent increase in earnings, such as might be associated with the introduction of piece rates.

Notions with regard to the existence of different grades of workers, such as the 'good' and the 'bad' worker, are of interest in this connection. The 'good' worker is one who maintains a consistently high standard of effort independently of earnings, and the 'bad' worker is one who has a low standard of effort whatever the incentive (13). In between there is the 'average' worker, whose standard of effort is believed to be dependent on the strength of the monetary incentive, and who can be persuaded by money to raise his level of effort. If workers differ in their responses to incentives, however, then any claim that worker productivity has risen by 30 per cent as a result of the introduction of incentives must refer to the 'average' worker and is not true of particular individuals. Wage negotiations must also refer to this fictional 'average' worker, which means that the effect of introducing incentives cannot be foreseen, as this must depend on how average the 'average' worker is in a factory and what his 'average' performance was on day rates (14).

A different type of notion which is of interest in this connection is the belief that there is a 'correct' rate for a job. This belief is apparently held by both management and workers, although their views as to which particular piece rate represents the correct rate often differ and have frequently to be reconciled by bargaining. A rate is 'correct' if it matches notions of the 'right' earnings with notions of the 'right' standard of effort, and it is 'loose' or 'tight' if it does not do so (15). The process of finding the correct rate involves a serious dilemma, because effort is a subjective experience and not a measureable quantity. Management tends to argue, however, as if effort were something like a quantity consisting of discrete additive units, and many firms use time study to obtain what they consider to be 'properly organised quantitative data' for setting the rate (16). While it is admitted that there always remains a residue of subjective judgements, even under time study, management representatives were found to believe that an experienced time-study man knows what is the right standard of effort and the correct rate for it.

Proceeding from the assumption that there is a correct rate for a given job, those entrepreneurs who were keen on time study next argued that there is a correct reward, not just for a particular job, but for a given standard of effort whatever the job. Most of them considered that the rate on jobs of similar skill ought to be adjusted so as to result in equal earnings for equal effort. In the light of these arguments time study becomes a technique of establishing an equitable wage structure based on the normative goal of providing equal pay for equal effort'. This implies that the rates for all jobs of the same level of skill can and ought to be related to the rate for one particular job by setting them in such a way that weekly earnings are the same as on that job for the same amount of effort. If a job is changed in such a way that it requires a different amount of effort, it is argued that the rate must be adjusted so that the same wage as before is earned for the same effort as before. For instance, when better methods of production or technical improvements are introduced, the worker's earnings must remain the same and the piece rate adjusted accordingly, so that 'a day's effort, if the same, is rewarded the same' as before. 'A pure methods change must involve no increase in pay because it does not involve a change in the standard of effort' (17). It is admitted that mistakes are made in setting the rate, resulting in loose or tight rates, but the incidence of such miscalculations is not considered a serious problem.

These notions are fraught with logical difficulties. If standards of effort are not measurable, then it is logically impossible to determine the 'rightness' of a particular work performance as a measure of the 'right' standard of effort. If effort is a subjective experience, then it is impossible to say whether two workers with the same work performance experience the same degree of effort. The naturally fast worker is likely to require less effort to perform a given task in a given time than the slow worker, and similar differences in the experience of effort may hold for the good and bad, the young and old worker. If each of these workers applies his own subjective standard to judge the 'rightness' of a standard of effort, then a rate which is correct for a slow worker will be loose for a fast worker and a rate which is correct for the fast worker will be tight for the slow worker. Thus, if workers differ in ease of performance and if effort cannot be measured, logically there cannot be one correct rate; there is no criterion for judging for whom or for what the rate is correct.

To make any sense of the proposition, one must postulate that it is correct for the average worker - which means, in practice, that it must be acceptable to a group of workers. This implies that the rate must agree with institutionalised (group) norms of effort. For the successful working of financial incentives, a group of workers as well as management must share the same conceptions of what constitutes the 'right' standard of effort for a given job and the 'correct' rate for it. If individuals deviate in either of these conceptions, there may be friction (18). If management and workers hold different conceptions, these differences may give rise to wage disputes if they cannot be bridged by negotiation or bargaining. This illustrates once more that the successful operation of incentive schemes depends on skill in effort bargaining. In practice, agreement on rates may be reached by the adoption of provisional rates for new jobs. If workers find with these rates that they cannot reach their earnings target with what they consider the 'right' standard of effort i.e., if they consider the rates are tight, provision is made for them to obtain an adjustment of the rate. If they find the provisional rate acceptable, it becomes established (19).

This suggests the curious position that the belief in there being a correct rate for a job appears to work satisfactorily in practice although it has no scientific validity. The worker's reaction to the rate, not scientific judgement, determines whether the rate is considered correct, loose, or tight. The worker's reaction, in turn, is an indication of the success of the time-study expert in estimating the worker's norms of effort. If he guesses correctly whether the standard of effort implied in his rate fixing will be tolerated by the worker and management, the rate fixed will turn out correct. That time-study officers make mistakes in judgement is evident from the statements made about the existence of loose and tight rates.

An interesting point to note is the fact that complaints about tight rates take the form of demands for adjustment of the rate and do not, in the first place, lead to effort adjustments. This suggests that workers are unwilling to adjust their standards of effort. Once they are on piece rates, they seem to have fixed standards of effort and to consider the rate for a new job to be loose or tight in relation to these standards. If rates which are considered tight or loose are not adjusted, however, workers may resort to restriction of output, as has been shown by Roy (20). This means that if the effort bargain involved in a system of payment by results is not made acceptable to the worker, financial incentives may not be effective; output may be restricted instead of increased.

In Great Britain payment by results schemes seem to have been effective in the past in raising standards of effort above day-rate standards mainly because management and workers have agreed in the past (and still agree) that this should be so. It is likely that financial incentives will continue to work reasonably effectively in practice so long as both workers and management believe in the bargain they have concluded and act accordingly. It is possible on the other hand, that the demands for extra money for a given standard of effort, which are constantly being made and conceded to, may alter the worker's attitude toward extra money for extra effort, and thus toward financial incentive schemes, and may affect his willingness to enter into or keep his part of the bargain (21).

FINANCIAL INCENTIVES AND MARGINAL PRODUCTIVITY

The foregoing discussion of managerial beliefs regarding financial incentives raises at least two significant questions for economic theory. First, how far does this system of beliefs correspond to that postulated by the marginal productivity theory? Second, what are the implications of the factors underlying these managerial beliefs for wage theory?

As has been shown, the managerial system of beliefs is composed of three basic propositions concerning the variability of the supply of effort, the importance of money as a motive to work, and the effectiveness of payment by results in harnessing this motive. At a lower level of generalisation, it is made up of notions of the existence of good and bad workers, of a correct rate for a job, of loose and tight rates, and of equal pay for equal effort.

There would appear to be no serious clash between the beliefs of managers and economists over the first three assumptions. The economist is aware that the supply of effort can be varied, although he normally - for the sake of simplicity - assumes a constant supply of effort per unit of time in the simpler wage-theory models. He considers that the financial motive for work is the most important motive operating in the labour market, and he assumes, as mangement does, that an entrepreneur must pay higher wages if he wants to increase his supply of labour. But while the economist thinks primarily of an increase in the number of workers when he speaks of a change in the supply of labour, managers in practice - especially in times of full employment - think in terms of increasing the supply of effort from their existing labour force. This possibility, although rarely discussed, is not ruled out by the economist. As regards the third notion, the managerial belief in the effectiveness of payment by results, the economist is neutral. The topic is seldom mentioned and seems to have aroused no theoretical difficulty or controversy. Insofar as the entrepreneur receives more output under a system of payment by results in exchange for higher wages, there would appear to be no clash with the marginal productivity theory. For greater physical productivity - if the entrepreneur operates under conditions of perfect competition - means greater marginal productivity and this means higher earnings.

It is only when one studies the lower-level generalisations of the managerial system of beliefs about financial incentives that divergencies from the marginal productivity approach become apparent. These arise from the goal, advocated by most of the respondents using time study, of paying an equal reward on different jobs for equal effort and equal skill. For equal effort does not necessarily represent equal marginal productivity. Two workers of the same skill, employed on different jobs and applying equal effort, may produce marginal products of differing monetary market values. Rewarding marginal productivity in this case would involve differential rates for equal effort. A policy of paying a standard rate for equal effort and skill may thus conflict with a policy of rewarding according to marginal productivity. It must be stressed in this connecton that the concept of the 'right standard of effort' (the 'fair day's work) operates independently of an evaluation of the market value of that effort. Production standards, as representing effort, are judged as fair and right in relation to each other and not in relation to the market value of the product (22).

Another example may be useful in illustrating the different effects of effort and marginal productivity evaluations. With better methods of production, worker efficiency (output per unit of time) may increase while effort remains the same or decreases. Marginal productivity, provided there is no change in the market value of a unit of output, thus increases while effort remains constant. Under such conditions, many employers who use time-study methods do not permit a rise in earnings to take place. They deliberately adjust the piece-rate price so that earnings on the particular job remain the same (23). In fact, they reward not marginal productivity but effort. They assess the effort cost of performing different tasks; they evaluate this effort cost, not in terms of money, but in terms of 'real' costs, of disutility or irksomeness. The managerial aim is to ascertain whether the effort cost of two operations is equal or not, and to try to equalise it or, if there are unavoidable differences, to arrange for compensation (24).

The manager's and the economist's system of beliefs are thus seen on closer examination to focus attention on two distinctly different elements in wage determination; effort evaluations, where standards of effort and their effort cost are assessed in relation to each other, as opposed to market evaluations, where labour productivity is assessed in relation to market prices as represented by the concept of marginal value productivity (25).

A wage policy based on effort evaluations reflects the disutility of labour, Marshall's 'real costs' (26). This means that economists may have been overhasty insofar as they have dispensed with the concepts of real costs and disutility of labour, in connection with wage determination (27). On the other hand, it would be equally hasty to dispense with the concept of value productivity. The two aspects of the problem of wage determination are interrelated: the wage rate must be right in relation to effort standards and right in relation to the market. It is thus likely that product prices set limits within which effort evaluations are made and that market and real cost calculations are interlinked (28).

The interviews on financial incentives provided little information about how economic judgements of profitability and market prices enter into wage determination. Statements made by management officals with regard to the share of management and workers in increased productivity (29) showed that they did not ascribe the division of the shares to economic forces; while they considered that the determination of the share of the consumer depended on market forces, they attributed the shares of management and workers to normative forces, to what appeared 'right' and 'fair' and to 'what should be done'. The concept of profitability entered only as a normative criterion - not as an economic one - as illustrated by the statement that 'a fair part of the gain should go to management and to increase the prosperity of the company'.

IMPLICATIONS FOR WAGE THEORY

The aspect of the problem which emerges from this study as most important is the preoccupation of management with the problem of effort standards and effort control. The managerial system of beliefs focuses attention on the variability of effort and on the evaluation and determination of effort standards. Underneath these evaluations is hidden a process of effort bargaining which appears to play an extremely important role in determining output and earnings.

The phenomena of the variability of effort, of the assessment and evaluation of effort standards, and of effort bargaining cannot, however, be considered as specific events whose occurrence is restricted to situations where financial incentive schemes are used; they must be considered as general phenomena which take place in any employment situation whatever the method of payment. The role they will play, the decisions to which they give rise, and the effect they will have on wage rates will depend to a considerable extent on the labour and product market situations, as well as upon the philosophy of management.

It was found in this enquiry, for example, that the entrepreneur, as long as he considered that his firm is in a fairly satisfactory position, tended to be content with his present wage policy, even if he believed that output could be raised and costs reduced by greater use of financial incentives. If, however, he became aware of external pressures, either from increasing competition or from rising market demand for his product, these pressures forced him to take action either to try to lower costs or to increase output. In this situation, the raising of effort standards and effort bargaining become important. If the entrepreneur holds the system of beliefs outlined above, he will consider that his best course of action, together with organisational and technical improvements, is to attempt to make better use of his labour resources by the use of payment by results. Through better plant utilisation, the use of financial incentives may enable him to reduce unit costs of production. There is no reason, however, why he should not try other methods of effort bargaining.

Effort bargaining is particularly important under conditions of full employment, where the shortage of labour exercises constant pressures upon management. In such a labour market situation, two types of bargaining - one initiated by management, the other by labour - go on side by side. Management will try to increase the level of effort which it obtains from labour without increasing costs per unit of output. Labour will try to increase the level of wages for a given level of effort. In trying to obtain a greater supply of effort from its labour, management, if under pressure from the market for its products, will be in a weak bargaining position and may have to make wage concessions. These may take the form of a deliberate toleration of loose rates - a disguised increase in wages to encourage an increase in the supply of effort. Labour, being in a strong bargaining position, may be inclined to lower its standards of effort, and this may necessitate the initiation of renewed effort and wage bargaining. Labour may also show a tendency to attack all rates as tight and to press for rate adjustments.

By contrast, in a situation of unemployment or underemployment, attitudes toward loose and tight rates will tend to be very different. In a situation where work is frequently slack, owing to seasonal fluctuations, for instance, management may tend to tolerate low standards of effort, allied to low pay, and workers may be content with this because they like a leisurely pace of work. This would explain why some small firms which pay time rates producing low earnings are able to keep their labour force and show a low rate of labour turnover.

The Effort Bargain

What are the implications of these phenomena for wage theory?

The variability of the supply of effort means that adjustments of the supply of labour to wage rates or of wage rates to the supply of labour frequently do not take the form of adjustments in numbers of workers nor of hours of work but of adjustments in standards of effort.

The phenomenon of effort bargaining indicates that we are dealing with conditions of monopolistic competition, even in the absence of trade union negotiations; each individual worker is a monopolist insofar as he is able to limit his supply of effort by restricting his output and to bargain for higher earnings by agreeing to increase his output. Institutionalised effort norms may reinforce this element of monopoly. This fits in with the arguments in favour of the bargaining theories of wages.

The role of effort evaluations has been discussed in connection with effort bargaining and rate setting and in connection with the evolution of an equitable wage structure. These, however, are not their only functions. Effort evaluations would appear to be of much wider significance. They are not merely relevant for the wage structure of a particular firm but also for the wage structure in the labour market outside the firm.

Effort evaluations can be used to explain the coexistence of different wages for similar jobs with varying standards of effort, for example, the coexistence of low day rates and high piece rates for the same operation in different firms. Furthermore, they would appear to make nonhomogeneous jobs comparable in terms of the wage required to ensure a given effort intensity.

The entrepreneur may argue that on day-rate effort standards a semi-skilled worker is worth a wage of £6 a week, but on piece-rate effort standards on the same job he is worth £8; that under the pressure of scarcity of labour the semi-skilled worker is worth this extra £2. Extra effort from the skilled worker is not required, hence his wage should remain the same.

The worker may make similar evaluations. He may be imagined as comparing different job situations in terms of the wage rate required to make him put in the same or a different standard of effort from his habitual standard. He has not only a notion of the effort if applied to a different job. He also has a notion of the effort adjustments

122

he would make in response to a change in the wage
rate or in response to the same wage on a different
job.

Changes in the employer's or worker's effort
evaluations may produce changes in the wage
structure. Changes in the product market, for
instance, which alter the entrepreneur's demand for
effort may lead to changes in wage rates in order to
adjust the supply of effort to the demand. Changes
in the worker's attitude to his job, rising
dissatisfaction for instance, may lead to effort
restriction. This fall in effort intensity may lead
to the offer of increased wages if the entrepreneur
has to meet urgent orders. In both cases, the
effort evaluations influence the wage structure
through effort adjustments or the demand for them.

NOTES

1. Statement made by the managing director of a
medium-sized firm. Compare D H Robertson, Economic
Fragments, 1931, p11. 'Under time work there is no
precise correspondence between the hourly wage and
the rate of expenditure of effort. If the hours of
work are fixed, therefore, there is no particular
reason why a rise in the rate of wages should
furnish any inducement either to increase or
diminish the rate of expenditure of effort'.
2. Forty-five representatives of management and 15
trade unionists were formally interviewed. These
included top executives (directors or managing
directors), other executive ranks (works or
production managers, personnel managers, company
secretaries), and a few time-study officers. The
trade union officials were national and branch
officials and factory shop stewards. The
interviewees were asked to express their views on a
number of set questions and were encouraged to
supply additional information. The amount of
information received from the various respondents
differed greatly because they were not all equally
conversant with the subject and because certain
questions were not applicable to the practices with
which they were acquainted. No statistical analysis
of the replies is therefore possible. The type of
information given, however, showed a striking
similarity of opinions; even the views expressed by
the trade unionists followed the same basic pattern
of response. The evidence suggests that the use of
financial incentives is associated with a specific

system of beliefs which incorporates the three assumptions just described and certain other generalised notions which will be discussed later.

The respondents worked for firms ranging in size from 27 to 17,000 workers, engaged in the manufacture of a wide variety of products, such as chemicals, metals, engineering and electrical goods, vehicles, textiles, food and drink. The degree of unionization varied greatly; some managers stated there were no unions in their firms or that they did not have official shop stewards; others adhered to national agreements with or without belonging to employers' federations; a few plants had negotiated factory trade union agreements.

Methods of payment used ranged from day rates and straight piece rates, fixed by rate fixers by rule of thumb, to highly sophisticated time-study systems of standard minute or incentive bonus payments, based on individual or group performance; none, however, used progressive incentive schemes. Most firms used several different methods of payment side by side. Thirteen firms had made recent changes, introducing or refining incentive schemes, and a number were expecting to make further changes. 3. In a further attempt to explore this question, 200 firms were approached by letter and 50 firms were visited; but this did not reveal a single case where the effectiveness of incentives could be isolated and measured.

The experiments conducted by Wyatt probably still represent the only positive results obtained on this question. The interesting point is that he found that the response to financial incentives differed with the type of work. When 10 girl operators engaged on the unwrapping of toffees were switched from a time rate to a bonus and then to a piece rate, there was no increase in output. When they were engaged on 4 other jobs and the method of payment changed, there was an increase in output, but the amount of the response differed considerably. See S Wyatt, assisted by L Frost and F G L Stock, Incentives in Repetitive Work, I H R B Report No 69, 1934. Wyatt's experiments thus show that there is no guarantee that the introduction of incentives will result in an increase in output. 4. The following comments may serve as illustrations:

'For many years we have been working on a piecework basis, and we have no doubt whatsoever of the effectiveness of incentive schemes on production, and I have no hesitation in stating that although our piecework rates are generally looked upon as being generous, the ultimate result is that we produce our car bodies considerably cheaper than we should on a day rate basis without incentive element'.

'Workers don't make effort until piecework price is applied'.

'Men will not put in effort on day-rates; they will start late and waste time generally'.

The general belief was that highly paid day-work could not achieve the same result as piece-work. Twenty people expressed this view without any reservations, and 10 of them were extremely emphatic about the impossibility of getting similar results from day-work.

5. In the focused interviews, management officials never stressed this point, and only one used the term effort bargain. Many respondents, however, made casual remarks indicating that it was a question of bargaining and that they were constantly engaged in negotiations with the workers on incentives. But awareness of the existence of a process of bargaining did not appear to be consciously integrated into the general system of beliefs with regard to financial incentives.

6. A detailed analysis of the concept of effort is given by W Baldamus in his book, Efficiency and Effort (published in 1961 by Tavistock Publications).

7. This does not imply that he gets higher earnings per unit of output (although this may happen) but rather that he gets higher earnings if he works harder and produces more output than before, as he has agreed to do. Compare Robertson, (note 1), p 11 'A rise in hourly wages which takes the form of a substitution for time-work of piece-work at (say) time-and-a-quarter rates, does not, of course, if the piece rate is fairly fixed, constitute an increase in the reward offered per unit of effort. It is simply a renewal of the offer of the existing rate of reward per unit of effort, coupled with a guarantee (absent under time work) that the rate will be paid for every unit of effort which the worker chooses to expend'. The managerial staff interviewed in this enquiry apparently thought usually in terms of earnings increasing proportionately with productivity i.e., of both increasing by 25 per cent or more, and increases in earnings of 30 per cent were interpreted as representing a 30 per cent increase in productivity. There were a few cases, however, where loose rates

(i.e., more than proportionate increases in earnings) were tolerated.

8. There seems to be a tendency for a belief in a generic difference in standards of effort for day rates and piece rates to become so well established that it obscures the fact that the aim of incentives is primarily a bargain between management and workers. There is awareness that workers ought to be consulted about the introduction of a scheme, but this consultation becomes an issue of 'maintaining good human relations', and not of agreeing on certain increased standards of effort. There is a danger that some people, prompted by their belief in financial incentives, forget that they are concerned with a process of effort bargaining and thus neglect the type of approach to workers and trade unions on which the effective functioning of incentive schemes depends. Solomon Barkin in 'Labour's Attitude to Wage Incentive Plans', Industrial and Labour Relations Review, Vol 1, No 4, July 1948, pp 553-572, argued that in the United States wage incentive schemes did not always produce higher earnings and were used as alternatives to wage increases, and that this produced unsatisfactory results. If this is so, it illustrates the point that the employers concerned overlooked that they were dealing with an effort bargain which must involve concessions on both sides.

9. A number of management representatives stated in the interviews that the shortage of labour had forced them to take on workers who were not incentive-minded, and to make wage concessions which meant that workers could achieve a high level of earnings with less effort than before, and that this had undermined the effetiveness of incentive schemes.

10. An interesting, but exceptional case covered in this enquiry was a wage agreement between a large trade union and several employers' federations covering a large section of a specialised industry, where the trade union had undertaken to try to ensure that standards of effort do not fall. The trade union argued that management had installed expensive machinery whose profitability depended on maintaining standards of effort equivalent to weekly earnings of £x a week. Workers who did not reach this target were reported by management to the trade union, which tried to get them to keep to their part of the bargain; if these workers did not heed the trade union warning, the trade union raised no objection to their dismissal.

11. Examples in Great Britain of the negotiation and maintenance of high standards of effort under a system of time rates are provided by the construction of he Esso Refinery at Fawley and of the Ford factory at Dagenham.

12. That this belief is held by many representatives of management can be seen from comments made during the interviews. A production director said that the purpose of introducing incentives was to raise effort, but the final effect was the stabilisation of effort at a higher level. A director of another firm argued that on day rates girls got into a certain speed of working. 'To raise this from 50 to 70 needed some extra stimulus' (i.e. a bonus). When this bonus had been in operation for some time, the girls got into the habit of earning their 30 per cent and the standard of effort settled down at this new level. Another director said that the purpose of their incentive scheme was to 'step up production and stabilise it at a higher level'. Effort levels cannot, of course, be raised ad infinitum.

13. This is illustrated by comments made in the interviews such as that young single girls and 'lazybones' are not incentive-minded and do not respond to financial incentives; skilled workers are not incentive-minded because they have a different outlook - they pride themselves on certain standards of performance; workers with the 'right' outlook have high standards of effort making financial incentives unnecessary.

14. It would appear that it is difficult in a situation of full employment to get labour with the 'right' outlook. Most respondents said that the type of worker they got only worked hard under a system of payment by results; only one production director stated that his firm had found by time study that their dayworkers were already working at 125-130 per cent, 100 per cent being considered normal. Thus their good day-rate workers might only be able to increase their speed by 10-15 per cent.

15. In the interviews, all the respondents acknowledged the possibility of the existence of loose and tight rates, thus demonstrating their belief in the existence of a correct rate - a belief which exists independently of whether time study is used or not. The majority of the firms had agreements with the trade unions (or understandings with the workers where the plants were unorganised) with regard to the adjustment of tight (and sometimes also of loose) rates. In practice, a considerable amount of negotiation and bargaining

may precede the setting of the rate. In a wage
agreement concluded in the Midland Hosiery Industry
the manufacturers' associations and the trade union
first negotiated and laid down 'what they believed
on a piece-rate basis to be the wage-value of what a
normal operative ought to earn. Having arrived at
that figure, they worked out what ought to be the
production on the job by this knitter'. This means
they argued first about the right earnings - the
wage value, and then about the right effort - the
production standards on the job. From this they
arrived at an agreed formula for rate-setting.
16. The following comment made by an influential top
executive provides a good illustration of the
attitude of management exponents of time study:
'They used to have some jobs where they paid a time
rate plus 2d per ton. This 2d was purely arbitrary;
it was not a properly worked out system so that the
bonus per ton was not strictly related to effort.
This sort of bonus system was simply a hit and miss
business which had no quantitative justification.
From the point of view of relating it to the real
effort the man put into it this was sheer horse
trading. One got a fairer approximation under work
study. Of course, in the long run, all wage fixing
was a process of bargaining. Someone has a service
to sell and someone wants to buy it. One had to
find out where the willing buyer and seller met. In
this process it was more satisfactory to have
properly organised quantitative data to do it with.
If one had not got these, then by mutual bargaining
one might arrive at the wrong figure. It might be
wrong because it was an insufficient incentive and
thus failed in its purpose. If the rate was loose
the workers would get more than was fair to the
other workers. This created the problem of
restoring relative fairness but the workers resented
and mistrusted adjustments. The workers must always
have confidence in the fairness of management and
their ability to keep a bargain once made. If
management had made a bad bargain it could not just
alter it. For this reason it was most important
that the bargain should be the right bargain; but to
be right it must be based on some kind of
measurement'.
17. See A C Pigou, The Economics of Welfare, 1920,
p529, 'in order that wages may be fair, the piece-
rates must be so adjusted that different outputs,
representing equal efficiencies shall receive the
same reward'. See also p530.
18. Hence the concepts of chiseler and rate-buster.

Compare F J Roethlisberger and W J Dickson, Management and the Worker, Part IV, Chap. 22, and D Roy, 'Goldbricking and Quota Restriction', American Journal of Sociology, Vol 57, 1951-1952.

19. All the firms visited claimed that this procedure worked smoothly and satisfactorily in their establishments. Trade union officials, too, claimed that they experienced few difficulties over rates. It is true that many strikes over this issue of rates attract public attention, but it is likely that these cases constitute an insignificant proportion of all rate settlements, for successful settlements are not reported in the press.

20. See note 18.

21. It should be noted that since the worker's part of the effort bargain is hardly ever precisely formulated, the worker cannot justly be accused of breaking the bargain if he restricts his output, as long as it is above day-rate level, for (as pointed out above) the actual level of output or effort has never been fixed. It is only implied in the wage value and may never have been mentioned openly. In practical terms, this means for management policy that financial incentives might be made to work more effectively in the face of rising wages if a minimum wage-earnings target is consciously agreed by both sides and is revised whenever wage concessions are made. If this does not work management may feel forced to adopt alternative methods of conscious effort bargaining. 22. The goals of the relative and absolute validity of production standards imply that the concept of a 'fair day's work' is not referred to any monetary arbitrator but judged as a phenomenon per se. The setting of production standards for different jobs must be considered as a separate problem from that of determining the standard rate for a 'day's work'. See T A Ryan, 'Fatigue and Effort in Relation to Standards of Performance and Systems of Payment', International Labour Review, Vol 65, 1952.

23. In the short run, earnings are thus unaffected, while marginal productivity has increased. In the long run, if there is an increase in productivity in the plant and if the market is favourable, bargaining may lead to an increase in the standard rate. For wage bargaining does not only take the form of bargaining in terms of effort, but it also takes the form of bargaining in terms of productivity (a term used in this connection in a much wider and less precise sense than the economist's concept of marginal productivity). But

if the standard rate rises, it rises equally for all
jobs, thus creating new discrepancies between
earnings on specific jobs and marginal productivity.
24. The term effort cost used here must not be
confused with Robbins' effort price. See L Robbins,
'On the Elasticity of Demand for Income in Terms of
Effort', Economica, 1930. Robbins defines the
'effort price of income' as the total amount of work
done divided by the total income. Under piece rates
this would be represented by the equation:

$$\text{Effort price} = \frac{1}{\text{piece-rate price}}$$

This makes effort a dependent variable, and
assumes that the higher the piece-rate price, the
smaller the effort price of income. For two
operations with the same piece-rate price, Robbins'
effort price is the same. Yet the effort cost may
differ. If one rate is loose and the other tight,
then the effort cost (ie, the intensity of effort)
involved in obtaining a given income will be
unequal; it will be low for the loose rate, and high
for the tight rate. The effort cost depends on the
number of units that can be produced 'comfortably'
in an hour; any output target above this involves
greater effort cost. This criterion of the strain
involved in the pace of work is independent of the
wage rate. Any increase in the pace of work
increases effort cost. Increased pay cannot
eliminate this; it can only compensate the worker
for it.
25. It would be ideal from the theorist's point of
view if these two elements corresponded respectively
to demand and supply factors, i.e. if market
evaluations could be shown to be the main force
underlying the demand curve for labour and effort
evaluations the main force underlyig the supply
curve of labour. Unfortunately, in practice the two
elements cannot be separated: in demanding labour,
managers have been shown to make effort evaluations;
in supplying labour workers can be found to argue in
terms of profitability. Both sides seem to consider
both aspects.
26. Alfred Marshall defined the 'real costs of
production' as 'efforts and sacrifices' for which
individuals must be compensated. Principles of
Economics, London, Macmillan, 1949 p339.
27. See J A Schumpeter, History of Economic
Analysis, New York, Oxford University Press, 1954,
p923, where the history of these concepts is

discussed.
28.   See E H Phelps Brown, 'Wage Policy and Wage
Differences,' Economica, Vol 22, No 88, November
1955. He considered that the market sets limits
within which the viable wage must lie and within
which notions of equity must operate.
29.   Of 24 respondents expressing views on what
proportion of productivity gains from methods
changes or technical improvements should go to
management, workers, and consumers, only one held
that distribution of the gains depended on economic
forces.   The others held that there were two
distinctly different problems: the determination of
the share of the consumer (which was a question of
market forces) and the determination of the share of
management and workers, which was never referred to
economic forces but always to moral values,
reflecting different philosophies of management.

8 Financial Incentives as the Expression of a System of Beliefs

First published in British Journal of Sociology,
Vol. X, No. 2, June 1959.

This paper discusses a problem which lies on the borderline of economics where the economist reaches the limits of his competence and the sociologist or social anthropologist may be interested to take over.

Expressed in general terms, the problem is this: when business firms experience the impact of strong economic (or other) pressures, their managements are forced to take steps to meet the pressures; how do managers justify the measures they adopt? Do they demand factual proof or do they rely on impressions? If the difficulties continue, do they stick by the measures they have taken because they are committed to a belief in them or do they abandon them? If they feel committed to the measures, do they build up a supporting system of beliefs? This paper examines these questions with reference to financial incentives.

In the post-war years the impact of full employment on managerial policy was particularly marked. British management was confronted with an acute shortage of labour, made worse by what management considered particularly low standards of effort. Many firms found that action was urgently required to deal with the problem of the shortage of labour. Under increasing pressures they tried payment by results as a solution. This trend is illustrated by the fact that the percentage of workers in British manufacturing industry who were paid by results rose from 33 per cent in 1938 to 40 per cent in 1951 (1). In the enquiry which I conducted in 1954 to 1955 and referred to in chapter 7, a third of the firms visited had recently made changes introducing or refining incentive schemes and others were in process of making changes. Various reasons were given for taking action, for example:

> 'The need to meet increasing foreign
> competition'
> 'The need to meet increasing number of orders'
> 'The desire to lower labour costs'
> 'The necessity of meeting trade union pressure
> for a shorter working week without loss of
> output'

Firms which, for some reason or other, were not
conscious of any particular pressures tended to
express satisfaction with their position and planned
no changes.

The adoption of payment by results has been
fostered by considerable publicity given to this
method of payment. The case for its use is based on
the following arguments. Under time-rates earnings
are not related to effort; it is plausible that
standards of effort could be raised if one related
earnings to effort. To do this one would have to
introduce a method of payment which acts as a
gearing device for effort and enables workers to
earn extra money for extra effort. The answer,
thus, must be payment by results.

We should note, however, that payment by
results provides only an indirect and rather
complicated gearing device. Simply to fix a price
per unit of output does not guarantee the
maintenance of a high level of output. How the
device is made to work will be discussed later.

Furthermore, we should note that practically no
valid statistical proof seems to be available to
demonstrate that payment by results raises labour
effort and maintains it at a high level.
Statistical data on the question of the relative
labour productivity of payment by results and time-
rates which stand up to scientific scrutiny do not
appear to exist (2). The reason is that the effect
of incentives on effort cannot be isolated. The
difficulties encountered when trying to isolate the
effects of changing one factor in an industrial
situation were amply demonstrated by the well-known
Hawthorne investigations. In the ordinary factory
situation, furthermore, managements do not as a rule
make isolated changes in a single factor; they tend
to make several changes in one go. The introduction
of payment by results, for instance, is normally
accompanied by organisational and methods changes.
Thus, the situations before and afterwards are
different, and no standards exist for comparing
labour productivity in the two situations. In the

course of an enquiry, in which I communicated with two hundred firms by letter and visited fifty, I did not find a single case where the effectiveness of payment by results in raising labour productivity could be isolated and measured.

In spite of this lack of statistical proof most of the managerial staff I interviewed believed that payment by results raises labour productivity. Twenty-five managers were perpared to estimate the difference, and twenty-two of these expressed the opinion that the productivity of piece-rates is at least 25 per cent greater than that of time-rates (3).

It thus appears that in most firms the use of incentive schemes rests on faith in - rather than proof of - the effectiveness of financial incentives; the results expected from payment by results have acquired the status of achieved results in spite of the lack of factual proof of the achievement. The following comments made by managerial staffs illustrate this:

> 'I have not been able to measure the effect but I am certain we should have been worse off without the scheme. Workers and everyone else'.
> 'For many years we have been working on a piecework basis, and we have no doubt whatsoever of the effectiveness of incentive schemes on production'.

There is evidence that the use of financial incentive schemes has become associated with a number of widely held generalised notions and beliefs, and that the people who hold these consider them to be connected and consistent.

I found, for instance, that the proponents of payment by results expressed repeatedly certain generalisations with regard to worker motivation. These concentrated on the importance of money as a motive and ignored or waived aside other motives. This showed up in statements, such as,

> 'Non-financial motives are of no importance'
> 'For men money is the be-all-and-end-all'
> 'Today the wage-packet is the thing'
> 'Money comes first, non-financial motives are of less importance'.

Implicit in the belief in the supremacy of the financial motive is the assumption that the worker is always interested in earning more money than he is getting on time-rates. The recurrent wage-claims of the post-war years have helped to strengthen this belief; nevertheless in many situations it may be unwarranted. As Max Weber pointed out at the beginning of this century 'one of the technical means which the modern employer uses in order to secure the greatest possible amount of work from his men is the device of piece-rates .... but a peculiar difficulty has been met with surprising frequency .... the opportunity of earning more was less attractive than that of working less ..... A man does not "by nature" wish to earn more and more money, but simply to live as he is accustomed to live and to earn as much as is necessary for the purpose'. Weber pointed out further that a worker does not necessarily ask: 'How much can I earn in a day if I do as much work as possible?' but: 'How much must I work in order to earn the wage .... which takes care of my traditional needs?' (pp59-60).

The notion that the worker has a definite wage-target is recognised by proponents of payment by results in a different context which will be discussed later; it is entirely ignored in this context where the worker's interest in extra money is taken for granted. Without such a treatment - ie. if one were to remove the assumption that the worker is interested in earning more money - one would remove the raison d'être of financial incentive schemes, for payment by results can harness only existing, not non-existing motives.

It is important in this context to draw a clear distinction between motives and incentives. While motives are internal forces which impel an individual to do certain things, incentives are external stimuli for action. The function of incentives is to harness existing motives for a particular purpose and thus control behaviour (4). The desire to obtain money is one motive for work; the money offered as a wage or bonus is one incentive to work.

If one believes that standards of effort can be altered and that money is the most important motive for work, one will tend to argue that one must use money as an incentive for securing higher standards of effort. We should note, however, that by itself this is not enough to justify the use of payment by results; for one can argue that it should be possible to use money as an incentive without payment by results simply by paying higher wages. But if one argues further (and this is what management does) that earnings act as an incentive

to additional effort only in conditions where they
are geared to effort, and that a piece-rate price or
incentive bonus provides a satisfactory gearing
device, then one will tend to believe that systems
of payment by results are the only effective systems
of financial incentives. This belief seems to be so
widely accepted that the terms 'payment by results'
and 'financial incentives' have acquired identical
meanings in industry.

The assumptions that a system of payment by
results gears the intensity of effort to earnings
does not appear, on first examination, to have much
justification. It is true that with piece-rates -
and similarly with incentive bonus and standard
minute payments - weekly earnings depend on weekly
output. The higher the output, the higher are the
earnings, but this does not mean that the size of
the weekly output (i.e. the product of the intensity
of effort) is uniquely determined by the piece-rate.
The piece-rate price merely defines a rate of
earnings per unit of output; it does not define how
many units of output are to be produced, i.e. it
does not by itself ensure the maintenance of effort
at a high level. As Weber pointed out (p59-60) the
worker can choose under this system how hard he will
work. Or as Baldamus (1957 p198) put it, under
piece-work 'the worker is left to himself' to decide
his own pace. Closer examination reveals that, in
practice, there is a hidden link between earnings
and the intensity of effort. When questioned about
the rate-setting process the managerial staffs I
interviewed frequently mentioned that they had in
mind a particular weekly wage-value, and that the
piece-rate price was set in relation to this. The
employer's image of the wage-value is assumed to
correspond with the worker's wage target, and the
worker is expected to put in the amount of effort
which will enable him to reach this wage-target.
The piece-rate price is set so that the worker has
to put in more effort than under time-rates if he
wants to reach the wage-value. The device of fixing
the piece-rate price in the light of a weekly wage-
value can thus be seen to represent a mechanism for
linking effort to earnings and determining
indirectly the intensity of effort. In this context
managers think in terms of a specific wage-target,
but knowledge of the role which the wage-target
plays in rate-setting is not consciously integrated
with other notions (for instance, those mentioned
earlier) which are expressed in relation to
financial incentives. No serious conflict with
these other notions arises, however, as long as the

wage value which the managers envisage is higher than the worker's time-rate earnings. In practice, the wage-value for many occupations is arrived at by multiplying the hourly base-rate (which is a time-rate) plus an agreed percentage (the piece-rate margin) with the hours of work. The incentive to work is thus built into the system: the worker receives extra money for extra effort. It is assumed that he will put in the extra effort because it is taken for granted that he wants the extra money.

As pointed out earlier, proponents of payment by results consider that financial incentives are effective in raising standards of effort. This conviction seems to have developed into the belief that workers have different habitual standards of effort on piece-rates (or bonus systems) than on time-rates.

This belief illustrates once more that the results expected from gearing effort to earnings have acquired the status of achieved results. The case for the use of financial incentives is strengthened by the proposition that on time-rates standards of effort are persistently low and on piece-rates persistently higher. It has been shown in chapter 7, that what the successful incentive scheme actually does, is to lay down agreed norms of behaviour. Through a process of effort-bargaining it leads to acceptance of the proposition that standards of effort on piece-rates ought to be higher than on time-rates. As mentioned earlier, many managers thought the standards of effort on piece-rates were at least 25 per cent higher than on time-rates.

From management's point of view the arguments just described seem to justify the use of financial incentives. Certain difficulties, however, arise in practice, and we find that subsidiary beliefs have developed to overcome these and to help to maintain the case for financial incentives.

For instance, managers may be found to divide workers into categories, such as 'good' and 'bad' workers. The good worker is one who maintains a consistently high standard of effort independently of earnings, and the bad worker is one who has a low standard of effort whatever the incentive. In between there is the average worker whose standard of effort depends on the strength of the monetary incentive so that he can be persuaded by money to raise it. The generalisation that workers work harder under a system of payment by results is modified at this lower level of generalisation by admissions that certain workers are not incentive-minded and do not respond to financial incentives. Thus, I was told young single girls see no point in working hard, as they have to hand their wage-packet to their mothers; they have the 'wrong' outlook and do not respond to incentives (5). Again, skilled workers are not incentive-minded because they pride themselves on certain standards of performance; they have the 'right' outlook making financial incentives unnecessary.

Thus the beliefs associated with financial incentives become hedged in with important reservations; they do not apply to particular individuals but refer to fictional 'average workers'. This means that managers can hold on to the belief in the effectiveness of payment by results even when there is evidence that there is no response to a particular financial incentive scheme or that the response is declining. The phrase 'these people are not incentive-minded' implies that lack of response to incentives is a function of the individual and not a fault of the scheme. Any post-war disappointments with regard to payment by results can be attributed to 'the sort of labour we get these days'.

The concept of the 'average worker' also plays an importat part with a different type of notion which operates at this lower level of generalisation. This is the belief that there is (with an incentive scheme) a 'correct' rate for a job. This belief (which exists independently of whether time-study is used or not) is apparently shared by management and workers although their views as to which particular piece-rate represents the correct rate may not coincide. A rate is correct if it matches notions of the 'right' standard of effort, and it is loose or tight if it does not do so. It is loose if comparatively little effort is required to obtain the right earnings.

It is clear that questions of the 'rightness' of rates or standards are not questions of fact but of subjective júdgement. Even if standards of effort were measurable (which they are not) there could never be any scientific criterion for judging the rightness of a particular standard of effort.

In reaching agreement on rates and standards the use of the concept of the average worker eliminates many difficulties; it implies that the standards laid down need not apply to particular individuals but only to the average worker. A slow worker may find the 'correct' rate tight because his normal standard of effort is below that of the average worker; by contrast, a fast worker may find it loose because his normal standard of effort is above that of the average worker. The postulate that there is one correct rate for each job is apparently never challenged. On the contrary it receives support from both management and workers. Management supports the concept of one rate and standard for one job because of the administrative and human problems that would arise if it dealt separately with each employee. Workers support it in so far as they hold institutionalised norms of effort, and thus share conceptions as to what constitutes the right standard of effort for a given job and the correct rate for it. This makes them judge the rightness of standards of effort and earnings in the light of group norms and not of individual performance. Where a job is condemned as too hard (ie. as requiring excessive effort) this is not the opinion of only one individual, it is usually a judgement accepted by the whole work-group.

It should be noted that rightness of a rate and standard can only be established after the event. As effort is a subjective experience, the worker can only decide after he has done a job whether the intensity of effort implied in the production standards and piece-rates are right or not. If he accepts the rate by responding to the incentive and producing the amount implied in the scheme, the rate is proved correct. If he complains that the rate is tight, and responds by restricting his output, the rate is proved incorrect. With a loose rate the incorrectness of the rate may show up either by the worker earning exceptionally high earnings or by the worker restricting his output for fear of rate cuts. The correct rate thus is the rate at which an incentive scheme works smoothly.

The belief in the existence of the correct rate helps managers to maintain their faith in financial incentives. If there is no response to an incentive scheme they need not attribute this to any weakness in the conception of payment by results, they can attribute it to bad execution of the scheme, for instance, to faulty rate-setting. The managerial staffs I interviewed admitted that mistakes in rate-setting occur, but they did not consider this a serious difficulty. They thought that the solution lies with time-study. Most of them believed that time-study (although it involves a residue of subjective judgements) provides them with 'properly organised quantitative data' for setting the correct rate, and that experienced time-study men know what

is the right standard of effort and the correct rate
for it.

These beliefs about time-study and time-study
officers introduce additional reservations that must
be taken into account when judging the merit of
financial incentive schemes. The four notions
concerning categories of workers, the correct rate,
time-study and time-study officers, imply that
proponents of payment by results admit that
incentive-schemes may not work if they are badly
applied by poorly trained or inexperienced staff, or
if they are applied to people who are not incentive-
minded. On the other hand, the managers believe
that incentive schemes will work if they are applied
properly by experienced staff to incentive-minded
people (6). Thus these notions underpin the case
for the use of financial incentives.

* * * *

We are now in a position to answer some of the
questions posed at the beginning of this paper.

It appears that most managers rely on
impressions and beliefs when making judgements about
the effectiveness of financial incentives. This is
necessarily so because of the difficulties
encountered when trying to measure the effectiveness
of incentives, but does not appear to worry
managers, as illustrated by the following comments

'We do not need the information'
'If one could measure the effect of incentives
this would be of little value'

The managerial staffs whom I interviewed showed
great faith in financial incentives, and justified
this by reference to a number of widely held beliefs
which seem to serve the·function of either
establishing or underpinning the case for the use of
financial incentives. The evidence suggests that
these notions form a supporting system of beliefs.

This system of beliefs, which takes the outcome
of financial incentive schemes - increased
productivity - for granted, has neither been proved
nor disproved by facts. Apart from occasional
comments to the effect that piece-rates or bonuses
are not as effective as they used to be, there is
little evidence to suggest that the system of
beliefs conflicts with prevailing British
experience, although the situation may be altering.
Moreover, it must not be forgotten that the facts in
this particular field are not independent of the

beliefs relating to them. As the effect of
incentives depends on behaviour and this, in turn,
on beliefs, it is likely that if everybody accepts
the proposition that under incentive schemes
standards of effort ought to be higher, they really
will be higher. Belief in the proposition is an
active force in its survival. For if everyody wants
the incentive scheme to be effective they can make
it work. The system of beliefs will thus tend to
prove valid to the extent to which workers accept or
share the belief that standards of effort ought to
be higher under piece-rates, and act accordingly.
As long as the managerial system of beliefs endures
we may assume that workers share it and that
financial incentives work reasonably well in
practice. In a recent book, Festinger, Rieken and
Schachter (1956, pp3-5) argued that lack of social
support and inconsistent information lead people to
discard a system of beliefs. Neither of these
factors appeared to be operative with regard to
financial incentives in Eritain in 1958. The use of
payment by results was widely advocated and
supported and there was so far no important
inconsistent factual evidence that might lead to its
abandonment. We must remember, however, that its
adoption in the first place was not based on factual
evidence.

It seems pertinent to ask whether a system of
beliefs, such as the one described here, requires
more than social support and the absence of
inconsistent information for survival. Must it, for
instance, fit in with other beliefs? An interesting
point to note in this connection is that the
managerial system of beliefs associated with
financial incentives conflicts with certain other
beliefs and ideas held by managers. What the
managers consider holds for the workers is quite
different from what many of them think applicable to
themselves. Many managers dissociate themselves as
regards their own pay from the principle of a scalar
approach where reward is proportionate to effort.
As one manager put it: he, himself, would hate to be
paid by the piece. The implication would appear to
be that managers' standards of effort are all right
and do not depend on pay. Managers are not
primarily interested in money, they are interested
in their work. The beliefs with regard to financial
incentives, thus, are applied primarily to workers
(7).

Does this mean that these beliefs exist as a
self-contained system, unrelated to other beliefs,
or can it be (in spite of the evidence just given)

Financial Incentives and Belief Systems

that they are part of a wider system, for instance that they are connected with notions regarding other managerial practices? We are not in a good position to answer this question because we know very little about beliefs associated with other managerial techniques. It should be of interest to examine how far these other techniques are associated with specific systems of beliefs; how far they are underpinned by beliefs rather than facts; and how far their adoption rests on the acceptance of a diagnosis and plausible solution independently of whether the solution has been proved to be effective or not (8). Also how far they are influenced by the scientistic approach which ignores the differences between the natural science and social science universe, and which likes to operate in terms of 'one cause - one effect' relationships.

In practice, many modern managerial techniques are used together; and few of them would appear to have been discontinued. Many large firms have a work-study and a training department, run a works council and welfare schemes, and use induction, selection, and financial incentives. Does this mean that beliefs in certain types of managerial practices go together? Has there developed among British management a managerial ideology which advocates simultaneously the worthwhileness of financial incentives, work-study, joint consultation, selection and induction, training and welfare schemes? If so, what is the structure of this ideology? Alternatively is the use of some of these techniques merely a question of fashion, not backed by much conviction? Are there variations in the degree of confidence in the various measures, or are most of the measures accepted uncritically? What is the relationship between committal, facts, and beliefs (9)? The economist is not an expert in studying these questions; what he can do is to point up the problems in the hope that - at a later stage - the other social sciences, through their specialised knowledge, may tackle them or else supply him with tools to examine them in greater detail.

NOTES

1. See Ministry of Labour Gazette, April 1958. The percentage was 40 per cent in 1953 and 1955 and 39 per cent in 1957.
2. Compare R Marriott, Incentive Payment Systems: A

Financial Incentives and Belief Systems

Review of Research and Opinion, Staples Press,
London, 1957, Chapter 5.
3.   These convictions are not confined to individual
managers. In a study made by the ILO (Payment by
Results, Geneva, 1951 pp138-9) it is reported that
'Various governments, and employers' and workers'
organisations have stated that the introduction of
systems of payment by results has generally led to
increased output per worker ..... Most of these
statements were in general terms'. This means that
they were based on opinions rather than facts. The
report continues 'In some cases, however, specific
instances were cited, together with quantitative
information on the effects on output of the
introduction of payment by results'. It should be
noted that scrutiny of this information reveals that
in no case is the effect of the scheme on labour
effort isolated from other changes, which included
simultaneous organisational and methods changes. As
methods changes can produce considerable increases
in output it is impossible to judge what changes may
have taken place in labour effort. The merit of
financial incentives schemes may well be that they
raise overall productivity through the
reorganisation of work and methods, but the benefits
from such a reorganisation could be obtained without
changing methods of payment. The specific feature
of financial incentives is supposed to be its effect
on labour effort, and this ought to be treated as a
separate issue.
4.   Compare M S Viteles, Motivation and Morale, New
York, 1954, pp76-7.
5.   Compare Max Weber p62, where he discussed the
difficulties of getting women workers to work hard.
6.   These findings may be compared with the
judgement expressed by A Abruzzi (Work, Workers and
Work Measurement, New York, 1956, p3) that claims
with regard to practices in industrial engineering
were often supported only by proof by proclamation,
'so that acceptance may be achieved by noise level
rather than by verifiable context. Proof by
proclamation must decree that results can be
verified but only "if properly applied" by "properly
trained observers" using "proper methods"'.
7.   These opinions and beliefs may be contrasted
with Weber's observation that business leaders,
higher technically and commercially trained
personnel, and upper ranks of labour were the people
most emancipated from economic traditionalism and
most impregnated with the spirit of capitalism, the
essence of which is the making of money, while the
more backward traditional form of labour (often

exemplified by women workers) did not respond to money (piece-rates)).

8. As regards other managerial practices, for example, a strong case has been made out for the use of induction schemes based, among other things, on the observation that labour turnover is highest among newcomers. In one firm I found that the management firmly believed that their new induction scheme had reduced their labour turnover. Their faith in induction was so great they had completely overlooked that workers who had not passed through the induction scheme also showed a statistically significant reduction in turnover. Compare H Behrend, 'Limits to a Firm's Control of Labour Turnover', Nature, Vol 173, February 27, 1954.

9. A table given in the NIIP enquiry, Joint Consultation in British Industry (Staples Press, 1952, p65) is of interest in this connection. It suggested that people who were in favour of the introduction of joint consultation and had committed themselves to the scheme expressed a more favourable attitude to the scheme after they had had experience with it, while those who were against the introduction of the scheme showed a less favouable attitude.

REFERENCES

W Baldamus, The Relationship between Wage and Effort, Journal of Industrial Economics, Vol 5, No 3, July 1957

L Festinger, H W Rieken and S Schachter, When Prophecy Fails, Minneapolis, 1956

Max Weber, The Protestant Ethic and the Spirit of Capitalism, published in German in two parts, 1904 and 1905, revised version 1920. English version by Talcott Parsons, London, Allen and Unwin, 1930. Page numbers refer to the translation.

9   A Fair Day's Work

First published in Scottish Journal of Political Economy,
Vol. 8, No. 2, June 1961.

Boulding (1953, ppxiv-xv) defined the task of the social scientist in regard to ethics as that of teaching us 'what moons we should not cry for; and he argued that 'The great object of social science, as of all science, is to find out what is possible'. For not all ideals are capable of achievement. And perhaps the vision of being able to base fairness on measurement is one of these. Yet, we find that work-study engineers often conceive their task as the measurement of a fair day's work (1). And the concept of a fair day's work, as well as that of a fair day's pay, plays an important role in modern industrial society, both in wage-negotiations and in industrial disputes. The phrase is bandied about freely by trade unions and managements and both sides think that they know what they are talking about. Yet the notion of a fair day's work is something of a will-o'-the-wisp - the more closely one examines it, the more elusive does it become.

This article examines some of the difficulties associated with the use of this notion. It sketches briefly the nature of the difficulties, and then explores the questions of how production standards are determined in practice, and how they are related to the ideal of a fair day's work.

A fair day's work may be defined provisionally as the amount of work which some ethical code demands ought to be performed; the amount which is neither too little nor too much, but right. Thus the concept of a fair day's work is an ethical concept concerned with setting a standard for work conduct. Within this ethical frame of reference work is viewed as an obligation, and the individual's contribution to society as an honest -

145

a fair - day's work. The existence of this goal makes itself felt in the form of strong moral pressures which may make us feel that we ought to be working when we are doing nothing (2). This does not mean that everybody necessarily accepts the goal of a fair day's work or experiences guilt feelings or responds to moral pressures. But all arguments about a fair day's work (such as are encountered in discussions between management and trade unions) imply a conviction that there is a level of work which is right. It is wrong to do less than this, and it is wrong (unfair) to ask people to do more than this. These judgements are clearly normative in nature.

But how much work is a fair day's work? Here we deal with an abstract concept which needs to be translated into concrete (preferably quantitative) terms in order to be useful as a guide to conduct. Can the notion be translated satisfactorily into standards for a day's work, and if so how? How should a day's work be envisaged, in terms of a given output of results, or a given input of effort, or a given input of time, or in terms of a particular combination of these variables? This is the basic problem and dilemma.

The problem of visualising what should constitute a day's work is encountered in all types of work, but it will be considered here mainly in relation to factory work.

It must be stressed that visualising standards for a day's work is not merely an ethical problem; it is also an important economic and managerial one. Production planning has to be based on some sort of estimates of standards of production. For production factors affect costs, prices and delivery dates, and it is vital for management to have control over these.

Yet the employment contract, concluded when a worker is engaged, does not define the amount of work a worker is expected to do; all it does is to fix a wage-rate, to lay down normal working hours, and to stipulate the type of work to be done. The reason for this lack of precision is uncertainty. The employer cannot define future tasks clearly in advance. He needs flexibility to adjust to changing conditions. Thus, what the employer purchases is not a given series of services but a supply of effort for performing particular types of services involving changing work-assignments. He cannot define beforehand the exact nature of these assignments, nor how often and how quickly the same tasks will have to be performed.

Again, he cannot define the amount of effort which he expects because effort is a subjective experience not a measurable substance (3). An individual can compare and judge whether the effort he expends on a job in a particular time-interval is greater or smaller or equal to the effort he has expended on that or another operation in the preceding time-interval but he cannot define the amount of the differences quantitatively. Only the product of his application of effort - output - can be measured where it consists of concrete output units.

Thus, while an ordinary sales contract can be quite specific with regard to the price to be paid and the quantity and commodity to be sold, the employment contract can only give a vague outline of the contractual obligations for which a price is paid. Simon (1957, Ch11) argued that the essence of the employment contract is that the worker agrees to accept the authority of the employer to select a given set of tasks for him out of a given area of tasks with the result that 'certain aspects of the worker's behaviour are stipulated in contract terms, certain other aspects are placed within the authority of the employer and still other aspects are left to the worker's choice'. Simon likened the acceptance of a job to the signing of a blank cheque. By accepting the authority of the employer the employee agrees to do what he is told to do. In theory this means that it is up to management to decide what shall be a day's work. In practice, however, the employee is often left considerable freedom as to the amount of work he will do. The lack of precision of the employment contract means that the standards of effort which are adopted in practice lie somewhere between the highest level which an employee can reach and the lowest level which an employer tolerates.

The amount of variation in effort which is possible differs from job to job and depends on type and organisation of work. It is small where the pace of work depends on technological rather than human factors, and it is great where the pace of work depends on human rather than technological factors. Thus, in a machine-paced job an operator may have little chance to alter his rate of working. For instance, in an engineering plant (3) I was told that effort could only be varied within very small limits because production was highly mechanised. And the executive of a textile plant reported that in spinning it was the machine which set the pace. Again, with continuous process production, as in the chemical industry, it is the·raw materials and time which determine the rate of output.

By contrast, there are many jobs where the pace of work depends mainly on the operator. For instance, in bricklaying where the brick-layer usually sets his own pace, a wide range of variation has been observed.

In jobs where the pace of work depends mainly on the operator and where management sets no upper limit to production (where - as management puts it - 'the sky is the limit') the question as to how much work should be a day's work is open to a wide range of interpretations. To be asked to do as much as one can is not a precise order; it is an unsatisfactory guide to conduct which cannot easily be translated into concrete terms (4). Where management realises these difficulties it often introduces work measurement as a tool for setting specific standards of production as a guide to conduct. This, however, brings with it problems which will be dealt with later.

The lack of precision of the employment contract means that both employers and employees are continuously confronted with the question of how much work (on the particular tasks chosen) should e a day's work. This question may or may not be interpreted as an ethical question. The worker may ask: how much am I expected to do? OR how little can I get away with? The employer may ask: What is it fair to expect? OR How much work is required to meet a given order at a given date?

THE EMPLOYEE'S APPROACH

The employee's approach to this question will tend to be shaped by his outlook and experience. How much work he does will depend on his conception of duty. It depends on whether he conceives this in terms of the fulfilment of specific contractual obligations, in terms of set tasks, or in terms of the input of effort or of time. Evidence from research into restriction of output has suggested that the effort criterion is often applied first, particularly by the factory worker. Most individuals, it seems, enter the work-situation with some idea as to what is the 'right' or expected standard of effort. They are aware that they have accepted obligations which imply that they should do a 'reasonable' (fair) day's work. Thus many employees show signs of guilt if they are caught doing nothing and many employees seem afraid of being censured for not working sufficiently hard. They are exposed to certain moral pressures which tell them that they ought to be pulling their weight. For a worker who is working too little is often **condemned** by his mates. Thus, as Roethlisberger and Dickson (1939 p522) have shown, the operators in the Bankwiring Observation Room in the Hawthorne plant observed a norm of conduct that 'you should not turn out too little work. If you do, you are a "chiseler"'. Again Roy (5), studying restriction of output in an American machine-shop, found that although workers set ceilings to production 'machine operatives not only held back effort; sometimes they worked hard'. 'Sometimes, when exerting themselves to reach quota, they expended effort to the maximum'. On really bad jobs where they considered that they could not reach 'normal' earnings, however high their effort, they deliberately dropped their effort to the minimum; but on jobs with a chance of 'making out' 'the machine operators with few exceptions put forth vigorous effort'. The study has shown that the workers evaluated each new job with its managerial production standards and rates in terms of effort. Where the effort-evaluations indicated that the production standards were attainable they set out to reach quota. The reasonableness of output targets was judged in terms of what the workers considered the right standard of effort. This right standard lay well above the minimum effort standard. Thus, what evidence we have suggests that workers do not habitually operate at the minimum effort level and that this is not merely due to fear of dismissal.

It appears also from these studies that workers do not normally operate at the maximum effort level. The level which they adopt usually lies somewhere in between. Thus, in the Bankwiring Observation Room there was another norm of conduct that 'you should not turn out too much work. If you do, you are a "rate-buster"' and the operators were aware of the fact that they were capable of turning out more work than they did. Similarly, the workers in Roy's study set a ceiling to production.

It would appear that the employee's notion as to what constitutes the 'right' standard of effort originates in the home and school and is, so to speak, imported into the work situation; here it is modified by experience, by managerial pressures, and by the social environment. The result is the establishment of an habitual standard of effort which workers tend to defend as right. The standard which is adopted may be affected by norms of output which have been evolved in the department and may reflect group conceptions as to what is the right standard of effort in a given situation. Each individual has to strike a balance between his own approach and that of management and of his co-workers. Thus Coch and French (1948, pp516, 519-20) reported that a new operator in the Harwood Manufacturing Corporation joined a group of girl pressers who were restricting their production to 50 units per hour, while the time-studied standard efficiency rating was equal to 60 units per hour. After 13 days in the department the new operator reached standard production. Thereupon she became the scapegoat of the group; this induced her to reduce her output to below 50. But when the group was broken up at a later date and the newcomer was left on her own she developed her own standard of production of 92 units per hour. In the Bankwiring Observation Room (see pp 112ff) the operators considered that the wiring of two equipments was a day's work, and observed this as a norm. But not all workers accept group norms. For instance, Dalton (1948 pp5ff) found that a certain number of the workers in the machine-shop which he was studying disregarded group norms and became rate-busters. Similarly Lupton and Cunnison (1957, pp234ff) described the differential output records of 'conformers' and 'job-spoilers'. Dalton characterised the rate-busters as economic individualists who considered the acquisition of money a mark of virtue and were keen on upward social mobility and on accumulating savings. By contrast, other workers in the same shop considered group loyalty a cardinal virtue and adhered to group norms of output. The study revealed that most of the rate-busters came from farms or urban lower middle-class families, most of the restricters from urban working-class backgrounds. Thus, it draws attention to the probable importance of the influence of outlook and social background on the response of individuals to managerial production standards and to group norms of production (6).

Furthermore, the economic situation may play an important part in determining worker standards of effort. Fear of unemployment may lead to restriction of effort in attempts to spread the work. Again, full employment may lead to effort restriction in bargaining bids for higher wages.

Dissatisfaction and grievances may also lead to restriction of output; unfair treatment, so to speak, absolves the worker from the obligation to do a fair day's work; for if management neglects its obligations, the worker does not need to adhere to his. Thus, if wages are considered unfair or piece-rates tight, the result may be a lower level of effort.

In addition to viewing a fair day's work in terms of effort standards and the output which these will achieve, the factory worker needs to take account of working-hours. When does he perceive these as being fair? One could argue that the evidence with regard to the enjoyment which the workers in Roy's study derived from loafing into the supervisor's face after completing the day's quota, suggests that they do not accept any obligation to put in a set amount of time. If they have completed their quota they feel entitled to loaf. They do not feel any obligation to work throughout the whole period of time scheduled for work. Other employees, by contrast, may feel that they ought to be working all the time while they are at work.

Claims by trade unions for a shorter working week challenge the rightness of existing working-times and show up the development of powerful value-judgements about the right (fair) length of the working day. These pressures may well have initiated a shift in the climate of opinion of our society as shown by agreements on reductions in the working week concluded between trade unions and employers' federations or individual firms in a number of industries.

THE MANAGER'S APPROACH

Like the employee, the manager tends to be influenced by his outlook and experience in his approach to the question of what should represent a day's work. Insofar as he comes from a different social background, however, he is likely to import different notions into the work situation and to draw on different experiences so that his image of a day's work may differ considerably from that of his employees.

Moreover, for the manager this is not merely a question relevant to his own behaviour, it is also relevant to his managerial function. For he is responsible for the work-performance of his subordinates; and often this is to him by far the more important problem; how much work can he expect from his workers? Are they working hard enough? The manager considers he has a right to demand that his employees do a good day's work. Thus, his attention with regard to this problem is of necessity focused on the question of effort control.

It is essential for management to set up and enforce standards of production which ensure the firm's survival and safeguard or increase its profits. For this reason it is plausible that management's main frame of reference for judging a day's work is economic. Often, for instance, so much work may need to be done and there may be such a shortage of labour that the question whether the worker is doing a fair day's work or not is irrelevant; what matters is that he must get through more work to meet the needs of the firm, either by putting in extra effort or by working overtime. Again, if certain orders are placed with the firm with fixed delivery dates it may be essential to ask for extra effort to complete the orders so that an important customer is not lost to a competitor. Thus, management's prime interest would appear to be that of securing as large a day's work as possible. From the economic point of view, the higher the level of effort which it can secure, the better.

This desideratum does not, however, solve the manager's problem of determining how much work should be a day's work. For he cannot ask the impossible. The target which he tries to reach must be realistic, that is, possible of achievement. The question with regard to his employees thus is: What is it reasonable, or fair, to expect from them?

This raises a similar question to that posed with regard to the employee: how does the manager perceive what should be a day's work; does he see it in terms of set tasks or in terms of the input of effort, or in terms of the input of time? The economic criterion makes it likely that he visualises it in terms of the completion of specific (though changing) work allocations. In envisaging output targets he will be guided by the record of past performance. He usually knows what the habitual rate of output has been. In addition he may have at his disposal work measurement data and often he may judge a day's work in terms of the standards set by work measurement. These imply the application of what is considered normal effort so that the day's task is viewed in terms of the output of results per unit of time obtained from the input of normal effort standards.

Furthermore, the working week is envisaged as consisting of a set number of working hours. Employees are expected to be at work for the full stint irrespective of whether they have completed their allotted tasks earlier or not. Thus speedier achievement of given results is not synonymous with reduced working hours. This seems to imply that the hours criterion of a day's work takes precedence over achievement and effort.

Insofar as management's conception of a reasonable day's work is based on past performance or on work measurement standards, it is liable to be conservative. Just as the employee tends to develop an habitual standard of effort and defends it as right, so the manager tends to defend as right the standard which he considers attainable normal performance. This may blind him to the fact that these standards are not the only potential standards (7).

CONFLICTING STANDARDS AND THEIR ADJUSTMENT

Management and worker conceptions with regard to the right production standards in a given situation may or may not coincide. In some cases workers may believe that they are doing a fair day's work while management does not think so. And this may be a genuine divergence of opinion. When such a difference occurs, management may accuse workers of restriction of output, and workers may accuse management of slave-driving (8).

In other cases management may be confronted with deliberate restriction of output. Again, management may consider that habitual standards of effort - be they fair or not - are too low to meet their economic needs: what the firm requires is an extra supply of effort from its existing labour force. For management must evaluate a day's work not only in terms of past experience but also in terms of present and future needs. These may demand the raising of the level of effort.

Management often attempts to achieve this by the use of financial incentives. Basically the question of raising the level of effort is a question of getting the worker to agree to adopt higher standards of effort. Such agreement can only be obtained through bargaining. It is not a question of individual bargaining but of negotiating with workers' representatives or whole work groups; this makes it possible to use group forces and group norms as a basis for agreement. Bargaining involves concessions on both sides, and one of the most important concessions management can make is in regard to wages. In return for wage-concessions workers may agree to raise their standards of effort. Financial incentive schemes provide

machinery for such barganining; their introduction
represents the conclusion of an effort-bargain in
which workers agree to raise their standard of
effort in exchange for the guarantee of higher
earnings (ie the agreed piece-rate margin).
Proportionate increases are assumed in earnings and
productivity. Where a piece-rate margin of 33 per
cent is agreed it is implied that productivity
should also increase by 33 per cent (9).

Alternatively an agreement can be concluded on
output targets for specific tasks. For instance, in
one experiment, it was shown that group-committal on
targets could raise productivity well above the
standard of 60 which had been 'efficiently set up by
time and motion analysis'. In this instance the
workers held three short weekly meetings to decide
on a definite production target. To begin with they
decided to raise production to 84 units per hour
although 75 was supposed to be the ceiling. The
goal was reached and the group set a new goal of 95,
but only reached 92. Eventually production
stabilised at around 87 (10).

Committal to production goals need not be
linked to payment by results. A wage-increase on
time-rates can be made into an effort-bargain by
linking it to an agreement on output targets.

It must not be forgotten, however, that
agreements on production standards refer to specific
situations and specific tasks. As jobs and
conditions change, conflicts arise, adjustments
become necesssary and new effort-bargains are worked
out. In a dynamic situation effort-bargaining is a
continuous process requiring constant managerial
attention.

IMPLICATIONS WITH REGARD TO THE NOTION
OF A FAIR DAY'S WORK

Arguments and agreements about standards of
effort raise an interesting question: which of the
possible standards represents a fair day's work?
This problem is perhaps most clearly illustrated if
one considers the effort-bargain which is contained
in a financial incentive scheme and which lays down
what difference there ought to be between output on
time-rates and on piece-rates (11). For it shows
that there is - by agreement - a standard of effort
which is considered right for time-rates, and a
standard of effort which is considered right for

piece-rates. Which of these two standards represents a fair day's work? Is the conception of what represents a fair day's work not something absolute but something relative, and if relative, what are the reference points? Is it a function of wage?

The concept of a fair day's work evokes the image of one particular right level of effort (the maximum effort point?) which is absolutely valid. It suggests a correct standard of conduct which is independent of any system of reward. Does not each individual owe the same contribution to society, to give of his best? (12) This interpretation of the concept is contained in such admonitions as 'we must work as hard as we can', 'we must do our share', 'we must do our best'.

In abstract terms some people may find it possible to accept and think in terms of an absolutely valid standard of effort. As pointed out earlier the problem is that of translating the abstract standard into action. The question then appears to become one of what is fair in given cicumstances to all concerned, to employee, management and society, and the answer to this seems to depend on the particular situation. It depends, among other things, on the particular goals of a society at a given time. Rules of conduct such as that of doing a fair day's work are means of achieving these goals and vary with them. In war-time, for instance, when survival is the over-riding goal, a higher level of effort than in peace-time is accepted as the right standard. In peace-time when adequate leisure may be one of the goals of society this affects the amount of work that is considered a fair day's work. As the concept of what represents adequate leisure changes (for instance, with the claim for a shorter working week) concepts of a fair day's work are revised. The goal of rising material standards of living (which is usually taken for granted in Britain) depends on high standards of effort for its achievement.

Furthermore, it is plausible that habitual standards of effort or habitual output norms often come to be considered as 'fair' standards. Certainly they become reference points against which injustice and unfairness is assessed. Thus, in practice, certain standards acquire the status of being fair not because of any absolute merits which they may have or because of any quantitative justification which may be produced but because they do not strike the workers as unfair and are not attacked by them as unjust. The evaluation is made

mainly in terms of subjective experiences of effort;
the worker judges whether the amount of effort he is
putting in is equal to his habitual standards of
effort or not.

Thus different answers seem to be given in
different circumstances implying that there is not
one right standard of effort but many right
standards according to circumstances. This would
appear to be a paradox connected with the concept of
a fair day's work: that the concepts of an
absolutely valid standard and of relatively valid
standards are held side by side.

Since a fair day's work is an ethical concept,
the question as to what constitutes a fair day's
work is not a question of facts but of subjective
judgements. These judgements seem to differ for
different people and for different occupations and,
as we have seen, for different circumstances; the
most important of these appear to be the level of
employment and wage conditions. It must be noted
that differences in value judgements cannot be
resolved by recourse to science; there is no
scientific criterion for judging the rightness of
any one standard of production as compared with
another. The differences can only be resolved by
mutual adjustment of incompatible standards.

IMPLICATIONS WITH REGARD TO THE ROLE OF WORK-MEASUREMENT

This raises the question how this problem is
resolved by work measurement. Foote Whyte (1955
pp17ff) has given the answer 'by guesswork'; he
explained that rate-setting is nothing but a
'guessing-game'. In my incentives enquiry it was
admitted by all management representatives that
there is an element of subjective judgement in work
measurement. That this must be so follows from the
fact that we have no means of measuring effort and
that time-study involves the assessment of what is
normal effort (13). Making this judgement is easier
if one can eliminate the technological variable.
This is where work-study helps. Work-measurement
makes it possible to standardise factors in the
situation other than effort so that the standard of
effort required may be judged more effectively, and
standards for different jobs set as fairly as
possible. This involves judging what standards are
acceptable to the workers and considered right by
them. In making these guesses mistakes may be made
and they show up, after the event, by the workers'

reactions to the time-studied production standards. The workers may find that the standards of effort which are implied in the time-studied production standards for the job are higher than their habitual standards of effort and that they cannot make normal earnings with what they consider the right standard of effort; the result is complaints about tight rates and demands that the job be restudied, usually followed by an adjustment of the standard. Conversely, standards may be set too low, making it possible for the workers to get exceptionally high earnings with their habitual standard of effort; as a result management is faced with loose rates. In practice, setting production standards and piece-rate prices is a question of getting agreement between both sides as to what is the 'right' standard and the 'right' price for it. As my incentives enquiry has shown agreement on correct rates and standards is arrived at by a process of bargaining which involves the adjustment of standards to each other. Many firms develop procedures for setting standards and rates which fit into the agreed pattern. For instance, there may exist provisions for the adoption of provisional rates for new jobs. If these rates turn out to be tight, workers can obtain adjustments; if they prove acceptable they become established.

If no procedures exist for arriving at agreement, and if tight rates are not adjusted, they may give rise to restriction of output. In such a situation, if there is no confidence in management, loose rates, too, have been found to result in restriction of output. As mentioned earlier Roy (14) found that workers on jobs where the rates were tight (i.e. on 'stinkers') decided it was not worth putting in any effort and let their standards drop to a minimum. On jobs where the rates were loose (i.e. on 'gravy' jobs) the workers set an upper limit to their effort for fear of rate-cutting (15). The evidence which we have on the operation of financial incentives suggests that, in practice, there is one 'right' production standard for each effort-bargain, that is one standard for each job which is acceptable at any given point of time and which works. The standard which is right because it works for a given job in one factory may be wrong in another, for different factories have among other things different traditions of speed and of human relations. As Ryan (16) has pointed out, a completely arbitrary standard may not work; it might be above everybody's achievement. Standards must bear some relation to the actual production rates of

A Fair Day's Work

a factory.

This raises the question as to what is the
relation of the standard that works (that is, the
standard agreed in individual factories) to the
ideal of a fair day's work? Does work-measurement
not aim to set up absolutely valid standards? It
seems to me that on this issue work-measurement is
caught in the same paradox that was pointed out
earlier: that two concepts are held   side by side;
the ideal of absolutely valid production standards
as well as the more practical ideal of relatively
valid standards (17).

Several research enquiries have drawn attention
to the inconsistency of different time-study
officers in setting production standards (18). This
inconsistency is serious if one believes that the
aim of work-measurement is to establish generally
valid standards of performance. In practice,
however, work-measurement is usually only concerned
with establishing standards that are valid in one
plant and, within the plant, the internal bargaining
process is the final arbiter of standards.

IMPLICATIONS FOR COLLECTIVE BARGAINING

However informal this internal bargaining
process may be, its importance cannot be
overstressed. Nor must its implications be
overlooked.

The setting, maintenance and adjustment of
effort-standards which take place continuously at
shop-floor level and which are so often linked to
the setting of payment by results rates represent a
process of bargaining which goes side by side with
national collective bargaining. Thus there takes
place a duplication of the bargaining process.
Certain issues are bargained about twice.
Sometimes, for instance, national agreements attempt
to deal with the problem of effort-standards and
restrictive practices. Thus, in 1957, in the
dispute in the enginering industry the Engineering
and Allied Employers' Federation attempted to deal
with restrictive practices by national bargaining;
it introduced the issue into wage-negotiations and
in the agreement which was eventually reached the
Confederation of Shipbuilding and Engineering Unions
agreed among other things 'to use their full
influence to bring to an end without delay all
practices which are contrary to the well-being of
the industry, including, for example -
1 Unconstitutional stoppages of work 2 Embargoes on

overtime 3 All restrictions on output or earnings
(19)'.

It can be argued that this type of national
agreement is too vague and remote from the shop-
floor to be effective; only in special cases where
identical equipment is used as in the knitting of
nylon stockings did I come across a meaningful and
comparatively unambiguous industry-wide collective
bargain about standards of output. In most cases,
the obstacles to the national determination of fair
production standards are formidable. Therefore,
most effort-bargaining must of necessity take place
within the firm. As Professor Phelps Brown (1960
p6) reported '....it has happened more than once
recently that the employers have asked for a
reduction of "restrictive practices" in return for a
wage rise; but with the best will in the world the
union leaders at those bargaining tables could not
commit their members up and down the country to
particular changes in working practices whose
significance could be evaluated only on the spot'.

On the spot evaluation, as has been shown in
this paper, arises all the time on the shop-floor,
and one can say that bargaining about standards of
production is part of the everyday life of the
plant. Even on the shop-floor, however, the
adjustment of manager and worker conceptions of
effort standards is not an easy process, but usually
it is a manageable process. Moreover, it is not
likely that it can be eliminated by national
bargaining (20). This fact strengthens the case of
the advocates of plant-bargaining, especially
because bargaining about effort is frequently not
independent from bargaining about wages.

If there is a case for plant-bargaining, and
this is not the only argument put forward in its
favour (21), this in turn has important implications
for trade union structure. For, as long as the
trade union branch in Britain is based on place of
residence rather than place of work, there exists
an important obstacle to plant-bargaining. A
structure in which the trade union branch is based
on the place of work avoids the need for two types
of union official (branch officers and shop
stewards), and thus eliminates the difficulties that
can arise from this type of duplication of
officials. Under the present structure, the
existence of in-plant bargaining increases the power
of in-plant leaders and this can seriously undermine
trade union authority as illustrated by many an
unofficial strike.

To meet this situation the place of the shop-steward in the trade union structure needs to be reconsidered and his bargaining powers defined and formalised.

CONCLUSIONS

This paper set out to examine how far it is possible to envisage, define and measure a fair day's work. It showed that the employment contract lacks precision and thus does not define a day's work clearly. The notion of a fair day's work introduces normative pressures which act as a guide to conduct in this ambiguous situation.

The concept of an amount of work which is right and which ought to be performed - of a fair and honest day's work - is, however, vague. It is abstract and difficult to translate into concrete terms. It is the expression of internalised value systems, and stimulates guilt feelings when a bad conscience is activated. Thus it is an ethical concept, and its definition depends on value judgements, not on facts. It follows that it is not possible to measure or ascertain scientifically how much work represents a fair day's work.

The essential point to grasp is that factory production standards are considered fair not because they are based on work measurement but because they are judged and accepted as fair by the parties concerned. It is the mutual agreement between management and workers which matters and which determines what production standards are accepted as right and are adopted. Work measurement is merely a tool for reaching such agreement, not a substitute for it.

Agreement is reached through bargaining about what represents a fair day's work. Such bargaining takes place continuously within the plant, and it is not likely that it can be eliminated. This raises the question of the wisdom of the duplication of the bargaining process that takes place when most formal collective bargaining is conducted nationally. It also raises the question of what is the most appropriate trade union structure in this situation.

In practice, it seems, the concept of a fair day's work acts as a dynamic regulative force round which management and workers bargain about working hours, production standards and wages.

NOTES

1. Compare for instance, P Carroll in the foreword to R Presgave, the Dynamics of Time Study (McGraw Hill Book Company, New York, 1945), pp xv and xvi: 'We continue to set up standards which purport to measure a fair day's work' and 'a number of time-study men, engineers and consultants are striving conscientiously to attain the fair measurement of "a fair day's work".' And T A Ryan and P C Smith, Principles of Industrial Psychology (Ronald Press Company, New York, 1954), p346: 'Jobs are timed and time standards set to determine what constitutes a fair amont of work to be expected from a worker in a day'.

2. Even when work is slack people may experience feelings of guilt because they are doing nothing. For having no work to do conflicts with the individual's conception of the work situation and makes him or her feel uncomfortable. Clerical staff, for instance, often feel restless and dissatisfied when they run out of work; yet they may refuse to go home because they feel they ought to be at work; there ought to be something they could do. Factory workers too have been reported to have reacted against such situations by changing their jobs.

3. Compare T A Ryan, 'Fatigue and effort in relation to standards of performance and systems of payment', International Labour Review, Vol 65, No 1, Jan. 1952, pp45-46. Ryan defined effort as 'an individual's experience of how hard he is working. At times he feels that he is working as fast as he can or is using as much strength as possible. This would be the maximum point of a scale, which would run from this point down to the point where he feels that he is just barely working at minimum speed or strength'. This is the sense in which the term effort is used in this paper.

4. It is plausible that many individuals find that the lack of a clear definition of their duties and of production targets involved in such a situation imposes considerable strain on them. They may feel a need for reassurance that they are doing what is expected of them. It may well be that there is justification for the opinion that it is just as unfair to provide no targets as it is to provide targets which are much too high.

5. See D Roy 'Quota Restriction and Goldbricking in a Machine Shop', American Journal of Sociology, Vol 57, March 1952, pp427ff, and D Roy, 'Efficiency and "The Fix": Informal Intergroup Relations in a

A Fair Day's Work

Piecework Machine Shop'. American Journal of Sociology, Vol 60, No 3, November 1954, pp255ff, and D Roy, 'Work Satisfaction and Social Reward in Quota Achievement: An Analysis of Piecework Incentive', American Sociological Review, Vol 18, 1953, pp507ff.

6.   From his evidence Dalton (1948) hypothesised that 'the rate-buster is likely to come from a family of higher socio-economic level than that of other members of the work-group, or if he is not, he is trying to reach such a level. He is ambitious and his immediate goal is money' (p18).

7.   For instance, J Montague ('The Integrated Rating System - II', Work Study and Industrial Engineering, Vol 3, No 5, May 1959, pp167ff), argued that work measurement tends to preserve the status quo because it is based on predetermined time standards which do not allow for the possibility of the existence of different standards of normality. Again, the Coch and French (1948) and the Bavelas experiments (see Note 10) showed that there were potentials not realised by work measurement.

8.   Compare O Collins, M Dalton and D Roy, 'Restriction of Output and Social Cleavage in Industry', Applied Anthropology, Vol 5, No 3, Summer 1946, pp1ff.

10. Research conducted by Alex Bavelas, as reported by N R F Maier, Psychology in Industry p151 (1958 edition).

11. In practice it is not possible to measure the actual difference, as the effect of financial incentives cannot be isolated.   See H Behrend, 'Effort-control through Bargaining', Nature, Vol 179, p1106, June 1, 1957.

12. To trace the influence of religion on this concept would lead outside the scope of this paper, but the influence is obviously very important.   See, for instance, Max Weber, The Protestant Ethic and the Spirit of Capitalism (1904), and R H Tawney, Religion and the Rise of Capitalism (1926).

13. This is dealt with by the so-called rating or levelling methods.

14. See Roy Note 5.

15. On this point compare also Roethlisberger and Dickson (1939) Ch 18.

16. See T A Ryan (Note 3).   Compare also A Abruzzi, Work, Workers and Work Measurement (Columbia University Press, 1956), pp24ff, and J Montague (note 7), p173.

17. Compare Ryan (Note 3), p45.   Ryan considered that there exist two goals under payment by results: the 'goal of relative validity or accuracy of the standards' which means that 'standards for various

jobs should be fair in relation to each other', and a second goal, namely that of 'absolute valididty or accuracy; that is, the absolute level of effort required at the standard pace should be fair to all concerned. This goal has also sometimes been called the "fair day's work".'
18. See, for instance, L Cohen and L Strauss, 'Time Study and the Fundamental Nature of Skill', Journal of Consulting Psychology, Vol 10, 1946, pp146ff. Winston Rodgers and J H Hammersley, 'The Consistency of Stop-Watch Time-Study Practitioners', Occupational Psychology, Vol 28, No 2, April, 1954. R Marriott, Incentive Payment Systems: A Review of Research and Opinion (Staples Press, 1957), pp95-98.
19. Compare Phelps Brown (1960) p5: 'The industry-wide agreement can deal only with situations that are common to many firms, and in a varied industry the highest common factors are not very high. Much that concerns the particular worker in his particular job has to be left out of the scope of organised bargaining altogether unless it is established within the firm as well as at the national level'.
21. See Phelps Brown (1960), D J Robertson, 'The Inadequacy of Recent Wage Policies in Britain', Scottish Journal of Political Economy, Vol V, No 2, June 1958, and D J Robertson, Factory Wage Structure and National Agreements (Cambridge University Press, 1960).

REFERENCES

K E Boulding, The Organisational Revolution, Harper Brothers, New York, 1953
L Coch and J R P French, Jr., Overcoming Resistance to Change, Human Relations, Vol 1, No 4, August, 1948
M Dalton, The Industrial 'Rate-Buster': A Characterisation, Applied Anthropology, Vol 7, No 1, Winter 1948
T Lupton and S Cunnison, The Cash Reward for an Hour's Work under three Piecework Incentive Schemes, The Manchester School, Vol 25, No 3, September 1957
E H Phelps Brown, The Importance of Works Agreements, Personnel Management, March, 1960
F J Roethlisberger and W J Dickson, Management and the Worker, Harvard University Press, 1939
H A Simon, Models of Man, John Wiley & Sons, New York, 1957
W Foote Whyte, Money and Motivation, Harper Brothers, New York, 1955

10 Some Aspects of Company Wage Policy

*Major points and details from: Some Aspects of Company Wage Policy,
Journal of Industrial Economics, Vol. VIII, No. 2, March 1960 and
An Assessment of the Current Status of Incentive Schemes, Journal of
Industrial Relations, Vol.5, No. 2, October 1963.*

This chapter deals with a question which frequently faces managers, namely, what is, in their case, an appropriate wage policy. Does their payment system and wage structure work well or are changes desirable? And if so what kind of changes? Before making hasty ad hoc changes it is important to examine carefully the claims made for different approaches. The paper looks first at the question of different methods of pay.

THE EVALUATION OF PAYMENT SYSTEMS

In the early 1950s the use of payment by results to raise labour productivity was widely advocated and many official statements encouraged its use (1). However, in the late 1950s doubts began to be expressed (2) partly because some managements became aware that the effectiveness of their incentive schemes began to wear off and partly because changes in industrial technology led to the abandonment of incentive schemes by a number of well-known firms. Thus the focus of attention began to shift to measured daywork. Cost savings schemes such as the Scanlon plan also began to attract attention and in the mid-sixties, productivity bargaining came to the fore to improve the quality and efficiency of employees.

During this period academic researchers with different outlooks and perspectives increased our knowledge with regard to the functioning of different financial incentives (3) and broadened our horizons (4). Their enquiries revealed that the question of work incentives has proved far more complex than originally thought; for this reason it is essential not to treat the question of methods of

164

wage payment as a problem with defined limits that can be separated off from other problems of wage policy and of motivation and efficiency and solved in isolation. We cannot apply successfully in this field a two-variable nor a simple cause and effect type of approach and analysis.

As Baldamus pointed out (1951,p8) 'one cannot isolate or separate motives and feelings into observable compartments'. Measures such as the introduction of a bonus-system are unlikely to affect economic motives only; they are 'bound to have repercussions on "non-economic" incentives'. Similarly non-economic managerial measures such as the introduction of joint consultation 'may affect a man's whole outlook on work, for instance, his appreciation of the job, which in turn could influence his pecuniary aspirations'.

In other words, there is a 'spillover-effect' in employee reactions to managerial behaviour which needs to be taken into account. If attitudes are favourable to management, reactions to a new method of payment may also be favourable; but if attitudes are hostile, their introduction may increase suspicion and set up resistance to the change. In the one case the change may be successful, and in the other ineffectual and disruptive. But the important difference between the two cases is not the method of payment, it is the total situation; the direction of the change - to or from payment by results - could just be a minor detail.

The implication of these arguments is that the value or effectiveness of systems of wage payment cannot be judged out of context. It is ·not a question of whether one system is a good system and the other a bad one; it is a question of which system is likely to be effective in a particular situation. Even when put in this form, however, we must remember that any answer that is given represents a value judgement, and such judgement must depend on the criteria used in the evaluation.

The criterion that is most frequently mentioned is that of output. However as mentioned earlier in this book it is almost impossible to find direct statistical evidence to support this belief. This is due to the difficulty of isolating variables; not only must we count with the spill-over effect in worker reactions mentioned earlier, but management action, too, does not take place in isolation; the introduction of payment by results is normally accompanied by other changes, especially by method study, and in many cases the latter may have more far-reaching effects on output than the former. The same difficulties apply if the criterion to be applied is labour cost.

In the absence of objective statistical data for judging the effects of incentive schemes we must fall back on the evaluation of behaviour and opinions. As discussed earlier, analysis of this type of evidence reveals that financial incentive schemes can work satisfactorily in the view of the users, but that they can also go wrong (5). Other methods of payment such as measured daywork can also work well in the view of the users and can also go wrong. The evidence all points in one direction, namely that there exist both effective and ineffective payment schemes. Furthermore, schemes that work well to begin with may lose their effectiveness and may become demoralised.

The problem for management, then, is one of assessing the effectiveness of its existing system of payment as a method of effort control and to decide whether it needs to initiate new effort bargaining methods or has to improve its existing bargaining procedures. Various aspects of the effort bargaining processes involved in the use of payment by results have already been discussed in detail in preceding chapters. In this chapter the focus is on the wider issues of how the chosen payment system fits into the company wage and personnel policy. In this context I would like to suggest the appropriateness criterion as a useful concept for reaching decisions.

THE APPROPRIATENESS CRITERION

It seems that often the crucial problem that faces management in dealing with labour is that of securing a high or sustained level of effort. Baldamus, for instance, argued in 1961 (p1):

> 'The organisaton of industry, with all its complexities and diversities, ultimately revolves on a single process: the administrative process through which the employee's effort is controlled by the employer. This means that the entire system of industrial production will be viewed as a system of administrative controls which regulate quantity, quality, and distribution of human effort'.

In some cases it may be sufficient to use close supervision as the main administrative control. In other cases it may be possible to control effort by the use of conveyor belts or by pacing the work by other mechanical means. Alternatively management may attempt to gain control by using a particular financial incentive scheme or measured daywork with agreed output targets.

The existence of alternatives raises the question of what factors need to be considered when evaluating the advantages which may be gained from a change to (or from) one method of effort control to another. It also suggests that the answer to what represents an appropriate method of payment has to be worked out for each specific situation; there can be no general answer. The choice in any particular situation needs to take account of such diverse factors as the type of work which is being performed, the production lay-out, the size of firm, the efficacy of existing effort-controls, the quality of management-worker relations, the objectives to be achieved by the firm's wage-policy, and the general climate of opinion.

The type of work most appropriate for payment by results is repetitive manual work where the product is standardised and easily measurable, and where the pace of work is controlled by the individual, not by the technology or the task. Variations in the incidence of payment by results in different industries are likely to be connected with differences in the possibility of applying it although that is not the only factor involved.

Even where type of work is suited to payment by results it may not be appropriate to install it. For instance, in a small firm, quantities produced may be too small and costs of administration too high to warrant its use; also management may find it possible to control effort by personal supervision. Again where trade is irregular, for instance where it is seasonal, it may be unwise to use incentive schemes as they are not suited to conditions where work is often slack. Nor are they particularly suitable when employees work on an assembly line; for instance, on the production line of a motor car factory (6).

Furthermore, where effort-levels are satisfactory or satisfactorily controlled there is no case for introducing payment by results. Usually the case for its introduction arises because management considers that production standards are unsatisfactory and need to be raised. It would be a misconception, however, to assume that the mere installation of a scheme is all that is required. As pointed out already, success depends on mutual agreement with regard to the effort-bargain, to fair standards of production and to fair rewards.

Slichter et al discussed certain prerequisites for success (7). They stressed that the schemes must have top management support, adequate personnel to adminster them, and continuous control on the shop-floor, and also that these schemes can only work effectively if management resists worker and trade union pressure tactics.

To sum up, advantages which can be gained from payment by results are not inherent but accrue in particular circumstances only. Nor do they last indefinitely. As Slichter et al put it (8):

> 'In no aspect of our study (of industrial relations) is the contrast between the "short-run" and the "long-run" more important. The establishment or revision of a single production standard on a particular day is of little consequence for costs and profits. The path of least resistance for management is obviously to give in a little, loosen the standard a bit, and avoid trouble with the union. Over the years, however, there is no surer way to develop a high-cost plant and poor labour relations'.
>
> 'Substantial demoralisation of an incentive plan results in an unstable situation. It leads eventually to abandonment, revision, or catastrophe'.

Finally it must also be stressed again that it is not merely the factual situation (and changes in it) which may affect the appropriateness of using payment by results; their effectiveness depends also on the outlook, the norms and belief-systems of the users of the schemes. It depends, for instance, on the acceptance of the ethical norm that standards of effort ought to be higher under payment by results. If people act by this norm, standards of production will be higher; thus if they want the system to work, they can make it work.

The question which we need to watch at any particular time is whether current thought and beliefs with regard to incentives are changing. If a new climate of opinion develops, this may influence managerial action and worker behaviour significantly. Thus, the history of modern managerial techniques has revealed certain fashion-trends. New techniques are publicly advocated; some firms adopt them and become fashion leaders; and eventually others follow. Management training

schemes and productivity bargaining are but two
examples of this type of development. The difficult
question for managers is to judge whether
fashionable techniques stand up to the claims made
for them, and if yes, whether it is appropriate and
desirable to use them in their organisation.

PAYMENT SYSTEMS AND COMPANY WAGE POLICY

The evaluation of existing methods of payment
in an organisation, it can be argued, should be part
of an evaluation of its pay policy. This means
that it must include an examination of how the
organisation's payment system fits into and affects
the organisation's pay structure and pay policy· as
well as its economic performance. Before carrying
out the evaluation it is important to clarify the
overall policy objectives so that priorities can be
defined and the appropriateness of possible remedial
measures assessed.

As possible objectives it would seem that a
company wage policy can aim to fulfil the following
functions:

> To attract and retain employees of the right
> quality and in the right quantity.

> To maintain or increase standards of effort.

> To avoid or reduce frictions and discontents by
> meeting expectations and conceptions of
> fairness, especially with regard to standards
> of living and differentials for status,
> responsibility and skill.

> To control costs and reduce administrative
> complexity.

However insofar as these objectives may clash with
each other the policy needs to evolve compromises.

Moreover, pursuit of the objectives may be
constrained on the one hand by national wage
agreements, the cost of living, the level of
earnings and the level of employment in the local
labour market and on the other hand by the firm's
ability to pay, its labour costs relative to its
total costs and the demand for the firm's product.

As regards the recruitment and retention of
employees, a firm which tries to evolve a pay policy
has to assess whether it can compete effectively in

the local labour market by paying nationally agreed
minimum or standard rates or whether it should add
various other elements to the base-rate such as
guaranteed overtime, bonuses or merit money; or, if
labour is scarce, whether it should try to attract
labour by offering higher rates of pay. In a period
of cost constraints it must assess whether it can
reduce or keep down labour costs by bargaining about
pay restraints, by changes in the method of payment
or by other means.

Problems connected with the second aim, effort
control, have been discussed already.

As regards the third aim, the prevention of
discontent with wages and salaries does not
necessarily lie within the power of a single
organisation. In Britain dissatisfaction with the
general level of pay is usually dealt with by
national collective agreements which deal with the
demands for pay increases and pay adjustments put
forward by the trade unions. Nevertheless there
would appear to be some scope for reducing or
avoiding wage discontents and frictions by a company
pay policy because many wage conflicts originate
within the firm, for instance, from anomalies in the
wage structure or from the effects of payments
received in addition to base rates. The resulting
differences in earnings often do not reflect widely
accepted and shared notions of fairness; for
instance that earnings should be commensurate with
status, responsibility, skill and effort. However,
no unanimity exists as to the figures which
represent an adequate reward for these factors in
particular situations. Conflicting interpretations,
changing relativities and growing anomalies can give
rise to constant friction.

Perhaps one problem in this area is that the
prevention of discontent is not necessarily a
conscious objective within a company pay policy,
merely a hidden one. Reforms may become necessary
because discontents are dealt with haphazardly as
they surface which can mean that discontents receive
little attention in policy formulation. Yet,
complaints with regard to the level of wages, wage
differentials and rate-setting can mar the success
of such a policy and can seriously hamper the
attainments of the other objectives, namely better
control of the supply of labour, of effort and of
costs.

As regards the fourth objective, the control of
costs has many aspects. Foremost among them is
control of the total pay bill. This is not only
important for economic viability but also as an aid

in production planning, though opinions differ
greatly as to the type of policy which will achieve
this. Labour costs need to be watched because they
may be inflated, in certain situations, by the use
of excessive or customary overtime and by loose
piece-rate or bonus schemes. In addition there is
the question of the cost of the administration of a
wage policy.

The more complicated the wage-structure and the
payment system, the more costly is the
administration (even in the age of the computer).
This means that payment by results schemes are more
costly to operate than straight time rates.
Moreover workers may experience difficulties in
understanding sophisticated schemes and this can, in
turn, affect the effectiveness of a particular wage-
policy and thus its costs (9).

Administrative problems often arise from the
untidiness of existing wage-structures. Sometimes
this has come about because small groups of
employees have successfully secured pay
differentials based on personal allowances or on
classifications of job differences which are
fictitious rather than real (10). Frequently wage-
structures become unwieldy in cases where national
awards have not been incorporated into the basic
rate but are treated as additions to it; for
instance, cost of living allowances (11).

The pursuit of any one of the objectives which
have just been outlined may lead to conflict with
the attainment of the others. Thus the offer of
high wage rates to attract labour can undermine the
effectiveness of payment by results. Or a new
piece-rate can represent a sparking-plug for a
dispute. Or semi-skilled piece rate workers may
earn more than skilled men or foremen who are paid
by time, upsetting accepted notions of fair
differentials for status and skill. This means that
in formulating wage policies managements must find
an effective reconciliation of such objectives as
controlling recruitment, effort, discontent and
costs. However, they must not expect that any
solution they adopt will hold for long. For
industrial life is not static but dynamic; and a
constantly changing scene requires repeated
adjustments. Thus different solutions are
appropriate in different situations and at different
points of time. When pressures of demand and
competition highlight the problem of effort control,
the use of incentive schemes may appear advantageous
but if increasingly bad feelings develop about rate-
setting and differentials the abandonment of payment

by results could be a catalyst and lead to improved industrial relations.

PAYMENT BY RESULTS AND INFLATION

An important change in our understanding of wage problems in the early 1960s was a growing awareness that the question of choice of method of wage payment is not just a problem of company wage policy but is one that affects national wage movements and has a direct bearing on the problem of inflation. It seems that up to that time many government officials and research workers approached questions of national wage policy and company policy as separate issues. Burkart Lutz, for instance, reported in 1961 that:

> 'According to commonly held convictions the problem of methods of wage payment has nothing to do with the macro-economic problem of wage movements. It is the concern of the individual firm' (12).

Thus the advocacy of incentive schemes by British government officials was usually associated with drives for raising productivity and efficiency. The fight against inflation by contrast led to the advocacy of policies of wage restraint. As far as I could ascertain British official pronouncements favouring a national incomes policy had not yet in 1961 taken account of incentive schemes as possible factors in inflation (13).

Again, academic research into wage-problems in the post-war period could roughly be divided into two types: studies of the movements of wages and prices in the whole economy (or in sectors of it) as opposed to studies of the operation of different methods of wage-payment in individual firms. The former with a mainly historic and economic orientation were more concerned with inflation than motivation; the latter with mainly psychological or sociological orientations were more concerned with problems of motivation than inflation.

Yet the evidence at our disposal already then suggested that the use of payment by results affected not only the wage-structure of a particular firm but also that of the labour market outside the firm. During the post-war full employment period, for instance, effort-bargaining initiated by employers to offset the shortage of labour led to the upward revision of piece and bonus rates. This tendency was reinforced by wage-concessions in the form of the deliberate toleration of loose rates. This increased the earnings of piece-rate workers and formed one element - and an important one - in the phenomenon of wage-drift.

Wage-drift (defined briefly as a tendency for earnings to increase considerably faster than wage-rates) began to attract attention. Thus, Turner (1960) was one of the first academics who argued that the interaction of productivity growth, wage increases and fluctuations in the level of earnings is highly complex and that the root of the problem lies in the wage-structure itself and in particular in the relationship between piece-rates and time-rates.

Phelps Brown similarly argued in 1962 (pp 344 and 350) that the problems of national and company wage-policy are interlinked. In discussing the upward trend of earnings under systems of payment by results, he pointed to three sources, firstly the tendency for improvements in equipment and processes to loosen rates, secondly the fact that in Britain piece-rates as opposed to time-rates are negotiated at the place of work and are frequently adjusted in response to local pressures, and thirdly that employers are more ready to raise piece-rates than time-rates.

The inferences Phelps Brown drew are of particular interest. He wrote:

'The contrast between the years before and since the Second World War suggests that one of the factors (e.g. common influences on drift) is the state of managerial expectations prevailing internationally in the post-war years; most drift could not have occurred if managers had reckoned a rise in unit labour costs more harmful than a loss of output. The contrast during the post-war years between the countries studied here and the United States suggests that another necessary condition for drift has been the need and the opportunity to alter particular rates at the place of work when only the broad lines of the wage-structure are prescribed by centralised collective bargaining'.

Phelps Brown concluded that action to reduce drift can only be taken by management. Managers need to accept responsibility for their domestic wage-structures and need to plan them rationally rather than extemporising and buying their way out of difficulties from day to day.

CONCLUDING COMMENT

What is needed then (at the present time just as in the past) is a constructive managerial approach to developing rational and consistent wage-policies which fit into the wider needs of our national economies by taking account of the fact that problems of company and national wage-policy are not separate issues but can affect each other vitally; and that the levels at which bargaining takes place and any duplication of bargaining at different levels (such as accompanies the use of payment by results) may be crucial in alleviating or aggravating these influences. It is therefore essential for managers to try to understand the problems confronting them and the potential consequences of measures they propose to take. As Shimmin has shown, past incentive schemes have often suffered from the effects of 'hasty applications made as a matter of expediency' (1959, p142). This is not a good basis for longer term measures.

When managers want to change an important aspect of the organisation's pay-structure or payment scheme they must strive through careful assessments to find an effective reconiliation of the contradictions which can arise among the four company wage policy objectives outlined in this paper. However, they must not expect that solutions they adopt will hold for long. Industrial life is not static; a constantly changing scene requires repeated adjustments. Regular appraisal as to whether the existing method of payment is appropriate should therefore be part of company policy.

Payment by results as a method of effort control offers certain advantages provided co-operation is forthcoming; for instance, the interest arising from the challenge of piece-work goals can contribute to worker morale and efficiency. However the gains need to be weighed against the disadvantages, among them the need for constant scrutiny to prevent a deterioration of relations and loosening of standards with their effects on the wage-structure of the firm and on the labour market.

A regular assessment of the climate of industrial relations would also appear important. If there is a lot of pay discontent, be it about differentials, rate setting or other wage issues (especially if they give rise to industrial

disputes) the climate of industrial relations can
deteriorate and action is needed to improve
management/worker relations and to create a more
favourable working climate. In such a situation
change may revitalize the atmosphere and workforce
but it could also have the opposite effect.

To sum up, the need to realign methods of
payments and pay structures to changed circumstances
(including the rate of inflation, the state of the
economy and of the labour and product markets)
involves the continuous reappraisal of the relative
importance of different objectives of an
organisation's pay policy. Managements must weigh
up which issues are most urgent in their
undertakings and must work out an effective
compromise.

NOTES

1. See, for instance, the British Ministry of Labour
pamphlet Wage Incentive Schemes, Industrial
Relations Handbook Supplement No 4, HMSO, London
1951, where it was stated that so long as certain
points are understood 'wage incentive schemes will
benefit the nation as a whole and give mutual
advantage and satisfaction to the employers and
workers concerned' (p2). Or see S H Slichter, J J
Healy, E R Livernash, The Impact of Collective
Bargaining on Management, the Brookings Institution,
Washington, 1960, p495, where it was stated that
during World War II 'government agencies encouraged
the use of incentives'. See also Payment by
Results, ILO report, Geneva, 1951, and Wage
Incentives in Australian Industry, Australian
Department of Labour and National Service,
Melbourne, 1959.
2. In Britain a one per cent decline in the
percentage of workers paid by results in 1957 was
described as a turn of the tide. (R R Hopkins,
'Incentives - the Turn of the Tide', The Listener,
July 10, 1958). In America, Slichter et al (see
Note 1) reported that we find '"a mixed picture" -
an important consideration (for changes) was growing
lack of confidence in incentives ..... While some
managements have abandoned incentive plans, a larger
number are dissatisfied and would like to do so but
see no way of accomplishing this objective on terms
acceptable to both union and management. Some
managements remain convinced of the fundamental
desirability of incentives even with a technology
and process that builds in considerable control of

Some Aspects of Company Wage Policy

production'. For an examination of the evidence
see: R Marriott, Incentive Payment Systems: A Review
of Research and Opinion, Staples Press, London,
Second (Revised) edition, 1961, pp 242-258; Garth L
Mangum, 'Are Wage Incentives Becoming Obsolete?'
Industrial Relations, Vol 2, No 1, October 1962.
3. R Marriott, (see Note 1). Marriott's
bibliography contains more than 300 items; yet it
does not cover publications in languages other than
English. Some of the French and Belgian studies are
recorded in the journal Sociologie du Travail,
Paris.
4. Findings of British researchers, for instance,
tended to supplement and not to contradict each
other. Thus, a continental observer surveying
British work on methods of wage payment concluded
that 'the true wealth of this survey rests in the
diversity of perspectives, and in their
complementarity'. Translation from Marcel Bolle de
Bal, 'Les Modes de Rémunération et les Sciences
Sociales du Travail en Grand-Bretagne', Sociologie
du Travail, Quatrième Année, Octobre-Décembre, 1962,
p394.
5. Thus Slichter et al, (see Note 1) reported that
in 1958 'There were extreme differences in the
success with which wage incentives were operating in
different companies and in different plants in the
same company. For example, a survey of 100 companis
indicated that 60 were satisfied with their
incentive plans, and 40 were not'.
6. See Sir Reginald Pearson, 'From Group Bonus to
Straight Time Pay', Journal of Industrial Economics,
Vol 8, No 2, March, 1960, where the reasons for
Vauxhall's changeover to measured daywork were
discussed.
7. Slichter et al (see Note 1) pp 519-520. Compare
also Marriott (see Note 2), Appendix on the Basic
Requirements of Incentive Payment Systems.
8. Slichter et al (see Note 1) p 503. With regard
to demoralisation the authors explained that the
term 'means more than just a poorly-functioning
plan. It implies: 1. substantial inequities in
earnings and effort 2. a growing average incentive
yield or bonus 3. a declining average level of
effort 4. a high proportion of "off-standard"
payment and time' (p497).
9. Compare Sylvia Shimmin, Workers' Understanding of
Incentive Payment Systems, Occupational Psychology,
April 1958.
10. An interesting example can be found in W H Sales
and J S Davies, 'Introducing a New Wage Structure
into Coalmining', Bulletin of the Oxford Institute

176

of Statistics, Vol XIX, No 3, August, 1957. The article reported that the examination of job classifications in the British coalmining industry revealed the existence of 6500 'different' jobs. A year's study of these jobs resulted in a standard list of some 400 jobs. Further investigation revealed that these could be classified satisfactorily into 13 grades in a national agreement between the National Coal Board and the National Union of Mineworkers.

11. An example from my incentives enquiry showed that a hosiery firm paid a base rate of 10 old pennies per hour in June 1955; this seemingly low rate was supplemented by a cost of living bonus of 18 old pennies.

12. Translated from Burkart Lutz, Hochmechanisierung und Lohnpolitik, Atomzeitalter, Europaeische Verlagsanstalt, Frankfurt am Main, Dezember 1961 und Januar 1962, p 280.

13. Governments in other countries, too, have been concerned separately with questions of incentives and low productivity (see ILO report, Note 1) and of national inflation and wage-policy (see, for instance, OEEC, The Problem of Rising Prices, by G W Fellner, M Gilbert, B Hansen, R Kahn, F Lutz, P de Wolf: OEEC, Paris, 1961, 12). Only in the United States did inflation not appear to be a major issue at that time.

REFERENCES

W Baldamus, Incentives and Work Analysis, Monograph A1, University of Birmingham Studies in Economics and Society, Birmingham, 1951

W Baldamus, Efficiency and Effort, Tavistock Publications, London, 1961

E H Phelps Brown, Wage Drift, Economica, Vol XXIX, No 116, November 1962

Sylvia Shimmin, Payment by Results, Staples Press, London, 1959

H A Turner, Employment Fluctuations, Productivity and Cost-Inflation in Manufacturing Industry, International Labour Review, Vol LXXXI, January-June, 1960

11 Research into Inflation and Conceptions of Earnings

Adapted from paper first published in Journal of Occupational Psychology, Vol. 50, No. 3, September 1977.

This paper presents a review of more than ten years' research by myself and my research staff which has been reported in detail elsewhere (Behrend, 1964 - 1975). Briefly, the research consisted of pilot studies, undertaken in the early 1960s, and of five national sample surveys carried out in Britain and two sample surveys of male employees in the Republic of Ireland in the years 1966 to 1973. Parts of the research were sponsored by the Social Science Research Council, and other parts commissioned by the Economic and Social Research Institute (Dublin), and the National Economic Development Office. The findings are summarised by topic so as to provide a map of the kind of evidence that is available in the publications which have resulted from the research.

PRICES AND PRICE MOVEMENTS

Early in the research it was found that past prices and not current incomes were the major frame of reference for judging the reasonableness of current prices. People did not apply the rather complicated kind of comparison which some economists would apply; this involves relating the past price to the past income, and then the present price to the present income, and assessing which relationship is more favourable. Instead the current price was usually assessed against the first price learned for the article in question. For example, in the early 1960s a young woman stated that she had seen a skirt costing £5, and had considered this price quite unreasonable because she had never paid more than £3. When asked whether she could not afford to buy the skirt she realised that she could easily manage to do so. It was interesting that respondents appreciated this fact only when it was pointed out to them. In other words, the awareness of a changed price to income relationship, it seems, occurred only as a result of an outside stimulus. It involved a learning process where individuals acknowledged later that life had become easier when they started to take their improved income position into account in making price judgements.

In 1963-64 respondents were inclined to believe that most prices were rising and by December 1966 (at the end of a six months' official price freeze) this tendency was considerably more marked. For instance, a fall in the price of meat had not been noticed, nor the fact that the price of bread, butter and some other commodities had remained the same.

The apparent failure to adjust notions of prices raised the question of how prices are learned. Any assumption that it might be easy to learn prices in times of inflation was confounded by the incidence of a widespread lack of knowledge of prices for certain commodities and services; this suggested that learning was often not taking place. People seemed to learn only a limited number of prices adequately; in addition they acquired certain vaguer, more subjective notions about prices to which we may apply the term 'price images'. There were considerable time lags in adjusting price images to new price levels and even more so in adjusting judgements of the 'reasonableness' of prices. Certain obstacles and aids to learning were identified, for instance the special effort which is often required to find out the prevailing price. For more details see chapter 12 and the original reports (Behrend, 1964, 1966, 1972b, 1974b).

VIEWS ON FAIR PAY AND LOW PAY

Views on fair pay for different occupations were obtained in our 1969 Irish enquiry (Behrend et al 1970b) when the sample of male employees was asked how much men in eleven occupations, and also how much men in four occupational groups, should be paid per week. The answers showed a very high level of agreement on the ranking of the occupations (1). This rank order corresponded to that of current rates of pay for the occupations. However, the amounts described as fair showed that the median figures for all but the salaried occupations were higher than the current rates.

Inflation and Conceptions of Earnings

A comparison of the views of the men in different social grades revealed that the median amounts were very similar for the floor of the pay structure but differed markedly for the occupations at the top of the pay structure. This evidence, together with the information on respondents' incomes, suggested that the higher a man's income, the greater were the differentials which he considered fair at the upper end of the income structure.

An open-ended question about low pay was included in four British surveys in December 1966, May 1969, January 1971 and January 1973 as well as in the 1969 Irish one. (Behrend et al 1970, 1970a and Behrend, 1971, 1974a) The question was: 'People talk about lower-paid workers. What does the term "lower-paid worker" mean to you in terms of pay? I mean for a married man before tax and deductions? Below £....per week?'

The British evidence showed clearly that ideas on low pay were adjusted upwards over time with inflation although at a slower rate than average earnings. The median views rose from £11 per week in December 1966 to £20 per week in January 1973 (2). The changes in the median views were similar to the adjustments of the Trade Union Congress targets for a minimum wage.

Another interesting feature was that 96 per cent of the respondents in 1966 considered that any amount below £10 per week represented low pay and 81 per cent in 1973 any amount below £18. This evidence suggested that it could have been possible to secure agreement on a floor to the pay structure.

In the 1969 Irish survey (Behrend et al 1970a) the median answer to the same low pay question was £12 per week. When respondents were asked later in the same interview what they thought would be a fair minimum wage per week for an adult married man, an adult single man, an adult married woman and an adult single woman, the median amount for both groups of women was also £12 per week. For single men it was £15 and for married men £18 which was similar to the average earnings of men at that time. This hierarchy reflected customary distinctions, for instance, that in certain occupations in Ireland married men received higher wage rates than single men, and in most occupations men received more pay than women. This means that the respondents accepted the 'need' criterion of fairness that married men required more money than single men and that men needed more money than women. However, as there were no precedents in custom for making a distinction between married and single women, the respondents were divided about this issue, 40 per cent of them naming the same amount, 39 per cent a higher figure for married women and 20 per cent for single women.

VIEWS ABOUT PAY INCREASES

Views about their last pay increase given by male employees in the February 1966 British survey were illuminating. Notwithstanding the fact that in Britain at that time a pay increase norm of three and a half per cent was in operation, the majority of the respondents described their last pay increase as an amount per week and only a very small minority expressed it in percentage terms. This was in marked contrast with policy-makers and negotiators (3). Similar findings were obtained in the Dublin 1971 survey.

How the respondents assessed their pay increases was not closely related to their incomes but depended on the amount of the pay increases. The great majority of the 1966 British repondents who had received less than £1 per week felt that it had made little or no difference. By contrast, the majority of the men who had received £2 a week or more considered that this amount had made a difference. Given that the majority of manual workers were earning less than £21 per week at that period, it becomes apparent that with a three and a half per cent norm a large proportion of the population was receiving pay increases of well below £1 and therefore fell into the category of those who perceived that no visible benefit had resulted from their pay increase. This frustration may well have been an important factor leading to the 1969 pay explosion and shows up one of the weaknesses of a percentage pay increase formula.

Our evidence suggests that there is at any given period of time a perceptual threshold zone for pay increases. The lower boundary of this zone is the monetary amount below which a pay increase is perceived by a clear majority of individual income earners as being not noticeable. The upper boundary is the monetary amount above which a pay increase is perceived by a clear majority of individual income earners as having made a noticeable difference. For instance, in the pilot studies as well as in the 1966 survey, the threshold zone in Britain was found to be between £1 and £2 per week. In 1971 in Dublin it was equivalent to between £2 and £2.50. Daniel

Inflation and Conceptions of Earnings

(1975 p36), who used somewhat different questions in
his survey, claimed that the 'critical point' (ie
threshold) was £4 a week in 1975.

Comparing the Irish evidence for 1969 and 1971,
it was found that pay increase expectations and
perceptions as to what represented fair pay
increases had been adjusted upwards. The major
frame of reference given for judging the adequacy of
the last pay increase, and for the amount considered
fair for the next pay increase, was the cost of
living. (For more details on the topics in this and
the next section see Behrend 1972a, 1973, 1974a).

PAY INCREASE IMAGES AND PAY INCREASE DIFFERENTIALS - TWO USEFUL CONCEPTS?

As a result of past experience and exposure to
two and a half decades of inflation, it appeared
that employees had come to expect pay increases at
regular intervals as a matter of right, not of
contribution. This right seems to have assumed the
property of a regular entitlement which is not
easily amenable to change and may account for the
intractable nature of inflationary income
expectations.

Pay increase expectations would seem to be
influenced by three interrelated factors which are
experience based: the size and changes in the size
of one's own past pay increases, the expected
protection against increases in the cost of living,
and the application of pay increase restraints.
More specifically this means that they are shaped by
the individual's own occuptional experience of past
pay settlements.

Ideas about the fairness of the size of pay
increases, on the other hand, seem to be based on
more generalised 'pay increase images' which are not
only influenced by the factors just mentioned but
also by other factors. For instance, they may be
based on past increases and the purchases these made
possible, and may embrace a judgement about the
adequacy of the last pay increase. Other images may
be based on amounts received by other workers or by
friends and acquaintances, on information from the
mass media, or just hearsay. Since such images are
often used as frames of reference for judging the
fairness of pay awards, it matters very much what
kind of images are being projected. For instance,
it seems likely that the images of 30-40 per cent
and of pay increase amounts of £20-30 per week often

182

projected in the media during the wage-round which preceded the August 1975 £6 limit fuelled expectations and pay claims. The pay-restraint limits of the 1975 and 1976 social contract put a temporary stop to the projection of two-figure pay-increase images. Early in January 1977, on hearing that in West Germany (with a lower rate of inflation) the IG Metall management were presented with a 9.5 per cent pay claim, I was surprised at my initial reaction; it sounded high even in the light of the counter-offer of 4.75 per cent. What I wonder will be the pay increase images we hold when this paper is printed or read?

Conflict over pay differentials is often considered as lying at the heart of the problem of cost inflation. But what about pay increase differentials? The differences between the monetary amount of one pay increase with the monetary amount of another increase? It seems to me that one should not assume a priori that the same ideas of equity are necessarily applied to pay differentials and pay increase differentials; for instance, equity of pay awards and of pay increase differentials may be judged by individuals in the light of pay increase images rather than of rates of pay.

Our research indicates that there is no consensus as regards fair pay increase differentials; many groups fight for an equalisation of the size of pay increases while others resist it or try to increase the differences. The question of the equity of pay increase differentials would thus appear to be one of the central problems facing negotiators and policy-makers in periods of wage-restraint, and one moreover which seems to require the ability to reconcile the conflicting pressures for equality of treatment and differential treatment by finding, each time round, new accommodations, new rules and pay increase norms. This point is illustrated by the changes made from one agreement to the next in the six national agreements which were concluded by the Employer Labour Conference in Ireland in 1970 to 1977.

PERCEPTIONS OF INFLATION

One of the most startling findings (early in the research in the mid-1960s) was that the term inflation meant so little to people, even to educated respondents. It was something abstract and remote which they read about in the newspapers but which had little personal significance. The apparent lack of any emotional dimension presented a marked contrast to the fear of inflation (Inflationsangst) which then existed in Germany where many people had experienced a breakdown of the currency twice in a lifetime. There was at that time a marked reluctance by German politicians and newspapers to refer in public to the creeping inflation which that country was experiencing.

Equally important was the finding that the process of inflation was not understood; namely that there is a relationship between pay increases and price increases. By 1973 a larger proportion of the population seemed to appreciate what inflation was about insofar as 60 per cent of the NEDO survey respondents stated that they thought that prices could not be stabilised without limiting the size of pay claims. However, those who were aware of a connection were caught up in the dilemma that they felt the only way to protect themselves from losing out was to agitate for pay increases although this would not stop the vicious circle. Daniel claimed in 1975 (p1) that people felt that inflation was harmful to the nation and that it was hurting them personally. However, Incomes Data Services claimed in 1976 (IDS Focus, p7) that recent surveys had shown that people still did not understand how their increases in pay affected their own and other people's shopping basket. In their view, what was necessary was an 'elementary understanding of the facts of the situation' and therefore 'every pay packet should contain a price warning', that is it should explain the effects of pay increases and taxation and other costs on prices; indeed 'employers should describe the impact of pay on prices as a matter of regular procedure' under the disclosure of information provisions. While this would be one way of drawing attention to the problem it is by no means certain that it would provide a solution.

THE SEARCH FOR A WORKABLE INCOMES POLICY

Can policy-makers expect to get public support for policies if they use words and explanations which are not easily understood? It would seem that a lack of understanding of the word 'inflation' and of the interrelation between pay and price increases, together with a lack of appreciation of the importance of curbing inflation, must be considered a major obstacle in the fight against inflation and in attempts to secure public support for an incomes policy. In 1975, more than eight years after the publication of our first evidence drawing attention to this type of communication problem, a major attempt to bridge the gap was mounted by the Government when an HMSO pamphlet 'Attack on inflation: A policy for survival' was printed for distribition to every household in Britain. There was thus a considerable time-lag before policy-makers began to respond to the evidence, or began themselves to become aware of the problem.

The findings from the Irish research, which had been expressly commissioned as an aid for policy-makers, were used by the Employer Labour Conference (as soon as they became available) in the deliberations which preceded the conclusion of their 1970 and 1972 national agreements. However, with independent research much time can elapse before the information is published and before insights relating to policy formulation filter through. This has meant with our research that opportunities for action have been missed by governments, and that time-lags in the use of information have led to 'mis-matches' because the evidence was related to changing, not to stable, situations. Two illustrations are discussed below.

If a new period of pay restraint were introduced, I suggested in the light of our evidence in January 1972, one might begin with a temporary holding operation. The basis of this would be a fixed weekly amount for pay increases - an amount which would be visible enough to bestow some benefit and yet not inflationarily large. It could be agreed by tripartite discussions between the government and the two sides of industry and a visible amount in the pay packet could be arrived at by different means - a sufficiently large increase before tax, or a smaller tax-free amount. For instance, if an amount of £2 per week in the pay packet were the aim, the personal allowance could be raised by £104 per annum, a relief which would accrue to every taxpayer. In the voluntary tripartite discussions, more than nine months later, the Conservative Government proposed a pay restraint limit of £2 gross rather than net, and this was rejected by both sides of industry. In the light of our research one could have predicted that £2 gross would not be an acceptable negotiating position; prices had been rising and the Irish Employer Labour Conference which had settled for £2 gross in December 1970 had had to settle for £2.50 in July 1972.

The tax concession idea was taken up four years later in the Labour Government's 1976 budget. However, it was linked to a percentage pay increase formula (with a floor and ceiling), not to a flat rate amount, and it was accompanied by increases in national insurance contributions. This raises the question: Could income earners identify what benefits they had derived from the combination of tax concession and pay increase? Since each individual case had to be worked out separately by the employers, no clear general information was available, and it seems unlikely that clear pay-increase images emerged of the benefits bestowed by the 1976 stage of the social contract.

These considerations indicate that it is important that insights gained from past experience, and from research related to past situations, should not be applied to the present without reinterpreting their meaning for the current situation. For instance, it must be remembered that in an inflationary period reference points change with the passage of time. Thus, the 1975 social contract pay increase limit of £6 a week was often referred to in 1975 as representing a reasonably moderate amount and yet for many employees it was the largest they had ever received. Could one have a better illustration of the adjustment of views to inflation between 1965 and 1975? and, at the same time, of the need to contain pay increase expectations regardless of what happens to the other variables involved in inflation? The 1976 social contract pay-restraint formula was more severe with its 5 per cent norm and a weekly minimum of £2.50 and maximum of £4.00 because the economic situation was still considered serious. Thus it seemed very important at that time that the 1977 stage of the pay policy should reinforce the process of lowering pay increase expectations so as not to lose grip over pay increase movements (4). Dampening pay increase expectations alone, it is true, cannot cure inflation but it can prevent inflation from becoming worse than it would be without pay-restraints. One can indeed argue that the less one can control the other variables, the more need there is to put brakes on those variables over which one believes one can exercise some control.

Opponents of incomes policies have often argued that the breakdown of past policies demonstrates that incomes policies do not work. Alternatively, it can be argued that past breakdowns resulted from lack of exerience in designing the policies as well as from inertia in adjusting to new circumstances. In more general terms, therefore, the search for a workable incomes policy needs to be looked at as a learning process where learning involves the ability to adapt the experiences and lessons acquired from the past to new and constantly changing situations. This means that continuous evaluations of past events are reqired. What mistakes were made? What unfavourable memories left behind? Is the present situation fairly similar or radically different? Does it require new remedies and the revision or abandonment of current policies?

In regard to new situations Schon (1971) argued that, where a public problem is new, there is no established solution or institution corresponding to it. Therefore the question is how a government can go about developing and carrying out an appropriate policy, when it is clear that the new problem has to be worked on but not clear what the solution is. It seems to me that the oil crisis, our high rate of inflation, our high rate of unemployment and the low rate of economic growth have created this type of new situation.

This raises the question: Can the government on its own solve new public problems of these dimensions and complexity? Can and should these problems be the responsibility of the government or of the community as a whole? Do we need more realism relating to economic problems and resources as well as to perceptions of the government's power and scope for action? The public, we found in our surveys, felt powerless and showed a tendency to pass the buck, saying that it was up to the government to deal with economic difficulties and to provide help.

The dilemma which faces us seems to be that the problem of inflation and therefore that of finding a viable incomes policy is difficult to solve because it has no technical solution. It belongs to a class of human problems which an American biologist (Hardin, 1968) described as 'no technical solutions problems'. Regarding this type of problem he reported:

> 'An implicit and almost universal assumption
> of discussions published in professional and
> semi-popular scientific journals is that the
> problem under discussion has a technical
> solution. A technical solution may be defined
> as one that requires a change only in the
> techniques of the natural sciences, demanding
> little or nothing in the way of change in human
> values or ideas of morality.'

With this type of problem, Hardin suggested, a
solution can only be found if 'morality is system-
sensitive', that is, sensitive to the needs of the
state of society at a particular point of time. It
is no good appealing to people's sense of
responsibility if it is merely an attempt to get
something for nothing. Responsibility derives from
social arrangements that create coercion.
Temperance can be created only by 'mutual coercion,
mutually agreed upon by the majority affected'.
Furthermore our choices in life are not between
perfect reforms and no action, but between imperfect
reforms and no action. Injustice therefore may be
better than ruin.
Ultimately one of the problems at present is
that of conveying a sense of realism to people's
understanding of economic life and of the restraints
imposed by scarce resources. Since psychologists
have special knowledge and skills relating to the
study of learning, this paper could perhaps spark
off some useful exchanges of ideas between them and
economists.

NOTES

1. The two pay structure questions were well
separated in the interviews and cross checks showed
a high degree of consistency in the replies; for
instance, very similar amounts were given for an
electrician and a skilled worker and for an
agricultural and unskilled worker. To obtain the
rank order, the occupations were arranged in order
of the descending size of the median amounts named
for fair pay for the eleven occupations. It should
be noted that the same rank order was obtained when
the mean amounts were used as a base.
2. In this context attention needs to be drawn to
what one might call the special appeal of certain
round figures. Thus £10, £15 and £20 were found to

be popular figures while £13, £17 and £19 seemed to be unpopular.

3. The majority of the male employees in the Irish surveys also named amounts not percentages. Similar differences in thought processes between theorists and the public would appear to apply to prices. Insofar as consumers can identify the size of a price increase, they tend to think of it in terms of the difference in amounts, often quoting both prices. To assume that they think of a specific price rise in terms of a percentage is unrealistic as percentages have to be worked out and most of us, as a little introspection will show, are not in the habit of working out percentages in everyday life.

4. 1983 comment. As it happened the Callaghan government lost control insofar as it could not get support for a proposed 1977 pay restraint limit and this marked the beginning of another pay explosion.

REFERENCES

H Behrend, Price and income images and inflation, Scottish Journal of Political Economy, Vol XI, No 2, June 1964

H Behrend, Price images, inflation and national incomes policy, Scottish Journal of Political Economy, Vol XIII, No 3, November 1966

H Behrend, What is lower pay? 1971 follow-up survey, Social Science Research Council Newsletter, No 12, 1971

H Behrend, Public acceptability and a workable incomes policy. In Frank Blackaby (ed), An Incomes Policy for Britain, pp 187-214, National Institute of Economic and Social Research and the Social Science Research Council, Heinemann, London, 1972a

H Behrend, Research into perceptions of price rises, Social Science Research Council Newsletter No 17, 1972b

H Behrend, Incomes Policy, Equity and Pay Increase Differentials, Scottish Academic Press, Edinburgh, 1973

H Behrend, The impact of inflation on pay increase expectations and ideas of fair pay, Industrial Relations Journal, Vol 5, No 1, Spring 1974a

H Behrend, Attitudes to Price Increases and Pay Claims, NEDO Monograph 4, NEDO, London, 1974b

H Behrend, Research into attitudes to inflation and incomes policy, International Journal of Social Economics, Vol 5, No 3, 1978

H Behrend, H Lynch and J Davies, A National Survey

of Attitudes to Inflation and Incomes Policy. Occasional paper in Social and Economic Administration, No 7, Edutext Publications, London, 1966

H Behrend, H Lynch, H Thomas and J Davies, Incomes Policy and the Individual, Oliver and Boyd, Edinburgh and London, 1967

H Behrend, A Knowles, What is lower pay? Findings from two national sample surveys, Social Science Research Council Newsletter No 8, 1970

H Behrend, A Knowles and J Davies, Views on Pay Increases, Fringe Benefits and Low Pay, Paper No 56, Economic and Social Research Institute, Dublin, 1970a

H Behrend, A Knowles and J Davies, Views on Income Differentials and the Economic Situation, Paper No 57, Dublin, 1970b

H Behrend, J Davies , E Paterson and E Rose, What does the word 'inflation' mean to you? and What is the connection between wage-claims and prices?, Industrial Relations Journal, Vol 2, No 3, Autumn 1971

A I Glendon, D P Tweedie and H Behrend, Pay negotiations and incomes policy: a comparison of views of managers and trade union negotiators, Industrial Relations Journal, Vol 6, No 3, Autumn, 1975

W W Daniel, The PEP Survey on Inflation, Vol XVL, Broadsheet No 563, PEP, London, 1975

G Hardin, The tragedy of the commons, Science, Vol 162, New York, 1968

IDS Focus, Every pay packet should contain a price warning, IDS Focus Quarterly 3, Incomes Data Services, London, 1976

D Schon, Change and industrial society, The Reith Lectures 1970, BBC Publications, London 1971

12 Research into Public Attitudes and the Attitudes of the Public to Inflation

Adapted from paper first published in Managerial and Decision Economics, Vol. 5, No. 3, 1978.

INTRODUCTION

The purpose of this paper, which was prepared for a colloquium on consumer behaviour (1), was to compare evidence about the attitudes to inflation of the British public with attitudes of British governments. The paper draws on the inflation enquiries which I directed in he 1960s and 1970s. The specific focus of the paper is that of perceptions of prices and inflation.

The inflation enquiries tried to fill gaps in knowledge in an area which, it seemed, had been neglected because the study of attitudes was often considered as the domain of psychologists while the study of inflation was looked upon primarily as that of economists. Moreover, it seemed that economic policy recommendations were often based on a priori assumptions about human motivation and behaviour rather than on empirical evidence and that some of the assumptions were open to doubt.

The national sample surveys which we conducted supplied empirical evidence as regards the attitudes of the public to inflation. The interviews used many open-ended questions and, where limited choice questions were used, prompts to help with the interpretation of the answers and to find out why people expressed a particular opinion. The answers provided insights into people's perceptions of inflation as it affected their lives in their various roles as consumers, income earners and citizens.

My earlier enquiries had suggested that the topic of conceptions of earnings, in which I was interested, had to be viewed within a wider horizon. It would have to take account of the movement of prices and attitudes to prices. As a first goal I examined the process of the individual's adjustments of notions of pay and prices to inflation. The section which follows discusses the evidence relating to prices.

THE ATTITUDES OF THE PUBLIC

Learning and Relearning Prices and Price Judgements

My first prices enquiries conducted in the early 1960s provided information about the process of learning and relearning prices and price judgements as well as insights with regard to the acquisition of price images and the impact of inflation on these images. (Behrend 1964 and 1966).

The studies revealed a widespread lack of precise knowledge of prices, suggesting that learning does not often take place and that people only learn a limited number of prices adequately. For example, in the second enquiry only one man and one woman out of 106 income earners and housewives were able to quote a reasonably accurate price for twenty everyday commodities and services. The prices remembered best were for daily papers and letter postage but, even for these, ten people did not give the price. Knowledge was fair with regard to milk, cigarettes, beer, bread and chocolates; yet many of the housewives did not know or had forgotten the price of toothpaste, toilet soap and washing powders. Very few respondents knew the price of coal and electricity. The evidence suggested that it is important for learning prices adequately that people make direct contact with the same price repeatedly and that they put in special effort to come to know 'normal' prices and to memorise them.

As obstacles to learning it was possible to identify the following factors which can cause confusion and encourage forgetting: low frequency of purchases; lack of direct contact with price through the habit of buying more than one commodity at a time; lack of interest; the incidence of different prices for the same commodity in different shops at different times; and the variety and number of articles on sale, especially as regards small goods. Conversely, learning was helped by regular purchases, direct contact with price, the existence of stable prices and conscious effort to get to know prices.

As regards price judgements, the evidence revealed that respondents judged whether prices were high, reasonable or low by past experience, using prices which they had learned (or thought they had

learned) as reference frames. Because of inflation
this necessarily provided unfavourable comparisons
and also gave rise to marked generation differences
in price judgements. The younger respondents who
had only recently begun to make everyday purchases
tended to accept certain current prices as normal
which the older generation considered unreasonably
high.

While many objective reference points which we
learn in life are unaffected by the passage of time,
market prices - although they represent objective
facts at a particular point of time - can and do
change. Thus inflation makes it necessary to up-
date our knowledge of prices and to dispose of
memories of past prices. How does this relearning
process proceed? Our evidence suggested that the
adjustment process is a painful one. It does not
proceed without friction and confusion; prices are
not necessarily remembered accurately nor relearned
properly. Thus, our evidence indicated that the
memory of past prices lingered on, perpetuating
feelings of resentment and frustration about distant
price rises, often producing a gloomier picture of
reality than was necessary or justified, certainly
in the case of those income earners whose pay had
risen faster than prices.

A professor of economics, for instance,
reported, that he was often annoyed when he had to
pay four shillings for his lunch in the university
refectory while he had only had to pay two shillings
as a student in Oxford; and suddenly he laughed when
he realised that this was an absurd attitude
considering his current salary! Other respondents
in the 1966 enquiry reacted similarly; they
considered that certain things which they wanted to
buy were too expensive; but when asked whether they
could not afford them, they began to realise that
their income had more than kept pace and that there
was no necessity to abandon the purchases or to
have a bad conscience about them. Thus, past prices
and not current incomes were found to be the major
frame of reference for judging the reasonableness of
current prices. People did not relate the past
price to the past income, and the present price to
the present income, assessing which relationship was
more favourable. However, having been sensitised
through our questions, individuals often began to
take their improved income position into account in
purchasing decisions and, as a result, stated later
that life had become easier.

To sum up, in learning, it seems, a picture of
the world of prices is slowly built up in our minds

Research into Attitudes to Inflation

from contact with a limited but increasing number of
market prices. At first, we learn isolated prices
and how one price among a range of prices is
considered the right one in given circumstances.
Slowly we evolve a more generalised picture which is
based partly on reality, on objective frames of
reference in the form of market prices, but partly
on subjective frames of reference for which we may
use the term price image. Price images are based on
our past experience of prices and of the properties
of purchased goods (for instance as regards quality)
and they are used for assessing the reasonableness
of market prices.

Attitudes to Price Increases

Awareness of the direction of price changes
were investigated by us in the pilot studies as well
as in two national sample surveys in the early and
mid 1960s. As already pointed out, respondents had
noticed and learned a number of changed prices but
not necessarily accurately. What they seemed to
notice and remember most after a time was the upward
direction of the majority of price changes. This
awareness seemed to develop with continued exposure
to inflation into a pre-disposition to believe that
all prices had risen. Thus falls in price which
occured during the 1966 price freeze escaped the
notice of the majority of the respondents. Many of
them showed a tendency to believe that prices which
had gone up in the previous winter had gone up
again, for instance, that the price of milk had gone
up again when it had actually gone down (Behrend,
1972b).
This belief that all prices had risen thus
produced a tendency not to register stable or
falling prices - a problem which was aggravated by
difficulties in recalling when the price of a
particular good had reached its current figure. A
stable price has, so to speak, no beginning and no
end; it does not make an impact, but is something
passive, overshadowed sometimes by the memory of
quite distant price increases.
In studying people's perceptions of, and
sensitivity with regard to, prices and price rises
it is important to differentiate between those
related to prices in general and those related to
specific prices. As regards the latter the early
price enquiries indicated that price rises in food
caused the greatest concern.
Our next major survey dealing with this topic

194

took place in 1973 when people had been exposed to inflation for eight more years, and to a much higher rate of inflation from 1969 onwards. The objective of the enquiry (commissioned by the National Economic Development Office) was to find out which specific price rises (if they were to take place) would be most likely to lead to pay demands. The opening question in the interview, HOW CONCERNED ARE YOU ABOUT RISING PRICES? served the function of easing in respondents and helped to make them talk about prices in general and how they felt about them. Next came simple YES/NO questions, followed by open-ended ones about specific prices, for instance: DO YOU PERSONALLY FIND ANY PRICE RISES WORRYING? followed by WHICH PRICES DO YOU FIND WORRYING? and HAVE YOU HAD TO CUT BACK ON ANYTHING BECAUSE OF RISING PRICES? followed by: WHAT HAVE YOU HAD TO CUT BACK ON? The aim of this strategy was that interviewees should come out with what was uppermost in their mind, because spontaneous responses would be most likely to represent their attitudes, their 'readiness to respond in a particular way'. To obtain a more overall picture, the final question on prices consisted of a list of major household items handed to respondents. They were first asked to look at each item and say whether they would like to see the price stabilised and then to say which items on the list they were not worried about. All additional comments they made were noted (Behrend, 1974b).

It was not surprising that the evidence on the general question revealed that the vast majority of the British respondents in 1973 said that they were concerned or very concerned about rising prices; it was perhaps more interesting that 10 per cent said they were not particularly concerned or not concerned.

Many people expressed the view that their incomes had lagged behind prices and many housewives (particularly those in the lowest income group) said that they found it difficult to manage, to make their money go round; the high prices of certain commodities had worried them greatly. However, the enquiry revealed that consumers were not worried about all price rises but had clear priorities as to which prices mattered most to them, specific food and basic non-food items heading the list. For instance the price rises which people selected most often spontaneously as those they were worried about were headed by meat and then fresh fruit and vegetables, fish, bacon, butter, cheese and bread. About half the respondents said they had had to cut back on certain purchases because of rising prices. People had economised by buying a little less of everything or by buying less of specific commodities, by switching to cheaper lines, by shopping around and by making or repairing things themselves. The most frequent item they had economised on was meat, and among other food items fish, bacon, butter, vegetables and fruit. Among non-food items, clothing, fuel and lighting and transport. They had also cut back on cigarettes, alcoholic drinks, sweets, entertainments and holidays.

A majority of just under 90 per cent of the sample wanted to see certain prices stabilised, meat again heading the list of the items mentioned spontaneously. Other items frequently mentioned were once again fish, milk, cheese, bacon, butter, fruit, vegetables as well as bread. Food and specific food items were mentioned two and a half times as often as non-food items. The answers to the final question using the list of various household items provided a similar picture. Respondents made clear distinctions between different commodities in their household budget. Overall priority was given to articles which were considered to be necessities.

Interpretation of the Word Inflation

Our prices studies in the early 1960s revealed that respondents did not appear to be bothered about inflation as an economic state of affairs; this was in spite of the frustration they expressed about the high prices of certain goods. This somewhat surprising observation (at a time when the government had been expressing considerable concern about inflation and had advocated pay restraint) led to the conduct in 1966 of our first British national sample survey.

As already mentioned in chapter 11, one of the most striking findings from this survey was that inflation meant so little to people. It was something abstract and remote which they read about in the newspapers but which had little personal significance. Moreover when asked about rising prices, only a few people stated that they had been badly hit by rising prices.

In 1966 many people did not understand the word inflation. Even in 1971, at a time when the mass media had been stressing the acceleration in the rate of inflation for months, 37 per cent of our respondents said they did not know what the word meant. The evidence suggested that there is a cleavage betwen the vocabulary used by economists and politicians on the one hand, and the rest of the population on the other. Typical of the responses illustrating this cleavage were: 'It is just a word they use on TV for the rise in prices and the cause of rising prices'; 'it is something to do with the government, with politics'; 'it is an economist's device for blinding the masses with economic science'. The communication gap was found to be greatest for the people who had received least education.

Problems of understanding go deeper than vocabulary. To find out how far the phenomenon of inflation was understood when non-technical terms were used, survey respondents were asked what they thought was the connection between wage claims and prices. The replies revealed that only a minority of 16 per cent interpreted the connection as a continuing process in which rising wages led to rising costs, and in turn to rising prices and further wage claims, while as large a proportion as 28 per cent did not appear to see any connection between wage claims and prices (Behrend et al, Autumn 1971).

Also striking was the finding that 81 per cent of the respondents in 1966 and 69 per cent in 1969 said that they themselves could not do anything to help the economic situation and expressed general feelings of powerlessness vis-a-vis Britain's economic problems. (Behrend et al, 1970b).

By 1973 the situation had changed a little. As mentioned in Chapter 11, a larger proportion of the population seemed to appreciate what inflation was about, insofar as 60 per cent of the survey respondents stated that they thought that prices could not be stabilised without limiting the size of pay claims (Behrend, 1974b).

How successful was the government in informing the public about its incomes policies? Our February 1966 survey showed that only a very small minority of the population were well informed about the policy goals and the pay guidelines; ignorance with regard to the policy predominated. The December 1966 enquiry showed, by contrast, that the vast majority of the population understood the prices and incomes freeze and accepted that the standstill had been necessary because the country was 'in the red' (as many put it) (Behrend et al 1967). They also stated that the price controls were an essential supplement to the pay controls. As regards the future, if the govenment decided to control incomes after the pay and prices standstill, 89 per cent of the respondents said it should also take powers to control prices. In the longer run, a majority of them felt, there should be a move away from pay restraint while price controls should be continued.

What was the impact of monetary measures? In this context, the use of purchase tax as a source of confusion should be mentioned because these increases are often quite large (the Conservative Government, for instance, increased VAT from 8 to 15 per cent after coming into office in 1979); this type of tax makes an immediate impact because it comes into effect at one point of time. Thus, measures taken to cure inflation may be more noticeable at times (and were perceived in this way by some of our respondents) than inflation itself. This means that the line between the disease and the medicine can become blurred so that citizens as consumers may feel disgruntled with both government measures and inflation.

To sum up: our surveys have shown that considerable problems of communication can exist between politicians (and experts) and the population. This suggests that it is very important for the success of economic and incomes policies that governments and experts should use words and phrases which can be generally understood. It would seem that a lack of understading of the word inflation and of the interrelation between pay and price increases, together with a lack of appreciation of the importance of curbing inflation, and sometimes of the measures to curb it, must be considered a major obstacle in the fight against inflation and to government attempts to secure public support for an incomes policy if and when they are using one.

BRITISH GOVERNMENT ATTITUDES TO INFLATION

I now come to the more difficult part of my paper, because it is more speculative, namely, the problem of studying 'public attitudes' to inflation and comparing them with our empirical evidence relating to the attitudes of the public. In Britain we tend to talk about the 'attitudes of the government' to this and that issue; in doing this we are using the word attitudes more as a label than a technical term. However, the usage suggests that it may be meaningful to define 'public attitudes' as the attitudes adopted in public discussions, the kind of arguments which are put forward with regard to the importance of fighting inflation and the choice of anti-inflation policies. These can be studied by an examination of official statements and policy recommendations and their implementation. A completely different research approach would be to study the opinions and attitudes of opinion-leaders by interviews or questionnaires (2).

This paper is confined to a discussion of the attitudes of British governments. What were their attitudes during the period in question? How far were they at variance with those of the population? What policies have they adopted towards inflation, especially as regards measures affecting prices? What do such measures mean for consumer studies?

The main objective of British governments after the second world war were those of full employment, rising living standards, price stability and better social services. However, we still do not know whether or how this combination of goals can be achieved. As a result, the goal of stable prices has been scaled down with time to the hope of containing price rises rather than containing prices themselves.

From 1948 onwards British governments have been pre-occupied almost continuously with the problem of inflation. They have decidedly held the view that inflation is harmful and have therefore tried to develop effective anti-inflation policies - attempts which found expression, particularly at times of economic crises, in the adoption of corrective fiscal and monetary measures and the introduction of incomes and prices policies.

The economic remedies of reducing the supply of money by withdrawing money through higher taxation and by credit squeezes in the form of increases in interest rates and hire purchase restrictions have been widely used in the ordinary April budgets as

Research into Attitudes to Inflation

well as in additional emergency budgets of which we
have had many. Cuts in government expenditure and
sitting tight on public sector expenditures have
also been employed at times. The use of these
measures has been accompanied by the problems of
judging when to stop deflating and start reflating
and the stop-go effects of these policies have often
been severely criticised. What has also been
criticised is that the policies have often been
accompanied by government borrowing and
overspending.

As regards incomes policies, successive
governments have at different points of time
introduced income standstills followed by income
guideline policies, most of them voluntary (but some
of them statutory), and returns to free collective
bargaining. However, the Conservative Government
which assumed power in May 1979 started off by
declaring that it favoured free collective
bargaining, ie it would not have an incomes policy.

Prices policies have been used in Britain
mainly as adjuncts to incomes and anti-inflation
policies. They have taken the form of freezes or of
percentage limits for price increases. They have
involved various procedures for price vetting; for
instance, advance notification of the intention to
raise prices and the permission or refusal to
proceed; also investigations into whether price
increases were justified or not. In this area, too,
there has been a change of direction away from
controls since 1979.

An assessment of the past history of prices and
incomes policies shows that the area which has
received most public attention in the media and in
expert discussions has been that of incomes policy
and the desirability or otherwise of having one.
The search for a workable incomes policy has taken
up much government time in the last few decades and,
when supported, has been based on the belief that
such a policy would be preferable to monetary and
fiscal measures because an effective incomes policy
would give rise to less instability and would
interfere less with economic growth. To be
successful, the policy would have to be based on
concensus; that is, it would need to have the
voluntary support of the trade unions and employers
and of the working population.

In practice, British governments have so far
only been successful in obtaining the voluntary
support and co-operation of the trade unions and
employers during the early stages of their incomes
policies in which the rules were usually fairly well

200

observed; in the later stages they have run into
considerable difficulties involving industrial
unrest and major strikes in vital sectors of the
economy - disruptions which could be considered to
be just as damaging for the economy as the 'stop and
go' effects from the monetary and fiscal measures.

Many people have therefore argued that incomes
policies are no use, that they always break down.
However, one can also argue that one major reason
for their breaking down has been that British
governments have been reluctant, not committed,
adherents to incomes policy. One can argue further
that an incomes policy, if one wants it to have a
chance to work, must not be seen as a short run
expedient but as part of a longer term coherent
strategy. The psychological effects of a policy
which is introduced as a temporary measure which
will be slowly relaxed prior to a return to free
collective bargaining is liable to defeat the
policy's longer term objectives. For, although the
policy will restrain expectations during the freeze
and constraint periods, it contains the built-in
expectation of bigger increases in the future and of
a 'free for all' at the end and thus the seeds for a
pay explosion.

It would seem that the successful development
of a prices and incomes policy and of an overall
anti-inflation strategy must depend very much on
government attitudes as well as on the attitudes of
the people who influence governments - trade unions
and employers' organisations and other pressure
groups, intellectuals, the press and the general
pubic. It is difficult to know in this context who
are the leaders and who are the led and more
information about the attitudes of these groups and
their interactions would be useful. What seems
particularly important is that we should have more
applied research in this area and less dogma. For
instance, one can argue that the search for a long
term workable incomes policy should be considered as
a learning process in which we must learn from past
mistakes, particularly perhaps from mistakes in the
assessment of the psychological variables which are
involved.

Research into Attitudes to Inflation

WHAT DO PRICES AND INCOMES POLICIES MEAN FOR CONSUMER STUDIES?

It is an interesting reflection that the two enquiries in our inflation research which were commissioned by outside agencies were both concerned with sources of discontent and the feelings and behaviour they may give rise to, one with people's reactions to price increases and the other with employee reactions to pay increases and pay differentials. The information was wanted in both cases to help policy-makers make up their minds on questions related to anti-inflation policies.

These studies revealed that consumer discontent spills over into employee discontent, expectations and behaviour. As already mentioned, the respondents in the 1973 NEDO survey were very worried about the rising prices of specific food items and other necessities and wanted to see the prices of these commodities stabilised. Insofar as they had been forced by rising prices to adjust their household expenditure they had changed some of their purchasing habits as a result of inflation. However, later answers in the survey revealed that the main remedy which they thought of as a means for coping with rising prices was that of putting in pay claims. Thus, 76 per cent of the respondents considered that price increases justified pay claims and only 16 per cent did not think so. The most frequent argument, put forward as justification, was that extra money would be needed to meet the rising prices. 65 per cent of the male employees not only said that price increases justified pay claims but also that they were prepared to back this conviction by personal action. Another finding was that many of the respondents who realised that pay increases can lead to price increases nevertheless considered that pay increases were the only way they had to protect themselves against losing out in the vicious circle. Only 6 per cent of the sample considered that rising prices did not justify pay claims because they would have a snowball effect and make things worse.

The Irish enquiry into attitudes to pay increases and pay differentials revealed that the male employees covered by the survey used the cost of living as the major frame of reference for judging the adequacy of their last pay increase and the amount that would be fair for their next pay increase. That the cost of living can play a major part in pay negotiations was a view expressed frequently in the 1975 Scottish postal survey (see

reference end of note 2). Thus, the trade union lay
negotiatiors considered that the cost of living was
what mattered most to their members; the cost of
living was also mentioned most frequently by them as
an effective argument in negotiations with
management. This assessment was borne out by the
finding that the management respondents, too,
mentioned the cost of living most frequently as an
acceptable argument in negotiations. These findings
indicated that the rising cost of living had become
an acknowledged source of discontent in industrial
relations and pay bargaining.

It would seem that prices and incomes policies
which depend on support from the general public, and
in particular from employees, cannot afford to
ignore anxieties about coping with rising prices and
low pay, and recognition of these anxieties has
indeed led at times to government measures which try
to deal with some of these consumer discontents.

This development raises many questions for
research: should consumer studies shift their focus
from satisfactions to dissatisfactions? Which
factors are most important in consumer behaviour in
times of inflation, the dissatisfactions and
problems connected with rising prices, or the search
for maximum satisfaction? Do purchasers believe in
consumer sovereignty, that they can get what they
want if they shop around? Or do they merely try to
minimise their discontents? Similar questions can
be applied to employee behaviour.

There is also a case for evaluating the
consumer responses to prices measures, to be able to
assess whether the cost involved is worthwhile. Do
consumers know what kind of measures have been
taken? Have they sought and used advice and
facilities that have been offered? A small pilot
enquiry which my research students conducted into
consumer reactions to the February 1976 price check
scheme suggested that few consumers knew about it or
had found it useful. In addition, quite a number of
Edinburgh shopkeepers still had the price check sign
in their shops some three months after the scheme
had ceased to operate!

CONCLUDING COMMENTS

I have presented in this paper some of the
major findings of my research into the attitudes to
prices and inflation of the general public and have
also discussed the attitudes of British governments.
In so doing, I have pointed to the communications gap

that exists because the public often do not understand what the policy-makers are talking about.

In this context it would appear important that policy-makers should understand the problems connected with the habit of 'compartmentalised thinking' which is often used in everyday life and which enables people to hold apparently contradictory views, each meaningful in its own context but not if related to the other. Often the arguments, which are kept in separate compartments, relate to statements at different levels; for instance, one set to a general phenomenon, the other to a specific aspect of the phenomenon. Compartmentalisation of thinking it would seem, impedes 'analytical' thinking and the recognition and acceptance of the interrelation of variables and events which are important for understanding problems of economic interdependence. The 1979 increases in oil prices, the economic recession and the high level of unemployment have created a new situation in which it is a matter of urgency to bridge this communication gap (certainly in Britain) and perhaps economic psychology can make a contribution towards our ability to impart the necessary understanding of economic resource constraints.

Finally, we should, perhaps, spare a thought for the predicaments which face governments and policy-makers in the fight against inflation. Does the public and do the pressure groups expect too much of them? Governments are guided by what their advisers, outside experts, pressure groups and the media tell them. In evaluating the various points of view they are confronted by the dilemma of whether the information with which they are presented represents beliefs or facts, especially as opinions are often stated with great conviction and expressed in factual terms. In the pressures which are put upon governments by certain groups there is often the implied belief that there is an immediate solution to the problem of inflation if only the governments had the courage to adopt certain courses of action.

However, the continued existence of inflation, in spite of many attempts at controlling it, suggests that control is not merely a question of listening to the right experts but a problem which one must work on continuously. It would seem that it is psychological attitudes and expectations and moral values which may have to be changed as well as economic strategies to deal with inflation and our other economic problems.

NOTES

1. This article is based on a paper presented at the Fourth European Colloquium in Economic Psychology held in Sweden under the auspices of the Economic Research Institute of the Stockholm School of Economics, August 29 to 31 1979. The major theme was consumer behaviour.
2. Our research included some experiments in this area. For instance, we started off the Irish enquiry with opinion-leader interviews. These provided information and insights which proved very useful for planning the enquiry and formed an essential basis for the work in a country other than our own. Our February 1975 postal enquiry obtained views from carefully selected groups of Scottish managers and from the Scottish trade union lay negotiators of two large trade unions. The evidence indicated, among other findings, that contrary to what had been widely assumed to be the prevalent attitudes to free collective bargaining, 79 per cent of the management respondents and 48 per cent of the trade union lay negotiators (when asked which of four possible policies for incomes they would prefer) opted for some kind of planning for incomes, an agreement between the CBI, the Government and the TUC, while only 6 per cent of the managers and 32 per cent of the trade unionists opted for free collective bargaining. See A Ian Glendon, D P Tweedie and H Behrend, Pay negotiations and incomes policy: a comparison of views of managers and trade union lay negotiators, Industrial Relations Journal, Vol 6, No 3, Autumn 1975.

REFERENCES

H Behrend, and H Behrend et al, see chapter 11 references

13 Inflation and Attitudes to Pay Increases: The Major Issues

Written for private circulation 1981.

INTRODUCTION

This paper presents an analysis of problems connected with inflation and anti-inflation policies which face pay negotiators and policy-makers by focusing on one aspect of pay policies, namely that of pay increases and pay negotiations. It is based on historical observation and insights from the empirical research enquiries summarised in chapter 11 (2).

Our inflation enqiries are relevant because they throw light on the thinking of the recipients of pay increases, that is, the parties most affected by the outcome of formal pay negotiations, incomes policy rules or other anti-inflation policy constraints. An understanding of their views can be of use in assessing the acceptability of pay increase offers and decisions and the likely effects on the industrial relations climate.

The paper draws on interview evidence from four of the seven national sample surveys which I directed, two of them in Britain in 1966 and 1973, and two in Ireland, one before and one after the 'pay explosion', in 1969 and 1971.

The pay increase questions in the first three surveys studied the respondents' assessment of what difference their last pay increase had made, and how far this judgement was related to the size of the last pay increase; also respondents' statements about expected pay increases and the amounts which they would consider fair next time round as well as their reasons for giving the answers (see Behrend et al 1970a; Behrend 1972a, 1973, 1974a). In the 1973 NEDO survey a different set of questions was asked (Behrend 1974b).

The evidence from these surveys indicates that

two interrelated issues which face pay negotiators relate to the choice of the type of pay award and the size of the pay award. In making these choices conflicting interests have to be reconciled, taking account not only of the problems within the organisation but also of those outside it. The choice of type of pay award is discussed first.

THE TYPE OF PAY AWARD - CASH AMOUNTS OR PERCENTAGES OR SOMETHING MORE COMPLICATED

As reported in chapter 11, the vast majority of our respondents, in replying to pay increase questions, described their pay increases in terms of cash amounts and not in percentage terms. Clearly this is so because a percentage has to be converted into cash terms before the employee knows how much extra money he will receive. Moreover, in relation to everyday life, he normally thinks in monetary units and not in percentages.

Percentage increases pose equity as well as conversion problems by awarding higher amounts to high income earners than to low income earners. This often gives, rise to discontent among the lower paid. For example, with a 6 per cent increase a man earning £50 a week only gets £3.00 while a man earning £150 a week gets £9.00. In connection with income structures and incomes policy norms this raises the ethical question: How can one justify that a man who earns three times more than a lower paid worker is allowed to receive a three times larger pay increase amount than the man who finds it difficult to manage? Who should carry the larger burden in a period of restraint?

Most of our respondents in the November 1966 survey considered that the July 1966 income standstill imposed by the Labour Government was equitable because it applied without exception to all employees. Can one make out the same case of equality of treatment for a percentage norm? It is in examining this question that it would appear necessary to make a clear distinction between pay differentials (that is, differences in the monetary incomes of different occupational groups) and pay increase differentials (that is, differences in the monetary amounts of pay awards to different occupational groups). It can be argued that one should not assume a priori that exactly the same ideas of equity are attached to both terms. As pointed out above, lower paid workers often resent the existence of pay increase differentials when the pay awards in their industry are based on percentages, while skilled workers defend them. Other high income earners also maintain that cash awards are unfair because they reduce pay differentials.

Our research has indicated that there is no concensus with regard to what are fair pay increase differentials: many groups fight for an equalisation of the size of pay increases while others resist it and still others try to increase the difference.

Therefore, the issue as to what form a pay award should take, quite apart from its size, is important in all pay negotiations and will remain so. Historically, in Britain there appears to have been a shift away from pay increases defined in cash terms towards agreements based on percentage formulae. However, arguments for fairer treatment for the lower paid led to some variations, for instance, incomes policy phases of a fixed pay increase amount introduced in August 1975 and a percentage norm with a floor and ceiling (e.g. with minimum and maximum amount entitlements) in 1976 as part of the social contract between the Labour Government and the Trades Union Congress.

It would seem that what is considered appropriate or is being fought for in terms of type of pay award depends very much on precedents, on the activities of pressure groups and the needs of particular historical situations. It would seem that in pay negotiations, flexibility and willingness to reconcile conflicting pressures are important pre-requisites for reaching compromise agreements. The variety of agreed formulae in successive Irish national agreements concluded by the Employer-Labour Conference in 1970 to 1977 illustrates that it was necessary to find new adaptations in every one of them.

THE SIZE OF PAY AWARDS

Evidence related to respondents' assessments of the difference which their last pay increase had made raised another issue which is highly relevant to pay increase negotiations. The findings showed that respondents who had received comparatively high cash pay increases considered that their last pay increase had made a noticeable difference and quite a few showed some degree of satisfaction with this.

However, in cases where the pay increase amounts fell below a particular perceptual size threshold, respondents felt that it was so small that they had derived no visible benefit, especially in view of rising prices and tax deductions. The individual's perception of the adequacy or inadequacy of the pay increase was found to be closely associated with the amount of the pay increase but not with his income level.

These findings suggest that with a really large percentage increase practically all employees may receive a pay increase amount which is perceived as adequate or good but with other percentage awards only some sections of the employed population may find that the pay increase amount makes a visible difference while others find it has made little, if any, difference. With a very small percentage award most employees may feel it has made no visible difference. Seeing no benefit can, in turn, lead to a demand for a further pay increase.

Thus our evidence suggested that pay increases can be indirectly inflationary because they are too small to make a noticeable difference and therefore may carry in them the seeds of another pay claim almost as soon as they are granted. They can also give rise to conflict and more frequent pay demands. However, two separate small pay increases were perceived by respondents as less helpful than a single large one.

The main frame of reference for the judgements was the cost of living and not the job. This provides another dimension to bargaining about pay awards and another source of discontent which should not be ignored in pay negotiations or in setting pay guidelines.

The evidence indicated that, to be acceptable to employees, pay agreements and incomes policies must aim (if the economics of the situation permit) to provide a visible benefit in terms of purchasing power and must not be too far out of line with expectations based on past experience. Many of the British pay increases received under incomes policy rules between 1966 and 1969 lay below the observed perceptual threshold and this may partly explain the 1969 to 1970 pay explosion.

In January 1972 I formulated a possible strategy to accomodate this 'visibility goal' in an incomes policy. I argued that the government could use taxation as a contribution to a tripartite agreement with the employers and trade unions on the permitted size of pay-increases by raising the personal tax exemption allowance; it could also use this as a bargaining counter. This approach was adopted by the Labour Government in its 1976 budget.

Pay Increases: The Major Issues

Up to then, and since, however, taxation has been
used mainly as an instrument of anti-inflationary
fiscal policies either by raising income tax or VAT
(or its predecessor purchase tax) or both.

PAY INCREASE IMAGES AND THE 'GOING RATE' OR PAY GUIDELINES

Our research has suggested that ideas about the
fairness of the size of pay increases (and of pay
increase differentials) are based on pay increase
images which spring to mind fairly spontaneously
through some association or other. For instance
they may be based on past pay increases and the
purchases they made possible and may embrace the
notion that the last pay increase was adequate or
not. Other images may be based on amounts received
by friends and acquaintances, on information from
the mass media or just on hearsay. It is therefore
a matter of considerable importance what kind of
images are projected in public discussions because
these images are often used by employees as frames
of reference for judging what would be fair in their
case. Particularly well publicised figures, whether
of pay demands or of actual awards, can become a
powerful influence affecting the level of pay
settlements during periods of free collective
bargaining.

In Britain this influence became very
noticeable once more in the free collective
bargaining wage round which started in 1979. Thus,
in January 1980 Incomes Data Services (IDS) drew
attention to he elusive role of the 'going rate'.

The 'going rate', they argued (p3) used to mean
the payment for a particular job in a particular
area or factory at a particular time but it had come
to mean percentage increases, that is popular or
chosen rates of increase for many groups at a
particular time; often it seemed to mean the pay
increase rate set by those who can go the fastest.

This definition or concept of the 'going rate'
represents a particular type of pay increase image.
It emerges from information about pay negotiations,
is projected by the mass media and picked up by pay
negotiators. Thus, during the 1978 to 1979 wage
round when the TUC had rejected the government's 5
per cent limit, contract re-negotiations were
deliberately delayed to see what 'going rate' for
pay awards would emerge.

It would seem to me that in times of inflation
a high 'going rate' for pay increases is likely to
raise the question whether there should be norms or

guidelines. The question may also arise in confused situations where it is not clear whether there is a 'going rate' and where even commentators may find it difficult to assess what is happening. The autumn of the 1980 to 1981 negotiations would appear to have fallen into this latter category. IDS repeatedly commented during that period that it was not clear whether a general pattern was emerging. In early 1981 in the public sector industries the miners' 13 per cent settlement emerged as a reference point and among public service workers the government's 6 per cent cash limit (officially on expenditure) was seen as a starting point for bargaining that must be exceeded.

DO PRICE INCREASES JUSTIFY PAY CLAIMS? THE QUESTION OF INDEXATION

Do individuals think that prices can be stabilised without limiting pay claims? And do they think price increases justify pay claims? These were questions I was asked to investigate in the 1973 NEDO survey.

As regards the first question, 60 per cent of the respondents stated that they thought that prices could not be stabilised without limiting the size of pay claims, giving as reasons that pay increases would lead to price increases; they would put up costs of production; it was a vicious circle; price and wage increases were closely linked so that they must both be controlled. However, many of the respondents considered that price increases justified pay increases. The major argument put forward as a justification was that extra money would be needed to meet the rising prices. Overall the survey evidence indicated that the only way many people could see of coping with rising prices was to put in a pay claim.

It is also of interest to note that in our postal survey in the first quarter of 1975, 55 per cent of the management respondents expressed the view that the cost of living was an acceptable argument in pay negotiations (A I Glendon et al, 1975).

However, in my view, compensating individuals for rising prices through indexation is not an answer to the control of inflation; it merely institutionalises and perpetuates it, as could be seen, for instance, in Italy.

In this context it is important to distinguish what is desirable and what is possible. For

Pay Increases: The Major Issues

instance, whether most of the people in the country can improve their standards of living without depleting resources or going into debt is not a question of providing extra pay but of producing the necessary goods and resources. The problem is that in times of recession production may be insufficient even to maintain standards of living. Thus one can argue that the only justifiable type of indexation of pay increases would be one linked to the ups and downs of real output growth and not to monetary prices, that is, linked to achieved or achievable increases in real living standards. This argument brings us back to the pay increase guidelines and norms based on the economic growth rate which have often been adopted in the past when there was still growth. Perhaps one of the failures of these past guidelines has been that the discussion was expressed in terms which the ordinary citizen found difficult to understand.

Looking at the indexation question from a different angle, the normative argument that price increases entitle people to compensation for the rising cost of living which has been widely and successfully used in pay negotiations poses many problems, and not only that of justifying awards. For instance, how often should such compensatory payments be made, what should be the form and the size of the award, should the award be the same for all employees or larger for some than for others; and if larger, should it be more for people with lower or higher incomes? These questions bring us back to the issues already discussed here as important in pay negotiations and shows how inter-related they all are.

In my view, it seems unwise to single out the cost of living as the major frame of reference for more permanent institutional arrangements as suggested by advocates of indexation. Moreover, there is one further, very different but important issue that needs to be discussed and not forgotten, namely that of whether regular pay increases can be a matter of right without obligation.

PAY INCREASES: A RIGHT WITHOUT OBLIGATION? THE 'GIVE-BACK' ISSUE

Our survey evidence has indicated that the inflation which has been with us since the late nineteen forties has created the expectation that every present pay increase will be followed by another pay increase and that this will happen as a matter of right not of work contribution - a right which seems to have assumed the property of a regular entitlement and which is not easily amenable to change.

However, with the deterioration in the economic situation, managements have been increasingly more conscious of the need to re-establish a closer link between extra pay and increased efficiency; they have shown much more determination in the pursuit of the productivity or, as Alistair Cooke has called it, the 'give-back' issue (2). In the 1979 to 1980 wage round this was a major issue in Britain. Often two pay increase figures were used in negotiations, a low one as a general concession and a higher one if the unions agreed to a 'give-back' from the employees, such as increased efficiency, better attendance, new work arrangements and reductions in manpower. The free collective bargaining battle for more money became linked to union protests against these demands; the 'going rate' was demanded without concessions. The changed approach to bargaining resulted in a number of bitter contract re-negotiation strikes but also, with or without strikes, in a number of pay increase agreements which included 'give-back' clauses.

The issue of the 'give-back' raises many different problems of interrelations, equity and misunderstandings. Employee efficiency cannot be increased without a change in outlook but the employees' willingness to co-operate depends on their interpretation of the economic situation and of the problems which face the country and their employers. It is in this area that there seem to be considerable communication gaps which hamper the drive for higher productivity in Britain.

COMMUNICATION PROBLEMS

All our surveys have highlighted that there can be serious communication problems between politicians, economists and the ordinary citizen. Often, it seems, only a minority of the population understand government statements, discussions of

current affairs and newspaper reports. In this
context it is important to realise that information
can only reach an individual who is motivated to
listen to it; also that the information needs to be
presented in a way in which it can be understood
once the individual's attention has been caught.
Our evidence, however, suggests that information
about economic issues and government policies is
often presented in a form in which it is
unintelligible to ordinary people.

Moreover, the manner of presentation is often
one which gives rise to confusion. For instance,
respondents were often unable to distinguish
inflation and measures taken to cure it. To them
inflation meant measures taken by the government to
combat inflation, the succession of 'ups and downs'
in the economy, or the recurrent economic crises
associated with balance of trade deficits. In
addition, respondents felt that politicians often
added to the confusion by a tendency to relate
economic problems to party issues; the following
comments illustrate this: 'they always seem confused
among themselves so I don't take a lot of notice of
them' and 'too much arguing against each other so
that I don't know who to believe'. A common
complaint was that politicians did not explain the
problems in simple language. The evidence suggested
that even apparently simple slogans needed more
explanation before they could be understood.

That communication problems continue to exist
has been high-lighted by recent research carried out
by some of my colleagues. It indicates, for
instance, that the vocabulary used in financial
disclosures to employees is not at all well
understood by many of the recipients. (Mitchell et
al, 1980 pp58-59).

CAN PAY INCREASE EXPECTATIONS BE CHANGED?

The Prime Minister, Mrs Thatcher, and her
ministers in repeatedly stressing the need for
'realistic pay settlements' have implied that the
worsening economic situation together with
persuasion will be effective in lowering employee
pay increase expectations. However, there are many
people who believe that more positive action is
required.

Our research evidence suggests that pay
increase expectations although difficult to change,
can be moderated at least for a time by the use of
formal pay restraints, and this would appear to be

better than no action. However, in the past it seems governments have undermined the longer-term effectiveness of their own policies by being reluctant and not committed adherents of incomes policy.

It is my view that an incomes policy, if it is to be given the chance to be effective must not be seen as a short run expedient but as part of a longer term coherent strategy. The psychological effects of a policy which is introduced as a temporary measure which will be slowly relaxed by a return to bigger increases and then to free collective bargaining is liable to defeat the policy's longer term objectives. For although the policy will restrain expectations during periods of constraint, it contains the built-in expectation of bigger increases next time round and of a 'free for all' at the end and thus the seeds for a pay explosion. Fear of the re-imposition of constraints adds force to the scramble for more. It is possible similarly that the experience of recession, insofar as it has an effect on pay claims, has only a temporary effect.

It would seem that in the longer run pay increase expectations cannot be moderated without a change in outlook by all concerned and without attempting to share the burdens of recession or the fruits of prosperity in a way which is acceptable to the majority of the population.

As regards the problem of inflation there is no consensus among economists (or politicians) about the causes of inflation and about measures for controlling it. The monetarists hold that the major factor on which attention needs to be focused is the money supply. Because inflation results from excessive monetary creation, it is the duty of governments to reduce and control it; and if they have the will to take the necessary monetary measures they can control it. Other economists, among them many British ones, do not agree (3).

The British experience of the 1969-70 pay explosion which was followed by an acceleration in the rate of inflation has demonstrated that high pay settlements can fuel inflation, and the high pay increases of 1979-80 have had similar effects. It is only one of the variables involved in inflation but it is an important one which we cannot afford to ignore. In my view inflation may become impossible to control if one allows the wage/price spiral to gather increasing momentum by accepting successive demands for full compensation for the rising cost of living as well as demands for awards based on fair comparisons as justifications for pay claims.

The situation is particularly serious when there is no economic growth to offset part of the monetary awards by real income growth. As long as some important trade unions (and the income earners they represent) continue their struggle for more in such a situation, ignoring the national problems and needs, inflation cannot be controlled by monetary measures alone. The industrial relations component of the problem also requires attention.

Inflation and anti-inflation measures and the way they are handled can seriously damage the quality of industrial relations and the industrial relations climate and can thereby worsen the economic situation. What is required is an improvement in these relations and to achieve this I believe we must continue the search for effective institutional arrangements to develop a workable incomes policy. In this context I would repeat the conclusion which I have stressed in the past that I do not see how there can be a purely technical monetary solution to the problem of inflation. What is required are changes in attitudes and outlook with regard to the rights and obligations of the various groups of society in the light of economic resource constraints and of the ethical dilemmas created by the differences in the situations of the well off and the needy.

NOTES

1. Since chapter 11 gave an overview of the inflation studies, there are some unavoidable overlaps with this chapter which looks at the topics in more detail and in a different context.
2. Alistair Cooke, (Letter from America, Radio 4, 13.4.1980) stated that the 'give-back' had become an important issue in the United States, for instance, in the New York transport strike. The term 'give-back', it seems, is easy to understand. Many of our respondents did not understand the word productivity.
3. See, for example, the statement signed by 364 university economists condemning monetary policies published in the Manchester Guardian, March 30 1982 pp 1 and 2.

REFERENCES

H Behrend and H Behrend et al, and A I Glendon et al, see Chapter 11 references

Pay Increases: The Major Issues

W W Daniel, the PEP Survey on Inflation, Broadsheet
    No 563, London, PEP, 1975
IDS Focus, London, 16.1.1980, The changing meaning
    of the 'going rate'
F Mitchell, K I Sams, D P Tweedie and P J White,
    Disclosure of Information: some evidence from
    case studies, Industrial Relations Journal, Vol
    11, No 5, November/December 1980

14 Bridging the Communications Gap with the Ordinary Citizen

Jointly with Elisabeth Gould, a psychologist, who has been involvd in a number of research projects. She is co-author of Stress in Youth, Oxford University Press, 1971.

Adapted from paper first published in Industrial Relations Journal, Vol. 13, No. 4, Winter 1982/83.

In 1981 I tried to obtain funds for a further enquiry into the problems of communication described in chapters 11-13 but money was tight and time precious. Elisabeth Gould (a former colleague) and I therefore decided to mount a small-scale enquiry without external funding. This chapter presents findings from this exploratory study of people's perceptions of the economic situation and shows that the problems had not disappeared.

The enquiry was carried out in October 1981. The evidence was obtained by Elisabeth Gould in interviews which covered 56 respondents of different ages, employment status and education and who lived in different districts of Southampton in pre-war, post-war and modern council houses as well as in owner-occupied houses, from Victorian to modern, of different sizes and potential selling prices.

To put respondents at ease the interviews started with two introductory questions about prices. The answers revealed, similar to our earlier enquiries, that people were very conscious of rising prices (more than half the respondents thought prices were going up faster than they had done) and that the price of 'food' and of specific food items such as bread, butter, meat and groceries affected them most.

Next, respondents were asked: WHAT DO YOU THINK MAKES PRICES GO UP? Answers differed widely but the most frequent and clear responses (given 22 times) referred to wage increases, a topic which came up spontaneously. Short answers were confined to 'pay rises', 'excessive wage-claims', 'high cost of labour'. Longer ones referred to the vicious circle, for instance, 'inflation - rising wages means rising costs - a vicious circle' and 'to start with, wages go up - as wages go up, you pay more, so

no better off'. Awareness of a connection between
wage increases and price increases seemed to be
greater than in our past surveys.

Other factors mentioned as giving rise to price
increases were the costs of materials affecting
manufacturing and transport such as petrol, diesel
and fuel and the world recession. On the other hand
seven respondents said that they did not really know
what makes prices go up while eight used the word
inflation mainly as a jargon word which they
associated with rising prices; for instance,
'inflation - mainly price rises' and 'inflation -
everything all round'. Finally there was the
attribution of blame to people and their policies.
Profiteering manufacturers and trade unions were
blamed twice while the government and its policies
were mentioned 12 times in a number of different and
often vague statements; examples are 'Maggie
Thatcher', 'reckon it is this government', 'the
government I suppose - government policies'.

Next respondents were asked: HOW DO YOU THINK
WE CAN STOP INFLATION? In reply, some picked up
their previous theme. Thus, seven of those who had
blamed the government for rising prices suggested
that the cure was a change of government or of
government policies as did eight other respondents.
Not a single one quoted government policy as a
solution, in spite of the fact that the government
had declared over two years that the reduction of
inflation was the major goal of its economic policy.
The nearest mention was a comment that it was 'up to
the government to try to do that; they were supposed
to have the power to deal with inflation'.

The wage increase theme was picked up as
important in the fight against inflation by 14
respondents, of whom ten had mentioned it already
while three had focused on the recession. The
suggested measures for stopping inflation were a
wages freeze or wage policy. Ten other respondents
stressed the productivity/efficiency theme as a way
of dealing with inflation. In a more pessimistic
mood nine respondents said that they did not think
we could stop inflation, a few adding qualifying
conditions such as that it could not be done without
a change of outlook. Finally five people said that
they did not know whether it could be done. Perhaps
they are not far out considering it is one of the
major unsolved problems of our time!

The answers revealed different levels of
approach by respondents, some being more conscious
of the complexity of the issue than others. While
many thought that some action was possible, at least

on one or two fronts, others were dubious about what could be done because it was too big a problem. Thus apparently simple questions were seen to be quite complex by more sophisticated respondents and yet we found it was difficult to distinguish their answers in terms of class, sex or education.

The next question was rather different in nature but respondents answered without hesitation even if it was just the word 'yes' or 'no'. The question deliberately introduced a technical term and asked: HAVE YOU HEARD THE WORD MONETARISM? 'Yes' answers were followed by: WHAT DOES THE WORD MEAN TO YOU? and 'No' answers by: HAVE YOU ANY IDEA OF WHAT CONNECTION IT IS USED IN?

Although the word 'monetarism' had been mentioned often since the present government came into power, 19 out of the 56 respondents said they had not heard the word before and 17 of those who had heard the word said they did not really know what it means. Only two of the 20 remaining respondents gave a reasonable description, namely: 'tight control on spending and borrowing - government policy' and 'a narrow way of controlling economy by money forces alone'. The others expressed vague associations such as 'something to do with Margaret Thatcher' or with money and economic policy such as 'good housekeeping' or 'the monetary fund'.

Following up the economic issues we asked next: WHAT DO YOU THINK ABOUT ALL THIS UNEMPLOYMENT? This gave rise to expressions of general concern such as dreadful, frightening, catastrophic, as well as of anxiety about the effect on young people. It also revealed that seven respondents had been affected by unemployment including a young graduate in mechanical engineering.

How then did the respondents view the future? To find out they were asked DO YOU THINK THINGS ARE BOUND TO GET BETTER? While six respondents said 'yes' 14 said 'no'. The remainder were rather doubtful, some hoping things would be all right but conscious that it was not certain and might take a very long time; others thought the situation could only improve if certain important changes were to take place in attitudes or policies. When asked: DO YOU THINK YOU CAN DO ANYTHING ABOUT THE ECONOMIC SITUATION? three out of four respondents said 'no' they could not do anything, not individually, some adding that it was up to the government to do something. This was in line with findings from two of our earlier enquiries which indicated that the majority of ordinary people felt that they were not in a position to do anything about the economic situation; they were caught up in it but powerless.

Two questions explored the way people obtained information about economic issues and how they thought communication could be improved. The main sources of information mentioned were television (39 times) and newspapers (38 times), only 12 saying radio and 2 books. Television was suggested as the main channel which would have to be used for making the information more comprehensible. An emphatic plea for the presentation of economic issues in simple English not using big words was made by 22 respondents.

Overall, summing up the evidence, our 1981 survey thus revealed, just as have our earlier surveys, that there is a communication gap between goverments, politicians, economists, news reporters and the general public. Our respondents considered that these other people lived in a different world; they used big words; they communicated with each other not with them. This suggests that the 'them and us' divide which is so often talked about as typical of the relations between managers and workers is also a great barrier between policy-makers, commentators and the public.

CAN THIS GAP BE BRIDGED?

Clearly, in our view, more research is needed to find out how people can learn to understand economic issues and how presenters of economic information can learn to make this comprehensible to a wider public.

Our respondents suggested that the specialists should not assume knowledge of technical words; they should use simple words and layman's language. If difficult words had to be used they should be explained every time they crop up. It would help if practical examples to illustrate problems were given and could make it more interesting for ordinary people. We would add that specialists should try to avoid the use of abbreviations such as RPI and PSBR which may be incomprehensible (and difficult to remember) even for well educated non-specialists.

Research would have to look at the problem in two specific contexts: what could be done for children, particularly in schools, and what could be done for adults. The interviews revealed that many of the respondents who found it difficult to understand economic matters would like to be able to do so and expressed willingness to learn. Whether television is the best way of tackling the task is an open question.

In our view, economists could be helped to convey their ideas more clearly if further research were to be done into the distinction between people's active and passive vocabularies, their ability to define words as against their ability to recognise words they have heard and their ability to put them into a relevant context. The word 'inflation' is a case in point. We found that this word is not part of the active vocabulary of ordinary people and that few of them used it spontaneously while they talked very readily about the problem of rising prices.

Readers should ask themselves how many of them can define 'monetarism'. We noted with interest that the 2nd edition of the Penguin Dictionary of Economics of 1978 did not yet include the word. It would appear important to us that people who are at the receiving end of a monetarist policy should not just have heard the word but should understand what it is about.

Furthermore, it seems to us that it is not the abstract concepts and fashionable labels which need to be understood but the problems to which they refer. Inded it may be easier to describe the problems in simple terms than in technical jargon.

As a measure of the problem of inflation the retail price index focuses on just one variable involved in inflation and yet it would appear very important that people, particularly employees, should understand that other variables are involved, such as wages and salaries, productivity, the supply of money and credit, consumption, investment, and expectations. Furthermore they need to understand the problems of the interrelations and interactions of these variables and the difficulties which arise in the pursuit of conflicting objectives.

Since communication is a two-way process it also seems important that policy-makers, economists and other specialists should learn to understand how people's minds work instead of basing their judgements on postulates about how people think or ought to think. One particular example that we have stressed in the past is that we do not in everyday life think in terms of percentages in relation to price or wage increases - the ordinary citizen thinks about them in terms of £'s and pence. Percentages are abstract artefacts which most people can only work out with the help of pencil and paper or a calculator. Thus, when we asked the respondents in our 1981 interviews whether prices were going up at the same rate as before, they did not make a sophisticated judgement such as that the rate of inflation was 11% and is now 14%; they made an experience-based judgement whether some items of food they usually buy cost 5 or 10 pence more or whether the week-end shopping had become much more expensive.

Finally, there is the question of whether it matters that there is a communication gap. Sometimes when we have reported on this problem people have shrugged their shoulders and said so what? It seems to us however that it does matter. It means frustration for those who want to get a better understanding of the situation which faces them. It affects employee perceptions of the world they live in and through this their attitudes to work and their pay increase expectations which, in turn, affect the climate of industrial relations and the state of the country and economy. What is required in this latter context is a better understanding of our problems of interdependence. It is also important for policy formulation, that decisions are not based on postulates about psychological factors but on a research and experience-based understanding of how people whose co-operation is needed interpret the situation and how they feel about it.

In our view it is important to make efforts, including research, for bridging the communication gap, particularly in the context of attempts to improve the climate of industrial relations. The provision for disclosure of information was a step in the right direction but seems to have done little to resolve the language problem, and the information supplied does not necessarily reflect what individual employees really want to know.

15   Concluding Comments

The purpose of this book has been to bring together my major contributions to the study of labour and inflation. The opening chapters have presented analytical evaluations of industrial relations problems and the remaining chapters the results of the three major empirical research enquiries in which I have been engaged, from the earliest carried out in the late 1940s to the latest in the early 1980s. The absence enquiries are discussed in chapters 5-6, the incentives enquiries in 7-10 and the inflation enquiries in 11-14.

In the 35 years covered by this research many important changes have taken place in this country in the economic, political, social and industrial relations scene accompanied by rapid technological changes. For instance, the years of full employment have given way to years of very high unemployment. Nevertheless I have become more convinced than ever when preparing this book that there are basic general issues and continuities which are important and will remain so in the foreseeable future. It is these perennial issues and considerations which I wish to emphasise here.

They may be summarised as follows:
a) In dealing with problems the first task is that of defining the nature of the problem. In this context, it is important to distinguish different types of labour problems; for instance, problems related to the individual's adaptation to work, and problems which face managers and trade union officials at the place of work and at the bargaining table. Some of these can be described as problems of everyday life which can arise at any time in all sorts of work situations. Economic problems, such

as inflation, are different in nature. This type of problem is concerned with economic conditions which affect the whole economy of a country and its citizens. What both types have in common is that they represent interrelation and interdependence problems.
b) The economic and industrial relations scene in a particular country at a particular point of time has to be viewed and understood in the context of a particular historical situation which is the product of the past. This 'heritage' includes problems created by past actions and policies and by attitudes acquired by people in past situations. Economic and labour problems are therefore place and time dependent. The specific existing situation affects what can be achieved (or what may happen) in the present or future. Nevertheless, situations which occur at different times or in different places can be very similar. It is therefore important to study the similarities and differences and their relevance for dealing with problems, and to adopt a historical perspective.
c) The analysis of the nature of the problem in one situation can help us to understand and interpret what is happening in another situation but not always; one must avoid mis-matches. Insights may nevertheless be relevant and they can also be useful for understanding changing situations.
d) Unemployment has become a major economic problem in the late 1970s and early 1980s. However, the working population of the United Kingdom at the end of 1983 numbered just under 21 million. This means that problems connected with work and with industrial relations at the place of work have not disappeared; they are still important. The rate of inflation has decreased markedly in the early 1980s but at the beginning of 1984 inflation was still considered to be a problem and its control a major government objective. However, the recession, unemployment and the question of economic recovery have added further dimensions to our economic problems.
e) In examining recurrent and long lasting problems it is important to look at the setting within which they take place and at the impact of changes and of resistance to change.
f) The most relevant visible changes which have taken place in the economic and institutional framework of British industrial relations in the last three decades have been changes in government economic policies and in our economic fortunes, in industrial relations legislation and technological

225

innovations and their impact on industry and commerce. We have witnessed that many things have changed; yet many have remained the same. 'Plus ca change, plus c'est la meme chose', as the French saying goes. What is striking is the continuation and reappearance of certain issues, controversies and problems.

g) Finally, people's perceptions of facts and their attitudes to them as well as norms and ethical codes are important factors which influence behaviour and must be taken into account. In this context it is important, if possible, to disentangle beliefs and facts and find out whether assumptions we make have a factual foundation. However, in the absence of reliable factual information, many managerial and political decisions, particularly those dealing with industrial relations problems, are liable to be based on judgements based on assumptions and beliefs.

In the remainder of this chapter I shall discuss some of the above points in more detail by focusing on the topics covered in this book.

PROBLEM DIAGNOSIS AND DEFINITION

The definition and diagnosis of problems, as well as the awareness of the existence of problems, is a question of perceptions and judgements. If something goes noticeably wrong, for instance if a machine we depend on breaks down, we know that it must be repaired or replaced and that this is a matter which must be dealt with. Prior to the breakdown we may not have noticed that something was wrong or, if we did, we may have felt it was 'sort of all right' and not yet a problem.

The identification of problems and the attention which is given to them therefore depends on their visibility and their perceived importance and this, in turn, depends on the type of problem which we are discussing and on the amount of publicity which is given to it. With work behaviour and labour efficiency problems, for instance absenteeism, it depends on evaluations of the perceived effects and on management's definition of what is a bad record. Thus, the absence rate in a particular firm may be above the average for the industry and the locality but it may not be considered a problem if the management believes that the incidence is 'normal' and has learned to live with it. However, if the firm is hit by adverse conditions, the managers may suddenly realise that they have an absence problem which they must tackle because they can no longer tolerate the existing level of absenteeism. Thus, the verdict as to whether managers think they have a particular labour problem or not depends very much on the situations in which they find themselves.

Having identified that there is a problem it is important to examine and diagnose the nature of the problem. In this context we find that there are not only different types of problems but also different ways of looking at them. From the economist's point of view, for instance, labour efficiency problems such as absenteeism and low productivity are resources problems; resources must be used efficiently not wastefully; from the manager's point of view, labour efficiency presents planning and control problems and from that of the psychologist it is a question of the individual's attitudes and motivation.

My own approach is that of formulating questions to which I seek answers. If one adopts this approach one can keep an open mind and does not fall into the trap of accepting as a starting point unconfirmed beliefs and hypotheses, for instance, mistaken definitions of the problem, erroneous assumptions about causality and suggested remedies. I would begin with simple basic questions, for instance: has the problem been properly identified? What is the problem? What are its implications? Two examples can illustrate that these questions are necessary. I have often been asked to give advice on an 'incentives problem' which it was believed could be tackled by payment by results; in one case, this turned out to be a manning problem, a question of how many men were required to monitor certain chemical processes. In another case I found the company had a dual problem: the trade unions demanded that their men, engaged in the laying of asphalt, should be paid by results to provide better earnings; however, the men could not increase their output because bottlenecks in the supply of asphalt meant that the gangs were often underemployed.

What makes the diagnosis of problems difficult is that we must take into consideration the nature of the variables involved. The problems may not arise from observable facts but from people's attitudes to work and their notions as to what is a fair day's pay and a fair day's work. It is possible to observe work behaviour directly; absence from work, for instance, can be recorded and so can output. However, people's perceptions, attitudes and motivation cannot be studied by direct observation; what we can record is what people say, the statements and opinions which they express, but these have to be carefully interpreted. This is an area, therefore, where interview-based social science research enquiries which study these variables can make an important contribution to our understanding of labour and inflation problems.

The diagnosis of the causes and effects of problems is also difficult because it involves perceptions and judgements. Moreover, the attribution of causes as well as of effects to certain factors poses the dilemma of assessing what are beliefs and what are facts; that is, whether attributions are backed by factual evidence or not. The absence survey in chapter 5 revealed, for instance, that many beliefs about the causes of absenteeism could not be substantiated by research evidence. On effects, the survey showed that although some people provided speculative estimates, the loss of potential output and the financial costs resulting from absences could not really be measured or predicted. The evidence indicated that disruption of production can be serious in some cases but is not in others; therefore the size of the loss is difficult to assess. If, for instance, absences do not give rise to bottlenecks in the production process or if absentees make up for lost time on their return to work there may be no loss. However, the employment of permanent employees as absence cover can be costly and so can delays in the execution of orders. If workloads have to be reorganised and allocated to other people this can become a source of irritation and frustration which affects not only managers and supervisors but also regular attenders who often like to see action against offenders.

The picture which emerges is one of unequal effects from absences. This finding may account for differences in managerial judgements as to whether the firm does or does not have an absence problem. Assessments of the effectiveness of payment by results revealed a similar state of affairs. In some cases managements were convinced that their schemes were effective while others were faced with restriction of output and conflicts over rates and standards. For a discussion of the unequal effect of strikes see chapter 4 pp 51-54.

At the time of writing, in mid March 1984, a comment about the on-going 1983/84 British miners' dispute is relevant here because of the contrast with the 1974 miners' strike mentioned on p53. So far the comparison illustrates the uniqueness of the two dispute situations; for instance, in 1974 the country was faced with an energy crisis and coal stocks were low; in the winter of 1983/84 we were still in the midde of a world economic recession and the National Coal Board held large unsold surplus coal stocks. Everyday life had not been affected by the dispute at the time of writing in sharp contrast with 1974. Among other differences were: changes on both sides in the persons occupying the top posts; differences in the union's dispute strategy - at present a non-ballot backed officially recommended strike following on an 18-week overtime ban; opposition to pit closures was a major issue in addition to a demand for a better pay settlement. It will be an interesting task for future analysts to make a more detailed comparison.

The uncertainty of the effects of labour problems makes prediction difficult and makes it all the more important not only to assess what one's problem is but also what the effect of measures of dealing with the problem could be. Potential repercussions and sources of trouble from alternative courses of action should be carefully evaluated.

There is no blueprint for dealing with labour problems once they have been analysed. Again therefore it may be best to start with questions such as: How can the problem be tackled within the given context? What courses of action are possible? What would be their repercussions? Or is it advisable to do nothing because the suggested changes would be too difficult to carry out?

Sometimes what may be required is simply a better understanding of the problem which can help the decision-maker to make better decisions and to get on better with other people. At other times when the problem involves the co-operation of groups of people with different backgrounds it is a matter of reaching agreement between the parties concerned. That is why collective bargaining can be so important in dealing with industrial relations problems. Similarly, with regard to economic problems there is a strong case for regular tripartite discussions between government, employer and trade union representatives to try to reconcile conflicting positions based on different economic and political considerations and to establish a constructive climate of co-operation for economic recovery.

Concluding Comments

THE QUESTION OF THE IMPACT OF CHANGE

The inflation studies in which I was engaged between 1962 and 1981 are the ones which were most directly concerned with the question of change. Some of the national sample surveys, for instance, monitored the impact of changes in the economy on people's perceptions of inflation and related issues by repeating questions in later surveys. My aim was to gain insights which would contribute to our understanding of economic behaviour and problems and would provide a basis for making more informed judgements and decisions.

The study of learning and re-learning prices in times of inflation showed that respondents adjusted their notions of prices in response to inflation but that this did not increase their knowledge of prices. It made a more noticeable impact on their expectations. They had become so used to the upward movement that they were inclined to believe that all prices had increased and this perception prevented their noticing stable or falling prices. Continued exposure to inflation, we found, increased the consumer's conscious awareness of price rises. The interesting question is whether the reduction of the rate of inflation to 5 per cent in 1983 has affected people's perceptions and attitudes and if so, in what way. We know that attitudes usually change very slowly. This suggests that the cost of living will still provide an unfavourable frame of reference in future years especially as many people feel that prices are so high already. As long as these perceptions persist, therefore, they will continue to give rise to inflationary pay demands.

As awareness of price rises increased, we found, concern also increased, especially when the rate of inflation accelerated. Thus, in April 1966 when there was still creeping inflation, 51 per cent of our respondents said they had been hit by rising prices but not badly and 85 per cent of them said they did not know anyone who had been badly hit. In January 1973, when the rate of price inflation had risen to 8 per cent, 65 per cent of our respondents stated that they were very concerned about rising prices and two years later when the rate reached 20 per cent, Daniel (1975, see ref p 190) reported that 73 per cent of his respondents said they were very concerned about rising prices and another 19 were fairly concerned. In October 1981 when the rate had come down to 13 per cent, the people we interviewed were still very conscious of rising prices and

230

thought the rate had accelerated although it had not. They were pessimistic about the outlook for the future and believed that it would take a long time before things improved. It will be interesting to see what responses Daniel receives to the repeat of his concern question in his 1984 survey sponsored by the ESRC; also whether younger people have learned to accept that rising prices are a fact of life and are therefore less inclined to express concern than older people.

The acquisition of knowledge about changing rates of pay and incomes is even more problematic than that of learning and re-learning prices. The beliefs or facts problem in this area is that only knowledge about one's own income is experience-based. Information about other people's incomes is difficult to come by and often based on hearsay or on income images projected by the mass media. These figures may refer to gross or net pay, to earnings or to take-home pay. To add to the confusion the regular use of percentage increases has increased already existing difficulties with regard to obtaining and memorising income information because they give rise to untidy amounts instead of round figures. Ask yourself how much information and what type of information you can give about your own income (and the income tax you pay) without looking it up and, if you are on a salary scale, how much you can remember about the whole salary scale.

My income images study revealed that respondents knew very little about other people's pay, and yet people's perceptions and beliefs about other people's pay play an important part in pay negotiations and in disputes about pay differentials. It looks as if income comparisons are liable to be based on inadequate information and that this state of affairs will persist.

Our pay increase enquiries represent another example of monitoring changes in perceptions by repeating questions in later surveys. The findings revealed that employees based their expectations on past experience and had come to expect that the next pay increase would be larger. The 'pay explosions' which followed periods of pay restraint in Britain in 1969, 1975 and 1978 have borne this out. The employees' major frame of reference for making pay demands was the cost of living and there are signs that many employees in 1984 still feel that they cannot keep up with this. It is difficult to assess therefore how pay increase expectations in Britain have been affected by the recession and the existence of unemployment. Even if certain groups of employees have accepted lower settlements than in previous years they may still expect higher awards in future years. As IDS Focus commented in August 1983 (p1) 'the level of earnings has been running at 7 or 8 per cent above that of twelve months ago, and there are few signs, if any, of the situation changing'. This in spite of the decrease in price increases to 5 per cent. Furthermore, the wage-round strikes which have occurred in the last three years have illustrated that the issues discussed in chapter 13 can still be the source of bitter conflict and that, among these, pay increase offers, described as too low by the trade unions, have often been the major bone of contention.

This suggests that the pay increase expectations which are a product of the past are now deeply rooted and may give another twist to the inflationary process in future years when, and if, an economic recovery gets under way. The size of pay demands, I believe, will remain an important issue for many years to come.

I now turn to a different set of findings from the inflation enquiries. The last two decades have seen what some people call a revolution in information technology; and yet communication problems between government ministers and economists and the ordinary citizen, we found, were as great in October 1981 as in April 1966. At that time the respondents did not know what the word inflation meant so could not understand the need for having an incomes policy, let alone the content of that particular incomes policy. In 1981 they did not understand the word monetarism and did not seem to realise that it was a government objective to reduce inflation.

It is a curious irony that the educational know-how required to help ordinary people to understand the content of communications about economic resource constraints and other economic problems has lagged so far behind the rapid technological advances in communication. I believe that it is important that we should learn to make progress in this area because the lack of understanding of the economic problems of interdependence can affect employee attitudes to work and their expectations with regard to standards of living and pay increases; these, in turn, can affect the climate of industrial relations and the working of the economy. There is a strong case for sponsoring research in this area.

I now turn to the industrial relations problems which were discussed in chapters 2 and 3. Most of

these are perennial problems. In my view the
maintenance of a reasonable climate of industrial
relations in an organisation and the improvement of
the quality of the relations is, and will remain,
important, both with regard to what may be called
small interpersonal frictions and wider problems of
co-operation and conflict. What matters to people at
the place of work are the interpersonal and
intergroup relations and it is these which remain
however much the nature of work itself alters.
However, the places where they occur and the form
they take as well as their frequency, may change.
It is unrealistic to assume that these types of
problems can be eliminated but there is, of course,
room for improvement.

Absence from work is one example of these
perennial problems. It has been a continuing
problem in Britain and other western countries in
the post-war period although the amount of attention
given to it by managers has fluctuated in line with
changes in the economic climate. Concern tends to
be higher in times of recession but can also be
great if a company is faced with rapidly expanding
market demand for its products or with tight
delivery dates.

The main factual change which has taken place is
that days lost by certificated absences (and
therefore the total absence rates) have been much
higher in Britain and other Western countries in the
1970s and early 1980s than in the early post-war
period. Some people, it seems, believe that this is
an intractable problem and that little can be done
about it and one can argue that without managerial
effort the likelihood of improvement is not great.
However, as our Scottish studies have shown, the
records of the majority of the employees can be good
or very good. The main attention should be focused
on the minority of employees with very bad records.
From the managerial and occupational health point of
view, the monitoring of absences to identify this
minority is important and will remain so. The
analyses described in chapter 6 provide an
appropriate method for this. It consists in a
simple technical innovation for analysing records,
namely a change away from traditional absence
measures to the use of frequency measures. It was
used as early as October 1975 by a member of the
Advisory Conciliation and Arbitration Service (ACAS)
and in the Post Office Annual Report on Sickness and
Medical Wastage 1977-78. But, as often with
research, there can be long time-lags before others
realise that this could be a useful change.

Concluding Comments

As regards productivity, this too has been a major and continuing problem area since the end of the second world war and one which will, I believe, remain important even although there has been evidence of improvements in some areas in the last few years. It must be stressed in any case that there have been great differences in the past and that it is likely there will also be differences in the future in the performance of different firms and industries so that the image that the whole of British industry has a bad record can be very misleading.

In the early post-war years much publicity was given to the need to raise productivity, particularly that of labour, as a means of recovering from the effects of the war and of raising standards of living. Thus, many official statements encouraged the use of payment by results and government funds were made available for research in this area. Payment by results, it was argued, would not only help to raise labour productivity but would also offset shortages of labour and reduce overtime which had increased in response to full employment. It is interesting to note that the existence of low productivity was considered at that time to be a sign of a difficult adjustment period and not a 'British disease' - the image so often projected in later years.

Although there has been some progress on the productivity front in the early 1980s the need for more and further improvements would appear to be even greater than in the past because of the world recession, the increase in foreign competition, especially from Japan and some third world countries, and the difficulties facing British exporters in producing the right goods at the right time and the right price when costs and prices are often adversely affected by changing interest and exchange rates.

As mentioned, the adoption of payment by results was recommended as one means for raising productivity in the early post-war years. The popularity of its use would not appear to have changed since then in spite of many other recommendations which became fashionable. For example, almost the same percentage of the working population was paid by results in 1951 (40 per cent) as in 1980 (42 per cent). However, this does not mean that the schemes are still used in the same organisations and industries; many firms have abandoned their schemes and adopted other approaches while others have introduced them. This indicates

234

that managements have felt they had to adjust their company wage policies in response to change and that the question of the choice of appropriate company wage policies and methods of payment will remain a problem in future years.

In this context, the problems of fairness resulting from the difficulty of defining performance standards which represent a day's work will also remain. The essence of the problem is that we deal wth an effort bargain, a fact which is often overlooked. However, an appreciation that it is agreement on the standards which matters, is essential for the effectiveness of the bargain and for the use of payment by results.

Similarly, our inability to define objectively what is a fair grade or rank for a particular job, and fair pay for it, will remain a problem in the future and one which makes it unlikely that job evaluation can ever play the role in national wage determination which some people apparently believe it can. When job evaluation is used as a means of ranking jobs and as a basis for an equitable wage structure, many subjective normative judgements must be made in choosing and defining the criteria for ranking and for weighting the qualities involved in carrying out a particular job. It is therefore important, when carrying out the exercise, to obtain consensus on what are acceptable criteria and weights for the evaluation, for instance, on how responsibility should be assessed. In this process the job evaluation becomes what one may call a status bargain which determines income levels within an organisation. Comparison with schemes in other organisations may reveal different rankings for jobs with similar names.

The concept of 'equal pay for work of equal value' has the opposite goal; it tries to establish which jobs have the same rank and should therefore receive the same pay. The same problems therefore arise as with job evaluation; but they will be greater if applied to jobs in different organisations where the quality and quantity of the work performance may not be comparable. Moreover one should not ignore the economic question of the price of the product of labour and what a firm can afford to pay. One can argue that the economic value of the work to be performed must be taken into account to establish the value of the work. In spite of these problems, an EEC directive has led to statutory legislation based on the concept; for instance, in Britain, The Equal Pay (Amendment) Regulation 1984.

Concluding Comments

Another issue which is relevant both to the discussion of labour productivity and absence from work is that of changes in the working week and attitudes to it. In the early post-war years the working week was much longer than now. The six day week was still widespread and the use of regular overtime began to take root. Criticisms of the excessive use of overtime began to be voiced in the 50s. It was frowned upon as an undesirable and costly habit and bad for the workers' health. However, many workers apparently wanted to earn overtime money and moved to jobs offering overtime opportunities. The result is that many organisations still use overtime while, because of the recession, others are working short time. It is likely that some employers will still prefer overtime to the recruitment of extra workers in the future, for instance because they are not sure whether an increase in orders is only temporary or not. Meanwhile trade union drives for shorter working hours continue. I believe that questions of shorter hours, part-time work, work sharing and overtime will still have to be weighed up in the future and tailored to the needs of specific organisations at a specific point of time in the light of external pressures. These include emerging norms with regard to what is a fair day's work in terms of the length of the working week, holiday entitlements and other demands for leisure. What must be weighed up against these are considerations of the economic effects of reduction in working time on the survival and viability of firms and the prosperity of the country. Whether reductions in working time necessarily reduce the output of a factory or other work organisation must be an open question.

Finally, we may conclude that with so many perennial problems the question of how to deal with them will remain important. It is in this context that the question of the uniqueness of situations is particularly relevant.

WAYS OF DEALING WITH PROBLEMS - THE SEARCH FOR SOLUTIONS

Labour problems, one can argue, are by definition 'no technical solutions' problems because they involve people. What can be achieved depends on the way these people look at the problems, on how they respond to them and on suggested ways of dealing with them. To obtain co-operation,

236

attitudes and expectations may have to be changed and if possible a sense of common responsibility developed to arrive at so-called 'solutions' which are usually compromise agreements about changes which are considered necessary or desirable. It is unlikely that long lasting solutions can be reached for this type of problem.

The search for a solution is place and time dependent and must be evaluated in terms of the unique historical situation in which the decision has to be taken. Nevertheless much can be learned from one's own past experience and that of others and from relevant research.

Thus, I am convinced that much can be learned by politicians who are interested in the search for a workable incomes policy or other anti-inflation policies from analysing mistakes made in the past and from studying research findings related to human non-technical variables such as people's perceptions of what it is all about, their attitudes to inflation, to standards of living and their improvement and to incomes and pay increases.

Many politicians, for instance, still do not appear to understand the implications of the evidence that people are not merely worried about price increases (a point which has often been recognised) but many of them also find that their pay increases are too small when a low percentage increase is applied to a low income, a point also relevant for state pensions. The 3.5 per cent increase in Great Britain in November 1983 for a single pensioner was £1.20, an amount which would have fallen 17 years ago into the hardly noticeable size of the pay increase threshold zone in our April 1966 sample survey.

Turning to the question of the industrial relations climate at the place of work it is widely held that the major responsibility for establishing a good climate rests with management; it depends on the outlook and quality of the managers and their social skills. However, in my view, a superficial layer of social skills is not enough unless it is backed by personal integrity. What matters is frankness and honesty and consistency in behaviour and attitudes; also tact and empathy; a respect for the indiviual in his own right which is not clouded by stereotyped images about 'workers' as a species. Furthermore, direct interaction is important to establish good relations and trust; perhaps some exchanges of opinions, not necessarily about work matters. What is also important is that managers adopt a democratic person-centred approach in their

237

Concluding Comments

relations with subordinates and not an autocratic hierarchical one and in addition that their statements are comprehensible.

There is no magical formula for improving work relations; success depends on continuous effort and on the outlook and attitudes of both managers and employees. However, training, if well done, can make a contribution to the improvement of interpersonal relations by sensitising people to the problem, and raising their awareness and understanding and their ability to learn from experience.

It is easier to do something about the problem of absence from work provided two pre-requisites are met: the existence (or establishment) of agreed disciplinary procedures and that of a record system which provides concrete evidence about incapacity or misconduct. Such evidence is needed should the ultimate sanction of dismissal be required, to refute claims of unfair dismissal. The records make it possible to establish criteria for classifying attendances and to identify the critical group with really bad records on which attention needs to be focused. Each case can be investigated and monitored. Whether management would need to do much more is an open question.

The survey of action taken by managements, discussed in chapter 5, showed that many different approaches have been tried. Some were successful and others found wanting. I would just like to comment here on some recent attempts. In the 1979-80 wage-round a number of British companies tried to deal with their absence problem by concluding self-financing productivity agreements in which, among other things, an attendance bonus was offered in return for reduced absence levels. The bonus qualifying standards of attendance were based on average absence rates or the average number of days lost. Because of the skew frequency distributions of absences, however, these standards must have been loose and therefore expensive. Well over half the workforce would have qualified for the bonus without improving their standards! It should therefore be noted that attendance standards as well as output standards can be loose.

Production control problems, such as loose output standards, point to the malfunctioning of payment by results schemes and these types of problems, it seems, are particularly time and place dependent. What can be achieved in a particular plant as regards output performance depends on its specific situation, on its past history, its

organisation and technology and the quality of the
industrial relations climate in the firm. What
works well in one situation may not work in another;
and what works well at one period of time may not
work well at a later stage. A change in
circumstances, such as the adoption of a new
technology or decreasing market demand, may make
existing schemes redundant. This is an area
therefore where imitation of what is being done
elsewhere can misfire badly although knowledge about
what has been done and what has happened elsewhere
can be useful in the assessment of what is
appropriate action in the specific situation. The
management concerned could learn something from its
past experience as well as that of others, for
instance, by identifying factors which hampered or
fostered the effectiveness of a particular payment
scheme and drawing up a balance sheet of plus and
minus factors.

Indeed one can argue that the need to adjust to
a changing environment makes it imperative that
managers should make regular assessments of the
functioning of their methods of payment and other
existing practices of dealing with labour efficiency
problems, particularly as regards company pay
policy, setting output standards, manning levels and
training, to see whether the practices are still
appropriate.

They must pay particular attention to the fact
that different employment policies are appropriate
in different stages of the life of an organisation,
that is, when starting up a new factory, when the
expansion stage begins, when it comes to an end, and
in periods of contraction and redundancies. This
means that, in a particular calendar year, what is
appropriate for a well established firm with a
stable product market may be inappropriate for one
that is expanding or contracting. This underlines
the point that it is a mistake to follow fashion
trends and use particular managerial techniques
because others are advocating them.

In the setting up stage, especially, I have
found that a lot of mistakes occur in the labour
resources and industrial relations area. To give
just one example, in one firm in the South of
Scotland, the managers' main attention in setting up
a branch factory was focused on meeting output
targets and building up the workforce; little
attention was paid to the adoption of an appropriate
pace of work. In addition, the management used
measured daywork without offering the equivalent
high time rates and only introduced method study and

239

Concluding Comments

work measurement much later. Towards the end of the
first year recruits were taken on at a pace of about
300 a week. The result was overmanning and the
establishment of a slow pace of work. The workers
could be seen to get into each other's way as I went
round the plant. In another factory management
introduced payment by results in the setting up
stage but discovered that this was inappropriate for
new entrants and it had to change to time-rates.

I concluded from a number of case studies that
careful attention to the establishment of a
reasonable pace of work is very important when
starting up new factories and that many other
lessons can be learned from monitoring problems
encountered in the different stages of a firm's
development. In times of recession and cut-backs,
for instance, it is important to assess the effects
on the managerial staff who remain and have to live
with the memory of the sometimes traumatic
experience of having to close a plant. In one case
I found that a manager was haunted by the fear that
similar problems might develop and affect the
viability of the plant which was in his charge. He
expressed the anxiety that there ought to be a way
to prevent it - a kind of 'we must avoid the Factory
X fate' complex.

FINAL OBSERVATIONS

I have argued in this chapter that it is
important to diagnose and define the different types
of economic and labour problems which confront us in
different situations, to assess whether and how they
are affected by a changing environment and to
examine what are potential alternative ways of
dealing with them before deciding what is the most
appropriate course of action. I have also argued
that it is an important pre-requisite for
understanding economic and labour problems to take
account of people's perceptions of the economic
situation, and of their work situation and role in
it. In this context it is not only the perceptions
of employees which must be taken account of but also
those of employers, trade union officials,
government ministers and other politicians.
Government decisions, for instance, are based on
economic as well as political considerations; they
are influenced by the ideology of the government
party and by the pre-election promises which
governments say they must fulfil.

This is an area to which well designed research

can make a major contribution. The question approach which I have used is particularly appropriate and so is the crossing of interdisciplinary boundary lines which can widen one's horizon. Working within the confines of only one social science discipline, for instance economics, can lead to the acceptance of restrictive and misleading assumptions and therefore inappropriate recipes for solutions. In my view, for instance, theoretical economists could learn a lot from empirical research and possibly also from introspection. An interesting question which they should ask themselves is whether economic theory has influenced them so much that they behave in the postulated way or not.

To understand people's perceptions it is important to study learning and thought processes. Earlier in this book (p204) I mentioned the habit of 'compartmentalised thinking' which is often used in everyday life and which enables people to hold apparently contradictory views. This in itself is a phenomenon one should watch and study. The other contrast one should be aware of is that between common sense, experience-based thinking and analytical, deductive thinking and the statements they give rise to. In everyday life many statements are based on common sense and this can give rise to misunderstandings. Much more research in this area is desirable. Margaret Donaldson's pioneering study on Children's Minds (Fontana 1978) is of particular interest for such research.

The mention of misunderstandings arising from different ways of thinking raises the more general question of problems of communication. What kind of messages do verbal statements transmit? At least four different types can be distinguished: statements conveying factual information; value judgements and opinions; persuasive statements which try to influence people to do something and expressions of feelings. However, the purpose of statements may be hidden, as with persuasion or when opinions and feelings are expressed in factual terms; for instance, if someone says, it is bitterly cold, he may really mean he feels cold and not that the measured temperature is low. The ability to recognise differences can be useful for evaluating printed information and in personnel work, for instance, for distinguishing statements which express feelings and statements about facts.

The differences must also be kept in mind when a researcher designs interview schedules to investigate perceptions and attitudes and when he or

Concluding Comments

she interprets the replies. Open-ended free choice questions are more appropriate in this context, and more likely to provide useful insights, than closed questions with pre-coded categories to choose from and tick. This is why it is important that this type of research is carried out by experienced and well qualified social science researchers.

It is also important that the reports prepared by researchers should be clearly written and should avoid unnecessary jargon and technical terms because these can give rise to communications problems between social scientists and readers.

However, the communication problem which I have been most conscious of has been that of providing speedy and easy access to the research results, particularly with topical material. There can be long time-lags in the publication of articles and books, and academic journals may not be easily accessible. To cope with this in our inflation studies we prepared preliminary reports for private circulation which we found provided an effective tool for reaching interested parties and policy-makers.

In this type of topical setting, I found, the researcher takes on the function of interpreter and commentator and his or her reports spell out the implications of the findings for specific historical situations. Only at a later stage is it possible to evaluate the longer lasting relevance of the findings and to identify the insights which have remained important and the lessons which can be learned from the evidence. In the light of these considerations, the original reports of the inflation enquiries, which described each survey within its historical setting, were not included in this book although they contain material which is of interest to specialists. Instead chapters 11-13 focus on the longer lasting insights and conclusions which have emerged from the evidence in our inflation enquiries, among them some economic policy implications. In this context I would argue that insights derived from my research into perceptions of, and attitudes to, past anti-inflation policies and to pay problems, are still relevant and can point to further questions and issues which are worth investigating. I believe that it will be important in the future that policy-makers and their advisers should have access to reliable information about what peple think and feel about particular economic issues and that further research in this area could be very useful. It is a disturbing thought that in 1981, when we tried to get funds, the British Department of Employment Work Research Unit was apparently not allowed to sponsor research in the pay area. One would have thought that pay was an important aspect in the study of work problems.

16   Index

a fair day's work (continued)
viewed in terms of working
hours 151
fair minimum wage, views on
180-181
fair pay, respondents views
179-180
fair pay increases, views on
182
fashion trends 168-169
financial incentives see
payment by results
financial incentives and
marginal productivity
117-120
future of the economy,
respondents' views 220

gearing effort to earnings,
problem of 110-111, 112,
133, 136-137
group norms of conduct
(output norms) 149-150

humanisation of work 32

incentives enquiry, author's
brief
description 4, 123-124n2
evidence 111, 124-125
n4n5, 126n9n10, 127n12
n13n14n15, 128n16, 129n19,
131n29
income images 231
incomes, knowledge of 231
incomes policy
search for a workable one
185-188, 201
see also pay restraint
policies
in-company criteria for
evaluating absences 92-99
derivation 92-93
use for classification of
absences 92-93
cross-tabulations 94-97
industrial relations
definition and scope 7-9
see also 23
industrial relations,
concern about 23-29

adequacy of rules and
institutions 25-26
interrelation with inflation
26-27
interrelation with the
working of the economy 26-27
quality of industrial and
human relations 27
question of diagnosis 29-31
industrial relations, criteria
of quality question 28-29
absence from work 28
strikes 29, 30-31
industrial relations,
institutional framework
of 12-13
industrial relations, images of
22-23, 27
industrial relations climate,
management's responsibility
237
industrial relations
problems 9-20, 23-24, 232-
233
conflicts 11-12, 13-14,
15-16
common and conflicting goals and
interests 14-17
co-operation 10-11, 13, 14-17
employee's share in income
of organisation 10-11
human efficiency 9-10
human relations 9
interdependence 23-24
motivation and incentives
9-10, 14
perennial issues 224-226, 232
question of facts or
beliefs 18-19
role of ideas and norms 12
industrial relations and public
policy 12
inflation, attitudes to 191-204
of British governments 199-
201
of British public 191, 192-
198
see also perceptions of
inflation
inflation, concern about 230-
231

Index

For Product Safety Concerns and Information please contact our
EU representative GPSR@taylorandfrancis.com Taylor & Francis
Verlag GmbH, Kaufingerstraße 24, 80331 München, Germany